T0268287

THE
REVENUE
ACCELERATION
PLAYBOOK

Creating an Authentic Buyer Journey Across Sales, Marketing, and Customer Success

BRENT KELTNER

THE
REVENUE
ACCELERATION
PLAYBOOK

FOREWORD BY
DAVID MEERMAN SCOTT

●● PAGE TWO

Some names and identifying details have been changed to protect the privacy of individuals and organizations.

Cataloguing in publication information is available from Library and Archives Canada.
ISBN 978-1-77458-101-8 (hardcover)
ISBN 978-1-77458-102-5 (ebook)

Page Two
pagetwo.com

Edited by James Harbeck
Copyedited by Steph VanderMeulen
Jacket design by Peter Cocking
Interior design by Fiona Lee
Interior illustrations by Michelle Clement
Printed and bound in Canada by Friesens
Distributed in Canada by Raincoast Books
Distributed in the US and internationally by Macmillan

22 23 24 25 26   5 4 3 2 1

authenticitywins.com

For my family: my wife, Ann-Marie;
son, John Henry; and daughter, Anna

Contents

Foreword

EARLY IN my career, I worked as a sales representative at a Wall Street economic consultancy. Back then, salespeople had the information and therefore the power in the buyer-seller relationship. If the buyers wanted information about how the product worked, they needed to come to me. If they wanted to negotiate a discount, they had to come through me. If they wanted to speak to a customer to learn about their experience with my company, they had to come through me. If they wanted to talk to the founder of the company, they had to come through me. I was involved from the very beginning of the relationship, and most of the leverage was with me, the sales rep.

We're in a new world!

As I see it, there are three important trends that have fundamentally changed the ways successful companies grow their businesses compared to when I was a sales representative. We are witnessing the biggest communications revolution in human history, and, as a result, your marketplace has changed. The vast majority of human beings, more than five billion of us, are connected instantly to each other via web-based and mobile communications devices. Information about products and services is available to buyers everywhere, 24/7, for free, and anyone can generate attention by publishing valuable content. With publishing essentially free, customers have a (loud) voice through social networks and review sites.

Because of the wealth of information on the web and social media, today's salesperson no longer controls the relationship the way I did thirty years ago. Now, buyers can check you out themselves. They can find your customers and read their blog accounts about what you do. They can reach the founders directly via Twitter and LinkedIn. Buyers actively go around salespeople until the last possible moment, and then come into negotiations armed with a glut of information. Now, it's the buyers who have the leverage.

The second important change in play right now is a distinct convergence of marketing, sales, and customer success. Today, buyers dictate how they choose companies to work with, and they don't really care what department your employees are in. Everybody on your team should be focused on business growth.

Here's a curious disconnect to illustrate how frustrating the old, siloed approach is for customers: many companies have completely different cultures and procedures for their customers depending on which department is interacting with them. The ways a company projects itself via its marketing messages are different from the way salespeople engage potential new customers when trying to win new business, which, in turn, is often light-years removed from how these same customers are serviced by the company only months later.

The third major trend is a return to humanity. A hundred years ago, our great-grandparents knew the people who sold them chickens, or nails, or cloth. Today, many people feel disheartened by the faceless companies they must interact with, which simply treat them as yet another customer number.

"Your business is important to us," says the on-hold message. Right.

We're all human, and we crave interaction with people who know us and respond to us as individuals. We all want to do business with other humans. We want to know there's a living, breathing person behind the communication. And we want reassurance that those humans on the other side understand and want to help us.

In my work over the past twenty years, I have analyzed how thousands of companies grow their business. Sadly, most organizations are built and run as if it were still 1989. The revenue acceleration model is broken.

Fortunately, Brent Keltner is a noted expert on how these important trends are playing out and is keenly aware of exactly what smart organizations must do to succeed in the new business environment.

The Revenue Acceleration Playbook is a deep dive into proven strategies for how to achieve remarkable business growth. Creating what Brent calls an authentic buyer journey across sales, marketing, and customer success means that an entire organization is aligned with buyers, rather than the usual disconnected approach. It's an attitude that recognizes how business has changed, including the importance of digital communications and the power of human touch.

This way of growing business is easy to learn, but you must overcome the status quo. Instead of "we've always done it this way," Brent teaches a new focus. *Adding value* to customers is very different from simply marketing and selling a product and then tossing the relationship over the cubicle wall to somebody in customer support.

Brent is the ideal person to write about these ideas. After a successful career working for RAND Corporation, a research organization that develops solutions to public policy challenges, Brent held a series of revenue leadership roles at several other companies. Using his years of experience, he then started Winalytics, a consultancy that works with clients on making the shift from a product-driven selling approach to the creation of an authentic buyer journey for customers that touches on marketing, sales, and customer success.

Brent writes, speaks, and advises VP- and C-level executives on these ideas. And now, for the first time, in these pages, he is sharing his ideas beyond his select group of clients.

I particularly love the playbooks that Brent teaches here. In the hundreds of business books that I've read over the years, I've never seen a concept as simple and as powerful as the playbook approach to revenue growth. Those ideas alone are worth the time to read *The Revenue Acceleration Playbook*— but there is so much more here.

Brent is super smart and has a PhD to prove it. But fear not, this book is no boring academic tome! It's a fast-paced read that lays out specific actions for your organization in a fun and approachable way. Brent outlines what you need to do to accelerate your organization's revenue in a step-by-step way so you can implement the ideas in your own business.

One of the best parts of the book is that you will read fascinating stories of dozens of companies that have implemented the revenue acceleration playbook approach. The stories, told from the perspective of companies that have implemented the ideas with success, clearly illustrate the value of this way of doing business.

As you read the stories, keep in mind that you will learn from them even if they come from a very different market, industry, or type of organization from your own. If you work at a nonprofit, you can still learn from the experiences of corporations. Those who work at big companies will find value in what smaller organizations are up to. In fact, in my experience, you will learn more by emulating successful ideas from outside your industry than by copying what your peers are doing.

Many of the people you will meet in these chapters implemented the ideas in this book and then enjoyed much faster business growth as a result. And now you can too.

There is no doubt that the best organizations lead from a customer-value perspective. Those who create an authentic buyer journey not only grow faster, but also have more satisfaction at work because they help their clients succeed.

Now it's your turn. Here's to your success!

DAVID MEERMAN SCOTT
Business growth strategist, entrepreneur, and author of twelve books, including the *Wall Street Journal* bestseller *Fanocracy*.

DavidMeermanScott.com
@dmscott

1

Discovering the Authentic Buyer Journey

I MOVED TO Boston late in 2002 to work for Kaplan Higher Education, the higher education division of Kaplan Inc., best known for its test preparation courses. After years of living in California, I wanted to have some time to find the right Boston neighborhood, buy a condo, and settle into a new life on the East Coast. So I spent my first year living in an apartment while I embarked on the search for my new home.

During this year, I worked with two realtors to find the right neighborhood and a condo to purchase. One struggled to really understand what I was looking for. The other became a great partner for me and earned a hefty commission!

I was introduced to the first realtor—we'll call her Elise—by someone in Kaplan's human resource group. Elise was a well-known Boston realtor and was well connected with all the various real estate groups, which helped her stay on top of the best current condo inventory. She and I had two Saturdays together walking through condos before I decided to put my search on hold for a bit.

I remember both of those Saturdays as a bit of a mind-numbing blur. Elise and I had agreed on a handful of Boston-area urban neighborhoods to target for our search, including Brookline, Brighton, Newton Corner, and Fenway. I was looking for a one bedroom with a den or a two bedroom, ideally with hardwood floors.

On the Friday nights before the Saturdays out with Elise, she sent me a list of all the condos in our chosen neighborhoods that met my criteria. We agreed by email to the top four or five to visit and picked one where we would meet up. Each Saturday felt like a footrace through condo after condo as we ticked through a requirements list: square footage, condo layout, a modern kitchen or kitchen needing renovation, quality of hardwood floors, state of appliances, number of bathrooms, and so on.

The conversations Elise and I had at the end of each Saturday focused on the steps and timeline to closing. There wasn't a lot of time spent on whether we were even tracking on my ideal outcome for a condo and living situation.

For me, the experience with Elise exemplified the classic product pitch or product-driven buyer journey. It was all about throwing product features and functions and hoping that something would stick. The idea of organizing the search around my ideal outcome seemed to get lost somewhere after Elise and I agreed to city neighborhoods and the number of bedrooms. After the second Saturday, I thanked Elise for her help and told her I needed to rethink my goals and timing for buying a condo.

About two months later, I restarted the condo search after being introduced to a second realtor, Susan. The experience with Susan could not have been more different from the experience with Elise. Susan started with a short intake interview, which included questions on the neighborhoods for the condo search and my desired number of bedrooms and bathrooms.

However, it also focused on a series of interesting experiential questions, such as, "What were your best and worst living situations in the past?" "What do you want to repeat or not repeat from these past living experiences?" and "Are there any deal breakers or must-haves for the next condo?"

On our first Saturday out together, Susan suggested we look at a maximum of three places and advised that they be different, rather than alike, so we could compare. As we walked through each condo, the checklist of things to review was the same as it was during the visits with Elise: square footage, condo layout, a modern kitchen or kitchen needing renovation, quality of hardwood floors, state of appliances, number of bathrooms, and so on. However, this time around, we stopped at the end of each condo visit to debrief.

These debriefs would go back to the things I had really liked and did not like, the must-haves and the deal breakers. After just a handful of condo debriefs, a few things became clear to both Susan and me. I really did want a second half bath in the common area for visitors. I really did not want to have to do any kitchen renovations. I liked the idea of living within walking distance of stores, restaurants, and supermarkets, but I really could not tolerate a lot of street noise—meaning the situation of the building and windows mattered a lot. I did not need pristine hardwood floors because I had a lot of oriental rugs I really liked that would cover a good bit of floor space.

I remember that after our first day together, Susan sent me a short email capturing these key learnings for both of us. We agreed to the best of our ability to use this information to add or remove condos from our list to visit. It took about two months with Susan to find the right condo. We didn't go every Saturday, but most. And while looking for a place was stressful and time-consuming, I really enjoyed the experience with Susan. I felt like I had a partner in identifying my ideal outcome for a condo and living situation in Boston. The "closing" conversation came up only toward the end, as we got to a handful of finalists for consideration.

The experience with Susan is what I think of as the *authentic buyer journey*. It starts, progresses, and ends anchored in what the buyer really values. The purpose of each interaction is to get more information on what the buyer is trying to achieve and explore the payoffs or positive impacts of partnering with a new company. The product itself has little standing. The purpose of the product is to help advance the buyer toward their goals. The product is presented and product demonstrations are conducted with the buyer's goal in mind.

The role of the go-to-market team—which in most companies comprises the sales, marketing, and customer success departments—is to partner with a buyer to explore options for moving from a current state to a future ideal state that supports goal achievement. "Closing" is not a phase of the sales process, but a natural outcome of finding agreement on a path to the buyer's future ideal state.

How an Academic Discovered an Authentic Buyer Journey

At about the time Susan was helping me close on my ideal condo and living situation in Boston, I was also transitioning into a new professional role. Kaplan Higher Education was my first job in the corporate world. I had spent the first ten years of my professional life as an academic, earning a PhD in social science at Stanford University, and then working as a researcher at the RAND Corporation, a leading think tank offering research and analysis to a range of federal and state government agencies, as well as to top corporations.

Kaplan was an amazing new environment for me, filled with firsthand learning about business, marketing, and corporate politics. It was also my first time doing actual business-to-business (B2B) sales. It was at Eduventures, however, that I truly became a revenue leader.

I joined Eduventures about fifteen months after coming to Boston. Eduventures is the leading commercial research and advisory firm in the education sector, and I joined to partner with a couple of their veteran executives to launch a new benchmarking research division for colleges and universities. In just over three years, we grew this new business into a $10 million division. We launched programs to collect benchmark data and operational best practices for all of the major colleges and university departments, including enrollment management, development and fundraising, student affairs, continuing education, academic affairs, and provost offices.

I had some experience with B2B revenue growth at Kaplan, but now I was quickly growing my own sales, customer success, and product teams, as well as continuing to manage marketing. I needed help and resources. So, I put out emails to my college and graduate school friends who had gone into business, asking for resources on positioning, marketing, and sales execution. Most of what I got back were things described as resources to build the "buyer journey" or "customer-centric selling" or "consultative selling." As I reviewed these materials, to my surprise, they took me right back to my condo search with my first "product-pitching" realtor, Elise.

The documents were labeled with terms like "buyer" and "customer." However, they were really just about the company's product. The focus was on questions like, "How does my customer or buyer perceive my product?" "How will they interact with my product?" "How do they think about my product's positioning relative to a competitor?" "What will they pay for my product and what discounts might motivate them to buy?"

The key gap in almost all of these documents was a focus on what the buyer was actually *trying to achieve*. There was usually some cursory discussion on "buyer discovery," with encouragement to ask about buyers' goals or pains, but little attempt to dig into what success really meant for the buyer. Typically, there was no real attempt to link a company's product to specific buyer goals or business outcomes. There was little focus on understanding the gap between a buyer's current or ideal state or how a partnership might close this gap. There was often little focus on the type of individual, organizational, or financial payoffs that might excite the buyer and lead them to purchase, or how they might see any money spent with a vendor as an investment in that payoff.

Ironically, I found myself building my go-to-market strategy and playbooks at Eduventures based on what I learned as an academic managing qualitative research projects at the RAND Corporation.

At RAND, I did a lot of projects on Air Force logistics as well as city and county government, but my favorite projects were on workforce development, the college-to-career transition, and corporate investments in building skills and career pathways. My dissertation research had been in this area, and, with another RAND colleague, I was successful in securing grants from the Sloan Foundation, the National Science Foundation, and others to continue this work. Our work focused on interviews with vice presidents (VPs) of human resources, and of training and development; chief human resource officers; and sometimes CEOs or senior general managers.

As I started interviewing corporate executives, I was acutely aware that corporate culture was very different from the academic culture I had grown up in. Not only were my first ten years as a professional spent earning a PhD and then doing academic-style research, but I was raised in an academic family, with a father who was in academic medicine and a mother who had been a teacher. So, in working to engage corporate partners for my research studies, I consciously adopted a set of what I thought of as "corporate behaviors."

When reaching out for interview requests, I was always very specific about what was in it for them rather than focusing on the content of the interview. I used a combination of email, call, and voicemail outreach to bring attention to my interview requests, remind the person I wanted to talk to what was in it for them, and use voicemail to let them know there was a human being on the other side of that email. In my emails and voicemails, I set a specific date for following up and then reached out on those dates to build their confidence in my reliability. I shared and referenced names of business colleagues or peer companies in my outreach to further underscore how an interview call could be of value to them.

I led all my interview calls with an agenda and then actively listened, recapping key points and follow-on questions. I wanted to make sure the executives knew I was hearing and capturing what they shared about their skills development strategies and the reasons for those strategies. I also followed up each call with an email to recap key points from my interviews and include any agreed next steps to collect further data or arrange interviews with members of their team.

As it turns out, in trying to align with what I perceived as "corporate behavior," I had developed my own version of an authentic buyer journey based on authentic conversations rather than product-driven conversations. And it was wildly successful.

At RAND, I secured not only hundreds of executive interviews but also many of the who's who of business leaders. For one project, I got all the major banks in New York, Los Angeles, and Chicago to participate and provide multiple interviewees. Another project was sponsored by John Reed, the iconic CEO who turned Citibank into a global brand. I also had a project with Gary Gregg at Liberty Mutual. Gary was an affable but hard-charging executive who made the company's mid-market business the dominant player for commercial insurance before becoming the company's CEO. A second partner on that same project was John Stankey, the legendary growth driver at Southwestern Bell who as CEO merged the company with AT&T.

The focus on an authentic buyer journey was also key to my success in my first true revenue leader role at Eduventures. Many things went right and helped us grow a new division from nothing to $10 million in revenue in three short years. We were relentlessly effective at sourcing, progressing, closing, and then expanding almost four hundred college and university partners. We were really good at hearing and responding to the goals of university leaders in a broad range of departments and offices. We listened and responded not only to the collective needs of a group of leaders in the same department at multiple colleges and universities, but also to the individual needs of each leader for their department at their college.

When I was first experiencing success at RAND engaging business leaders, my friends in the business would ask kiddingly, "How does this academic geek get so many top business leaders to engage?" The question often came from those same friends who later provided me with the documents on building a buyer journey or customer-centric selling when I moved to Eduventures. At first I thought, "Well, RAND has a great reputation for research, and I'm just leveraging the RAND brand."

Over time, I realized there was more to it. After RAND, Kaplan, and Eduventures, I had two more experiences as a go-to-market and revenue leader, with CollegiateLink and Plus Delta Partners. In both cases, I again set in motion rapid success in shifting the growth trajectory to drive faster revenue acceleration.

The reality was, my success was the result of *not* being trained in traditional corporate go-to-market and sales strategy.

Had I been trained in the corporate approach, I would have been steeped in a product-oriented buyer journey rather than having the opportunity to build a go-to-market approach that focused on an authentic buyer journey.

Authentic Conversations Lead to Better Outcomes

After more than a decade as a revenue leader, I started Winalytics in late 2014 to share this approach on shifting from a product-driven pitch to authentic conversations with more revenue leaders. I have now worked with hundreds of companies and revenue leaders as a consultant, advisor, and mentor.

In the course of all of this, I have learned a few core principles that I have put into practice as an executive and a consultant, and then finally turned into this book. If you put these ideas into practice, you will not only experience greater professional success, but also find your work more fulfilling. You will have happier buyers and customers, more collaboration with your peers, and the opportunity for your job to become an endless learning opportunity. Here are those core principles:

Shifting from product-driven selling to authentic conversations leads to faster business growth. I have seen this shift contribute directly to turning early-stage companies from mediocre growth trajectories to exceptional trajectories with

250–300 percent growth gains for multiple years running. Even if an early-growth company has a transformational product, selling the transformational product is a lot less successful than helping buyers understand how transformation can help them with key business goals. For more established companies or companies that are in more established markets, I have seen gains of 30 to 40 percent revenue productivity.

Shifting from product-driven selling to authentic conversations leads to happier buyers and customers and much higher work satisfaction for you. When your buyers or customers perceive you as a partner or trusted advisor in helping advance their key initiatives, the friction goes out of buyer or customer conversations. It is more about qualifying for fit on both sides. Buyers and customers will give you more of their time and bring more positive energy to each interaction.

Shifting from product-driven selling to authentic conversations leads to improved revenue outcomes across all of your go-to-market teams. When your customers are more engaged and sharing more information, you win more and quicker at every step of the buyer and customer journey. For marketing and sales development teams, it means the same pool of prospects to yield a lot more quality opportunities. For sales teams, it leads the same set of sales deals to yield more closed-won dollars. For account management and customer teams, it leads the same installed base of customers to yield more expansion and upsell dollars.

Shifting from product-driven selling to authentic conversations leads to faster learning and growth in your job role. Each buyer or customer conversation becomes an opportunity to find the pattern for aligning buyer goals with company products in ways that will not only thrill and delight your buyer or customer but also move you faster toward booking revenue on a new or expansion deal.

Here is what I have also learned about the chief barrier to realizing the benefits of an authentic buyer journey:

The main barrier to adopting an authentic buyer journey is in your mind. In Winalytics's own client conversations, we are often asked by CEOs, chief revenue officers (CROs), and sales and customer success leaders, "What leads your engagements to be successful or unsuccessful?" My response: "If your team is receptive to learning, collaborating, and pushing themselves to continually up their game, and you will hold them accountable for this, then we will be successful." In the current B2B environment, top-performing teams learn how to better solve customer problems continually from their customers and other team members. Top teams look for opportunities to continually get better at things they have already done hundreds of times.

When it comes to revenue acceleration, "Zen mind, beginner's mind" wins every time. Unfortunately, there are still a lot of revenue leaders and go-to-market team members who become satisfied with the status quo and stop focusing on learning or getting better. They often go into a buyer situation convinced that they know the answer before even having the conversation. They lead with their product, believing if they share enough features and benefits, they will find one that wows the customer and leads to a deal. They approach training and coaching sessions with an "arms folded" posture, convinced they have "done all of this before" and "know a lot more" than the others in the session.

Some individuals stuck in the traditional go-to-market mindset may be high performers, but the reality is that their resistance to continually learning from their customers and peers is still leading them to underperform.

In this book, you will learn how to accelerate your revenue growth by moving from a product-driven pitch to an authentic buyer journey at every single phase, from initial buyer engagement, through prospecting, early sales discovery, and first meetings, and on to closing new buyers, expanding buyer and customer relationships, and identifying the fastest way to grow in target market segments.

If you are excited about driving faster revenue growth by constantly collaborating and learning from your buyers and team members, this book is definitely for you.

If you believe you are already at the top of your game and have little to learn from the revenue leader stories or the authentic buyer journey model shared in this book, I would still encourage you to continue reading for those nuggets that may help raise your performance.

When I met Susan, the realtor who helped me find my Boston condo, she was a new real estate agent. Because of the way she approached my condo search, I ended up purchasing a condominium with her guidance. I was very happy with the search, and I lived in that condo for years until I met my wife and moved up to Boston's North Shore. Susan was happy too, because she made the sale, which was lucrative for her, and she also had a great reference client. In a profession with a high fail rate, Susan quickly emerged as a successful, established relator because of the way she approached working with real estate buyers.

Susan achieved her revenue and business growth goals because of her focus on an authentic pursuit of buyer understanding and openness to learning, listening, and adapting through the buyer-seller relationship. Many of the revenue leaders and go-to-market team members we have coached to greater success at Winalytics have used the same process to achieve phenomenal performance gains. The ideas in this book can help you secure your goals as a revenue producer or leader as well.

Sharing Company Stories on an Authentic Buyer Journey

In my work with go-to-market teams, I always say, "Do not just claim you bring about an outcome for your buyer or customer. You need to offer evidence." I'm practicing what I preach: in this book you will be able to read more than twenty company stories with examples of how an authentic buyer journey drives faster revenue growth.

In the next chapter, I show in practical terms how an authentic buyer journey drives faster revenue growth with a direct comparison of two companies in the corporate learning market. Both companies use an immersive virtual reality (VR) platform to capture human resource budgets previously spent on classroom-based training on soft skills like leadership, sales, services, and diversity. One of these companies has grown five times as fast as the other by using an authentic buyer journey, while the other has used a more traditional, product-centric selling approach.

With that foundation laid, I show in a three-part progression how to build and use a revenue acceleration playbook.

Part I shows, in three chapters, how to build a value narrative playbook across your go-to-market team. It shows how the most successful go-to-market teams understand that the real purpose of buyer discovery is to get the buyer to define a very specific statement of value or impact that can motivate a purchase. It shows how deeper value discovery allows go-to-market teams to move from generic product pitching to tailored product discussions that build momentum by mapping directly to a buyer's or customer's top goals and desired impacts. It also shows how a value narrative playbook needs to be translated to team-specific playbooks for marketing, sales, account management, and customer success to bring an authentic buyer journey into practice.

Part II shows the specific revenue outcomes that result from an authentic buyer journey built around overall value narratives and team-specific playbooks. Its four chapters each focus on a specific revenue outcome: prospecting as a trusted advisor to produce more new opportunities; selling into buyer value to win a higher percentage of sales opportunities; closing and expanding on value to raise account values quicker; and using customer success as a revenue driver to grow into target markets faster.

Part III focuses on changes to organizational processes, measurement, and skills development to make an authentic buyer journey sustainable. The first chapter shows how top-performing go-to-market teams create shared revenue accountability by adding a new set of measures to team-level goals and processes so you can connect each team's goals to the next team's goal achievement. The second chapter shows how top-performing go-to-market teams can advance from a traditional training model to a team-based learning model.

As you read the stories, you will start to understand that an authentic buyer journey works for companies in all sectors and growth phases. Growth stage companies can learn from enterprise go-to-market teams, and vice versa. Software-as-a-service companies can learn a lot from old-school product companies selling food products or even car rentals. It is quite possible you will learn as much or more from the companies outside your industry or at a different stage of growth than from the peer companies that are most familiar to you.

YOUR NEXT STEPS IN EACH CHAPTER

- **Put it into practice:** Each chapter ends with practices you can put in place immediately. A complete authentic buyer journey involves five different playbooks and more than two dozen plays, but each individual play stands alone and creates value.

- **Support to implement plays:** To support moving into practice, the end of each chapter guides you to a specific set of questions and resources for use individually or with your team.

You can access these resources at winalytics.com/theplays.

2

The Revenue Impact of an Authentic Buyer and Customer Journey

"WE HAVE amazing stories of impact at a blue-chip list of clients that includes Best Western, Coca-Cola, LinkedIn, T-Mobile, and the Air Force Academy," Mark Atkinson, CEO of Mursion, told us. "I am not sure why these successes aren't translating into faster sales growth."

Mark was meeting that day with his VP of Sales, Brentt Brown; VP of Marketing, Christina Yu; and the senior sales team to kick off the next phase of Mursion's growth. The team was sitting in a conference room in Mursion's head office in San Francisco on a late spring day planning for the next fiscal year, which started on July 1. I had the opportunity to join the meeting to support the team in building the next phase of growth. The meeting was the beginning of a process to fully incorporate Mursion's first-mover advantage and unique value proposition across marketing, sales, and account management.

Mursion started the market for immersive VR simulations that blend artificial intelligence and live human interactions to support essential training for skills such as leadership, diversity and inclusion, sales, and customer service. Companies spend tens of billions of dollars each year on essential skills training, often also called "soft skills" training. Mursion's immersive VR helped shift away from generic classroom training or e-learning to an authentic, personalized training experience that could cost-effectively scale across a large group of learners.

"Many first movers lose their market leadership as 'lookalike' competitors copy their success," Mark said. "That is not going to happen to Mursion. I want to be able to take our customer successes and write them down in a way that sharpens our buyer conversations and helps us effectively scale our sales and marketing processes."

Mark wanted his team to create an authentic buyer journey by leading not with a truly transformational product but, rather, with how that product could create a very different outcome from other training offerings for buyers. The conversation began that day with a focus on the sales process.

Mursion Commits to an Authentic Buyer Journey

"How do you currently draw on existing customer successes to support discovery in your sales conversation?" I asked the group.

Brentt spoke up. "You know I've led teams that start with discovery of a buyer's goals and priorities. But, at Mursion, our product is new and different from anything our buyer has ever experienced. We really need to start with a product demonstration so they understand what we are talking about. Also, our buyer goals are pretty much the same in all cases:

they are looking for a way to scale the impact of their investments in soft-skills training."

"I'm wondering," I said to Brentt, "how often you find your team is doing multiple demos to different stakeholder groups without really understanding what the buyer is trying to accomplish."

Brent paused for a moment and looked down in thought. "You know," he said, "you're right. Too often, we have multiple demos before we even know if we're talking to a qualified buyer with a specific problem. It would be helpful to filter out the ones who are curious but not really buyers early on." He looked around at his team. "I bet we could take a blended approach: start with a demo so they understand the power of the platform, and then ask them what training goals immersive VR could help improve or scale." Several of the others nodded thoughtfully.

"That blended approach sounds like a really good evolution," I said. "Staying focused on the buyer does not mean having to be slavish about when and how we get to good 'discovery questions' on their goals and priorities. It means to stop very intentionally a couple of times in conversation to ask if the buyer acknowledges a specific goal or priority that our product can help advance."

Brentt nodded. "That makes sense. And I can see now why it will get all of our teams more conversational with our existing client success stories. It's in the existing stories that Mursion's potential impact on specific priorities or goals is the clearest. I know those stories well. When a prospect is not a hundred percent sure of how to respond to Mursion as a new product category, I can use the stories to suggest a direction and nudge the conversation forward."

"That's exactly right," I said. "And that's why it's so helpful to distill the story Mark is referencing into specific buyer goal areas and buyer impacts. These buyer goals and impacts can be used by every go-to-market team to 'nudge' a buyer or existing customer to understand how Mursion helps them."

Connecting Authentic Conversations Across Go-to-Market Teams

At this point, the conversation shifted from sales to marketing and securing new buyer meetings. "How's it going with prospecting and demand generation to get more initial buyer calls?" I asked. "Are you leading with VR as a transformational new training product, or are you focusing on business outcomes?"

Christina took that question. "The majority of our leads right now are inbound from individuals who have reached out to us, and"—she added with a hint of frustration—"often, these are less senior individuals who are focused on our product demo." She leaned in slightly. "We have started to shift to more proactive outbound outreach to senior buyers focused on Mursion's unique training outcomes—things like scaling participation in leadership training, or diversity and inclusion training, or providing ongoing reinforcement of classroom training."

"Okay, that is a great direction," I said. "When we work with teams on building an authentic journey that puts buyer goals first, product second, we generally start with good discovery and sales execution. Then we move to add fuel to the fire by accelerating prospecting for new opportunities and, where appropriate, focusing on building a more intentional sales-to-customer-success handoff."

Christina looked around at her colleagues. "Can I suggest as a next step that after this meeting we record Mark and take notes on the CEO perspective on a dozen of these key customer stories? In selecting the stories, we can make sure we have good ones for our leadership, diversity and inclusion, customer service, and sales to cover all of our training use cases. We can also pick examples of our successes in key industry verticals like financial services, retail, hospitality, and others."

"I love that approach," I said. "When we think about building an authentic buyer journey, it always starts with telling stories about buyer value—we call these 'value narratives.' The great thing about value narratives is that you can create consistent discovery questions, capability talk tracks, and success stories for each narrative that can be used by all of your go-to-markets. It makes for a more consistent, engaging buyer experience."

A couple months after this spring meeting with Mark, Brentt, Christina, and the sales team, Christina and I had a follow-up call on the success stories. Christina and the team had developed a library of a dozen stories and seeded these stories into all of their go-to-market processes.

"You made quick work of that," I said to Christina. "What were the keys to success?"

"After recording Mark for the CEO's perspective, sales team input was a key part of our process for developing our success stories," Christina said. "I didn't want to spend time on these customer stories and then have them sit on our company website and never be used. I wanted to understand the format that was most likely to fit directly into a sales or account management conversation."

"From what I'm reviewing in the shared folder on success stories, it looks like you came up with a variety of different formats," I said. "I'm guessing sales team input was important for that."

Christina smiled and nodded. "That's right. I wanted to make sure the stories could be used in every phase of buyer and customer interactions. We now have success case snippets along with webinars and research snippets on our website.

The snippets are also used in prospecting outreach. We have short spoken success stories, and three or four bullet points for each story that can be used verbally during a sales call. And we have success case slides that can be used in sales or account management calls where there is an interest in a more detailed walkthrough of a specific client story."

The meetings with the Mursion team that spring started an almost two-year project to build an authentic buyer journey across all sales, marketing, and customer success processes. As CEO, Mark Atkinson set this direction for the team, and the go-to-market leadership team responded. The team's commitment to an authentic buyer journey paid off. Even as new competitors entered the market, Mursion went on a dramatic growth run.

Why an Authentic Buyer and Customer Journey?

As the Mursion example shows, a company focused on an authentic buyer journey trains and enables its go-to-market teams to begin and end each buyer interaction by focusing on what is most important to the buyer. An authentic buyer journey focuses a go-to-market team on speaking to buyers in the language they understand best—namely, the goals, pains, and expected results that shape their work. In an authentic buyer journey, a company's product, story, and mission are valuable and important to buyer interactions to the extent that they support a buyer's specific goal achievement.

An authentic buyer journey works for a simple reason: it keeps the buyer at the center of every interaction in a buying environment saturated with information and distractions.

Today's buyers are overwhelmed with information. They have unlimited amounts of information about a company

Your buyers have access to almost unlimited information about your products. They don't want more product information from your team; rather, **they want to quickly understand how your product helps achieve what they value most.**

and a company's competitors from websites, peer review sites, social media platforms, industry reports, trade magazines, and multiple other sources. Most companies make the problem worse by organizing the buyer journey around their product and company story.

PRODUCT-DRIVEN SALES APPROACH

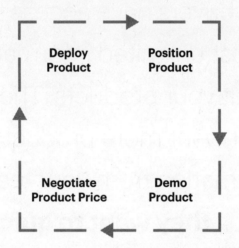

What buyers want most is not more information on your product or company: they want your help cutting through information overload to see how you can help achieve a critical goal or remove a key pain point. This gap, between the old approach of companies pitching their product and buyers wanting an authentic experience anchored in their goals, has been growing for years and is only getting worse.

The challenge emerged first in the sales experience. Almost a decade ago, Forrester Research did a study that found that 80 percent of executives believe meetings with sellers are a waste of time, and three-quarters said sellers are "not knowledgeable about their business" or "their specific business issues."

Even as the information-abundant environment has changed buyer behavior, most sales teams have not adapted. Gartner's research on the new B2B buyer journey shows an expansion of individuals contributing information and inputs in the buying process. The typical buying process now has more than seven people involved. Gartner also found that two-thirds of the time in the buying process was spent looking at product alternatives, with just 20 percent of the time spent with vendors. Yet, most sales people squander this narrow window of time to make an impact. Sales teams over-share product options and information, believing buyers need to "consider all options" and that "more information leads to better decisions."

It is not just in sales but also in marketing and customer success where there is a growing disconnect between buyers who want authenticity and go-to-market teams who focus on product. Go-to-market teams have responded to the demand for information by doubling down on content development, but this content too often has an inside-out perspective, focusing on the company's product and story rather than on the buyer's journey. In fact, a recent article on Medium.com shared research showing that while 91 percent of B2B companies use content marketing and 56 percent increased content production in the last twelve months, only 30 percent have a defined buyer journey that motivates their content strategy.

The drift back toward a company's product and product pitching is strong across sales, account management, and customer success teams. There are two reasons: 1) buyers and customers are often quick to ask for more details on a product or to insist that they need a product demonstration, and 2) go-to-market team members in marketing, sales, and customer success are comfortable with their product and standard product talk tracks. Conversations on buyer or customer goals, by contrast, are fluid and can be unpredictable.

To build an authentic buyer and customer journey, you need to begin and end every conversation focusing on what matters most to that buyer or customer. **Resist the temptation to drift back into product pitching mode.**

As we will see in the company stories throughout this book, investments in enabling an authentic buyer journey are well worth the return. The commitment to putting buyer goals first and product second accelerates growth at each phase of the buyer journey.

Mursion Versus Salento: Two Different Growth Trajectories

To begin to understand how an authentic buyer journey can drive revenue growth, let's compare the growth trajectories of Mursion and Salento (not its real name), another company offering immersive VR. Mursion is a client of Winalytics; Salento is not. I analyzed both companies with the same go-to-market diagnostic I use when I begin a comprehensive review of a company's commitment to an authentic buyer journey.

The diagnostic review starts with the website and screen captures of the home page, as well as any pages related to product and services, how it works, resources, content, community, and About Us pages. I sign up for the company's newsletters and wait to receive prospecting outreach emails. I then use the website to book a demo. During the demo, I take screenshots of their sales deck structure and presentation, and I take notes on the structure of questions, product discussions, and offers made in the call. I look at the follow-up email to the sales call. In all cases, I am comparing the weight of leading with a buyer's goals and desired impacts that might result from a partnership with a new company against that of a focus on leading the buyer experience around the company's product.

With Mursion and Salento, the comparison using this diagnostic was straightforward. Mursion and Salento both use immersive VR training to help companies deliver experiential learning at scale for soft skills like leadership, customer service, sales, and diversity and inclusion. Both have developed their immersive VR offerings to tap into a huge market for corporate training that is variously estimated to be between $87 billion and $142 billion. Some of that investment is to train and onboard new employees so they quickly understand their job roles, acquire new skills, and learn the company culture. Other training focuses on existing employees the company wants to upskill to improve the employees' performance, job satisfaction, and career prospects, as well as the company's own performance. Managerial training to make leaders more effective is also a common form of investment.

Traditionally, corporate training has been done in an instructor-led classroom environment. Classroom-based training builds consistency in the learning experience and makes interactive learning from peers and instructors possible. However, there is a very high coordination cost to getting all learners to the same physical or virtual space, and opportunities for an individual learning experience are limited. As an alternative, many companies have started to invest in self-paced e-learning solutions, involving video or digital learning as well as coaching solutions. These newer forms of training allow each learner to move at their own pace and for instruction to be individualized, but they make it difficult to create a consistent learning experience, and they miss the social and interactive elements of learning that are so critical for skill and behavioral retention in employees.

While both companies offer the same category of product, their growth trajectories could not be more different. Each company first launched their immersive VR platform for soft-skills training in 2014. Nearly a decade later, Mursion has become the market leader for immersive VR, with around

$20 million in revenue, a plan to become a $50 million company, and inclusion in the *Financial Times*'s 2021 list of the fastest-growing companies in America. In contrast, Salento has reached only a fraction of Mursion's revenue.

It's About Us Versus It's About You

While there are many factors that shaped these two very different growth trajectories for Mursion and Salento, one of the important factors is a very different buyer journey.

Salento uses a very traditional, product-centric approach to the buyer journey. At the top of the company's website home page, there is a nod to experiential learning being linked to a superior workforce. However, after this mention of a potential buyer goal, the home page immediately focuses on Salento's award-winning technology, followed by a section on the award they received, then a section called About Us, and a section called Our Products. The product-centric focus continues in prospecting outreach to new potential buyers. Prospecting emails focus on their branded immersive platform as the ultimate training and development platform proven to improve business results. The emails focus on options for VR-only training packages and blended, instructor-led training packages that make training deployments turnkey and also offer a 100 percent unconditional satisfaction guarantee.

Mursion's website and initial prospecting emails to a new potential buyer are completely different. The header on Mursion's home page focuses not on the company or the company's product, but on a series of goals and challenges a buyer may be working on that Mursion can help address. The header rotates through a series of panels on "difficult

PRODUCT-DRIVEN SALES APPROACH
Old Approach

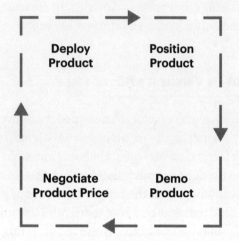

AUTHENTIC BUYER JOURNEY
New Approach

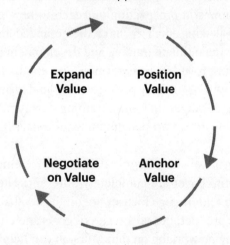

leadership conversations," "making inclusion a reality," "becoming more empathetic," and "upleveling the customer experience through stronger customer success skills."

Like the Salento home page, the Mursion home page continues with a list of top clients. Then it pivots to inviting the visitor to join its peer community. The peer community offers an opportunity to stay abreast of the latest trends and best practices in using virtual reality to build essential skills. The visitor is also encouraged to start the process of building their own custom simulation to reflect the reality of their specific workplace.

The focus on the buyer and the buyer's goals continues into email outreach. Most of Mursion's outreach to new prospects begins with questions like, "Are you working on scaling leadership training? Or building the soft skills in your workforce to create a more diverse and inclusive culture?" The prospecting emails continue by sharing names of other companies that are working on a similar challenge and inviting the new prospect to a value-added mutual discovery call to share some lessons from these peer customers.

Intentionally or unintentionally, Salento is communicating to potential customers, "This is about us, our product, and our success." Mursion, by contrast, is very clearly saying to potential customers, "This is about you, your goals and challenges, and the learnings we can share from our work with your peers."

Authentic Conversations Put
Buyer Goals First, Product Second

The difference between Mursion's focus on an authentic buyer journey and Salento's product-oriented buyer journey, first evident on websites and in prospecting emails, becomes even clearer in sales team interactions. A sample sales conversation with Salento starts with an agenda for the call and then a cursory discovery phase. It then takes a deep dive into Salento's product and the company's available learning modules. The discussion of learning modules is followed by different packages and pricing options.

The Salento sales team has been exposed to enough consultative selling or value-based sales methodologies to start their conversations with a reasonable set of questions. Those questions might include, "What problems or priorities are you working on?" "What are your biggest challenges and pain points?" or "What issues are on your road map for the year?" The questions lead to a discussion of goals and priorities, but they do not necessarily lead to the discovery of anything that will engage a buyer deeper into continuing the conversation.

A sample sales conversation with the Mursion sales team is quite different. The call also starts with an agenda, then moves to a short demo so a buyer understands the potential impact of immersive VR, and then moves to a much deeper discovery phase on buyer value. Mursion's discovery starts with a question like, "Now that you have seen the platform, are there current training or development initiatives that might benefit from this type of learning?"

The questions continue along the lines of, "In the training areas you just mentioned, what are you doing currently?" "What is your ideal state, or what would you like to be doing differently?" and "What's keeping you from moving to that ideal state?" The team is probing to find out if there really are meaningful challenges to solve. The questions also include a focus on the impacts that would result from solving those challenges. For example, "If you could solve your current training and move to your ideal state, what would be the main benefit? Who would be really excited?"

Value narratives support authentic conversations that put buyer or customer goals first and your product second during every single interaction.

As the call continues, it becomes clear that the reason for this deeper discovery is that the Mursion team wants to move from a generic to a very targeted product discussion. By doing deep discovery, the Mursion team is able to build buyer engagement and excitement. Rather than a generic product pitch, they share information on their product and their company that maps directly to a buyer's goals and targeted improvements.

One of the most important reasons for the difference in buyer journey and growth outcome between Mursion and Salento is the presence of a *value narrative playbook* at Mursion and the absence of this playbook at Salento. Value narratives are go-to-market frameworks that accelerate revenue growth by putting buyer goals first and product second in every sales, marketing, and customer success interaction.

As we will discuss in more detail in Part I of this book, a value narrative uncovers a specific route to buyer value through deep discovery, and that discovery is then used to map the company's product and capabilities to what each buyer values most.

Mursion has built a buyer value narrative for each of the four essential skills areas that its immersive VR platform helps its corporate partners scale: leadership, customer service, diversity and inclusion, and sales. Each value starts with several levels of discovery questions to probe for buyer goals, gaps, and targeted impacts. The narrative continues with product talk track and client success cases that provide evidence on a buyer's goals and targeted impacts. The value narrative ends with confirmation questions that allow the buyer to share in their own words the principal points of alignment they see.

AN AUTHENTIC CONVERSATION

Value Discovery
Start with your
buyer goals

Value Mapping
Map product and
content to this goal

Value Confirmation
Confirm your buyer
sees alignment

Authentic Conversations and Buyer and Customer Engagement

Mursion uses a value narrative playbook as the foundation of authentic buyer and customer conversations to help its go-to-market teams avoid three common pitfalls that hurt engagement and revenue growth:

1 They avoid "shallow" discovery by shifting go-to-market teams to the much deeper value discovery needed to identify an impact that can motivate a purchase.

2 They avoid mind-numbing product pitches by moving to product discussions that thrill and delight customers by mapping to specific goals and targeted impacts.

3 They avoid the tendency for marketing, sales, and customer success to have disconnected, unaligned playbooks by having each go-to-market team link its playbooks to the same company-wide value narratives to build consistency for buyers.

Most sales conversations, as well as many account management and customer success calls, start with a "shallow discovery" phase focused on the buyer's goals and priorities. More often than not, this discovery phase is a bit rote, with

An authentic buyer journey will lead to improved revenue outcomes across the buyer and customer journey: more new opportunities, more won opportunities, higher account values, and deeper market segment growth.

a series of polite questions designed to show that the go-to-market team member is interested in what the buyer thinks—without really digging into what the buyer cares about most. A value narrative playbook moves from shallow to deep discovery with several levels of discovery questions to focus not only on a buyer's goals but also on current gaps to goal achievement as well as specific impacts or improvements that might motivate a buyer or customer to take action on a new purchase.

A key to Mursion's growth trajectory was building a "habit of discovery" in its go-to-market teams, whether marketing, sales, or customer success. They expect every buyer interaction to start and end with a focus on discovery, rediscovery, or clarification on what a buyer values most. Good value discovery takes the guesswork out of the purpose of the buyer interaction. It lets your buyers build, in their own language, the target and the bull's-eye that might motivate a purchase.

Most marketing and sales enablement teams have gotten very good at building product-oriented collateral—things like product capability summaries, product battlecards, or competitive positioning documents. Linking product capabilities and customer success stories to specific buyer goals and targeted impacts, however, is a common pitfall for most go-to-market teams. Generic product discussions and demonstrations often bore buyers and lead to disengagement. Overcoming the focus on product is a critical role played by a value narrative playbook.

In many companies, playbooks to guide each go-to-market team's buyer interactions typically do not exist, leaving each team member to develop their own language and approach to managing buyer interactions. Where team-level playbooks exist in marketing, sales, or customer success, they have often been developed independently by each team without a connected sense of buyer value. This leads to higher variability in the buyer journey and limits a company's ability to scale growth.

Mursion has used its value narrative playbook to foster an overarching philosophy and approach to buyer value creation across all go-to-market teams. It has developed revenue playbooks specific to each go-to-market team that suggest individual or coordinated actions to guide specific buyer- and customer-facing situations. All of these playbooks connect to the key discovery questions, capability talk tracks, and success cases in the company-wide value narrative playbook.

An Authentic Buyer and Customer Journey and Specific Revenue Outcomes

Building an authentic buyer journey does not just happen on its own. It takes three key investments of time and attention from go-to-market and revenue leaders:

1 Identifying clear buyer goals and targeted impacts to support the shift from product-driven to authentic buyer and customer conversations.

2 Building the company-wide value playbook and then team-based playbooks to bring an authentic buyer journey into action.

3 Investing in the processes, measurements, and skills development needed to sustain cross-team execution of an authentic buyer journey.

The reward for these investments is higher performance and higher revenue growth. In Part II of this book, we will see how an authentic buyer journey drives better revenue outcomes at every phase of the buyer journey: it generates more new quality prospect conversations and more new sales opportunities; it leads to faster deal velocity, with more of the new opportunities that are produced converting to closed won and becoming new customer accounts; it leads to higher account value with less price negotiation and a faster path to account expansion on those new customer accounts; it leads to deeper market segment expansion in the customer success phase by helping to identify success patterns and peer best practices that engage more buyers in key target market segments.

More New Opportunities

To go back to our comparison of Mursion and Salento, when a prospect goes to Mursion's website or receives a prospecting email, they typically hear an invitation to a value-added conversation around their goals and challenges.

Buyers are a lot more likely to commit to a discovery call with your sales team if you make it clear that you plan to provide a ton of value in early discovery. Buyers expect that, if nothing else, they will take away insights and best practices. I call this "prospecting as a trusted advisor." In fact, Mursion was able to increase discovery calls and sales-qualified opportunities from the same lead pool by 65 percent in about six months after committing to shifting their prospecting to a focus on buyer value.

Salento, by contrast, prospects around its product, product awards, and "money back guarantee." What they are telling buyers is that if you commit to a call, it is going to focus heavily on Salento and their product. This doesn't work as well because no one wants to sit through a product pitch.

Mursion's success in raising the productivity of new opportunity generation was dramatic but not atypical. As we've learned by analyzing our customer data at Winalytics, companies that use buyer value narratives to shift to an authentic buying experience in early discovery raise their new opportunity production from the same set of leads by an average of 45 percent or more. Buyers are simply a lot more interested in engaging in a discovery call with a new vendor when they believe they will take away something of value in managing their own business.

More Won Opportunities

An authentic buyer journey leads to more closed-won deals with higher conversion rates from an initial discovery call. By committing to starting and ending every sales conversation around the buyer's goals and targeted impacts rather than around their product, the Mursion sales team positions itself as trusted advisors and problem solvers. A buyer experiences their interactions with Mursion's sales teams during discovery or stakeholder calls as value-added to their overall decision-making process. The calls help them refine and prioritize their goals and targeted payoffs. The calls also help buyers think critically about return on investment (ROI) and improvement, and actively evaluate alternatives. Buyers appreciate the focus on finding the right fit and so engage more deeply.

If you build your sales process around an authentic buyer journey, it does not mean your team will win every deal, but it does mean they will win a lot more deals. When a sales team focuses on buyer goal achievement first, they get invited to more follow-on calls, have greater access to decision-makers, and receive more collaboration on the buying process. In fact, Mursion raised their discovery call to closed-won rate by almost 60 percent—from the low teens to the high teens—in just under a year.

The buyer experience with Salento's sales team, by contrast, is much more likely to be perceived as a product pitch. The early focus on the modules a customer can buy as well as finding the right package and price can lead the buyer to perceive that the seller's main focus is on "closing a deal" rather than helping the buyer figure out the solution to their critical business goal.

From analyzing our customers, we have seen that companies that anchor sales conversations in buyer goals and payoffs experience average gains of 40 percent or more in deal velocity to closed won. We have seen companies that were closing new opportunities at a 12 percent rate jump to 17 and 18 percent. Teams closing new opportunities at a 25 percent rate have increased the rate by as much as 10 percent.

Higher Account Value

An authentic buyer journey leads to higher account values. By using its buyer value narratives to explore a range of buyer goal areas, the Mursion team has found it easier to target the goal with the highest urgency, strongest ROI case, and least price pushback. Mursion also shortens the time between an initial sale and an upsell. Deep discovery across value narratives helps sales and customer success teams shift from thinking about individual goal areas to focusing on continually expanding buyer value by linking one goal area to a new set of buyer goals and payoffs. It also results in less price discounting and a shorter time frame to land, then expand, both of which increase account values.

By contrast, as mentioned earlier, Salento's prospecting emails offer a "money back guarantee" or "comprehensive instructor-led package" as their introduction to the company. The sales team conversation quickly pivots to modules and pricing bundles. The go-to-market team at Salento is saying, "This is all about making a deal," which naturally leads the buyer to think about pricing and price discounts. Similarly, these buyers have not been educated about or given time to think about a range of goal areas that Salento can address. This means that each time the sales or customer success team introduces a new product, it will be treated as a new purchase rather than a continuation and expansion of value in the existing relationship.

In analyzing Winalytics's clients, we have seen teams that use an authentic buyer journey to align closing an initial sales and account expansion raise overall account values by an average of 20 percent. Exposing buyers to deep discovery across multiple goal areas during the sales or customer success process changes the buyer experience in several ways and leads to higher account values for several reasons.

When buyers have had a chance to consider and prioritize a variety of goal areas, they have a clearer understanding of the payoff and ROI outcome to a company partnership and are less likely to push back on price. Similarly, when your buyer knows you can help them with a variety of goals, they are more likely to see you as a strategic partner who can expand to goal achievement in several areas rather than offering a point solution focused on a single problem area. As well, a buyer who has been educated on multiple goal areas is more likely to consider upsell or cross-sell opportunities that address new goal areas.

Deeper Segment Growth

Finally, an authentic buyer journey leads to deeper growth in target market segments. Your buyers are most interested in hearing from, and seeing evidence from, peers in their direct market segment or other buyers "just like them." The way buyers talk about their goals, pains, customers, and markets vary in important ways from segment to segment.

Mursion has used its buyer value narratives to create versions of discovery questions, capability statements, and evidence of buyer impact in the specific voice of the customer for specific market segments. They have used case studies with clients such as Best Western, Coca-Cola,

Investments in new organizational processes, cross-team measurement, and a shift to a team-based skills model are all necessary for an authentic buyer journey to be sustainable.

LinkedIn, Nationwide Bank, T-Mobile, and the Air Force Academy to highlight specific skills use in areas like leadership, diversity, or customer service and to show success in specific market verticals like financial services, retail, hospitality, and others.

Another very clear way in which Mursion and Salento are sending different messages to their potential clients is through their blog and blogging practices. Both companies' blogs do a nice job of featuring use cases for the type of soft skills that their platforms can develop. All but one of Salento's blog posts are written by someone at the company or a company executive. Many of Mursion's blog articles, on the other hand, are written by thought leaders, experts, and company executives who are not Mursion customers. Mursion is very directly saying to its potential buyers and current customers, "We want to invite you into a peer community focused on best practices for building key skills."

Organizational Supports for an Authentic Buyer and Customer Journey

To make an authentic buyer journey sustainable and to secure the revenue gains it promises, Mursion also needed to invest in new organizational processes, measures, and skills. Sales, marketing, and customer success have different DNA and different roles in building an authentic buyer journey. Many companies stop there. They say marketing is good at identifying and engaging buyers, sales is good at working deals, and customer success is good at customer care and account deepening, so those specific things are what they measure for each. Unfortunately, focusing only on team-level goals and processes leads to slower revenue growth. It makes the buyers do too much work in moving through the buyer journey, creating friction that leads to lost deals and fewer upsells.

After building value narrative playbooks across its go-to-market team, the Mursion team also developed new measures and processes to create shared revenue accountability. The focus was on adding a new set of measures that connect each team's goals to the next team's goal achievement. The cross-team measures are the most important for faster revenue growth by keeping buyer value at the center.

Mursion also shifted from traditional skills development with a focus on stand-alone training to a team-based skills model. In an environment where buyers have access to a large number of alternatives and need to sift through large volumes of information, go-to-market teams need to continually sharpen their skills to anchor on buyer goals and payoffs.

Without that, there is often a drift back to product pitching. Customers frequently ask for more product information or demonstrations. The product discussion is easier and more stable. The go-to-market team member can walk through a very scripted set of talking points. Product enablement with sell sheets and battlecards is often well developed; enablement related to anchoring on a buyer's goals and targeted impact, less so.

Mursion's team-based model combined developing shared playbooks, team training to introduce and socialize best practices around these playbooks, and then individual application and coaching. In making the best practices of top performers more fully available to middle performers, team-based skills development was a key component in raising the performance of Mursion's prospecting and sales teams.

Now that we've seen an example of how an authentic buyer journey can lead to dramatic growth gains, let's jump into Part I of the book. We will start with foundational pieces around how a value narrative playbook can shift from shallow to deep buyer discovery, from product pitching to buyer value mapping, and from a friction-filled buyer journey to a seamless buyer journey with clear hand-offs from one go-to-market team to the next.

YOUR NEXT STEPS ON VALUE PLAYBOOKS

- **Identify your value narratives:** What are the three or four revenue, cost, process improvement, and user experience goals that connect all of your buyer personas?

- **Link buyer personas to value narratives:** Which value narratives do your C-, VP-, and director-level buyers as well as your user buyers care about the most?

The supplemental content for this chapter will help build your value narratives to position your unique value to your buyers or customers. You can develop value narratives as an individual contributor or as a team. Access this content at winalytics.com/theplays.

PART I

A Value Playbook and an Authentic Buyer and Customer Journey

3

Value Discovery as the Foundation

"OUR BUSINESS success has come from focusing on the idea that the customer does not buy a product or a feature, but a solution to a business problem," stated Jarin Schmidt, chief experience officer at Credly. Jarin and I were speaking via videoconference, but his broad smile and entrepreneurial excitement for his work at Credly were palpable even in the remote format. I remember thinking, "This call is going to be fun."

"Our challenge is that skills badging is such a new idea that our buyers and team can get focused on badging as a 'cool concept' and forget to do good discovery on the business problem it solves," Jarin continued.

In the e-learning ecosystem, a *digital badge* is an indicator of an accomplishment or skill that can be displayed, accessed, and verified online. While relatively new, digital badging has been growing in popularity since a standard for digital badges was first developed in 2011. Organizations ranging from professional associations to employers to learning institutions have adopted digital badging, sometimes called *skills badging* or *digital credentialing,* to enable people who participate and successfully complete their programs to communicate their achievement online in a recognized and verifiable format.

In 2018, when Jarin joined Credly, the company was a nimble start-up with about twenty employees. Jarin came to Credly as part of its acquisition of Pearson Education's badging business, called Acclaim. Prior to joining Credly, he had spent more than seventeen years working in various roles at Pearson, including four years on the Acclaim team.

I asked Jarin why he had made the move from a "safe" corporate job to an entrepreneurial venture. "The Acclaim badging system had been just one element of a large portfolio of education services at Pearson," Jarin answered. "At Credly, the focus was on doing that one thing really well." He smiled slightly and added, "I certainly did stop to wonder if this cool concept of badging could solve enough business problems to turn a start-up into a successful stand-alone business!"

Jarin began to share the reasons he was confident that Credly could solve enough business problems through its digital credentialing to become a successful growth company. "Whether it is a big or small company environment, at the end of the day, business growth is all about 'problem finding.' In the years I worked on digital badging at Pearson, I had gotten really good at problem finding. I was always able to show human resource executives a wide variety of talent management challenges that digital badging can help solve. So, I knew the market opportunity was huge."

Jarin was drawing on a key best practice in building an authentic buyer journey: starting not with his product, but with a problem or, even better, several problems the buyer is working to solve.

Credly Uses Deep Value Discovery

Jarin elaborated on how good buyer discovery was key to Credly's early success. "There are many business challenges that result from skills not being effectively documented," he explained. "A professional skills credential can be an abstract idea, but it gets a lot more concrete when we link to specific, desirable business outcomes."

He then gave me several examples of specific challenges that he used to focus conversations with corporate buyers. He shared that better skills badging can improve new employee recruiting by increasing brand awareness among passive candidates. Or, it can increase employee retention with better internal career paths. It can also support higher training completion rates by showing the promotion opportunities that result from training participation.

Jarin's instinct that skills badging could solve a range of buyer problems was on target, as evidenced by Credly's consistent and rapid year-over-year growth since 2018. With a focus on solving identified business challenges, Jarin and his team signed up a lot of top corporate buyers, including places like KPMG, DocuSign, and Tableau.

"After proving we had identified a broad market problem, we next had to make 'problem finding' repeatable," Jarin said. I nodded and smiled: Jarin clearly had a strong entrepreneurial instinct for the need to build an organization to execute an idea. "So often," he continued, "an early leader's vision and instincts fail to take hold in a sales team. Knowing this, we trained all of our sales team members to start each prospect conversation by sharing a 'buffet menu' of common use cases and then asking the buyer to identify the most important use cases for their own situation."

Jarin's team draws on best practices for buyer discovery by opening their meetings around this "menu" of business

You can quickly focus a buyer or customer conversation by offering a "menu" of business goals you can address together. Alternatively, you can share a short overview of your product and then pivot to the menu of goals.

goals and challenges. Rather than open-ended discovery, or focusing on just a single goal or challenge area, they use a structured opening to probe on several potential buyer goals. Broad discovery on several goals leads to quicker identification of high-urgency problems.

"When a sales team member starts to talk about the badging features that appealed to a buyer," Jarin continued, "we take them back to buyer goals by asking which use cases got them most excited and what talent management problems they needed the most help solving."

Drawing on several levels of buyer discovery is another best practice used by Jarin's team at Credly that you can implement in your own sales process.

"As we move deeper into the sales process," Jarin said, "and identify specific goals, we then ask more about how a gap in skills badging can hurt that goal achievement. If a buyer is focused on talent recruiting, we ask about goals and obstacles to recruiting passive job candidates. We ask if they believe skills credentialing will raise their brand with passive candidates. If a buyer is interested in training completion rates, we want to know how training and career promotion are linked for employees, and if digital badging can create a stronger linkage."

Many teams stop at first-level discovery on a buyer's goals. They ask polite questions about goals as a warm-up to start talking about their product. However, they never ask a buyer to explain what may be keeping them from achieving their goals or how the buyer might define success around a goal. Your conversations with your buyers and prospects really do not turn into sales conversations until you get to a specific outcome that a buyer cares about deeply.

Jarin knew this, and he confirmed it. "We found that buyers with a specific goal and a known gap to achieving this goal are more motivated purchasers," he concluded.

Credly created a growth juggernaut by having its sales team start each prospect conversation focused on value discovery rather than Credly's product. By committing to doing high-quality discovery before talking about their product, the Credly team makes it possible for its buyers to tell them directly the goals, gaps to goals, and impacts that are most likely to lead to a closed deal and successful partnership.

How Deep Discovery Leads to Buyer Engagement

Sellers do not close deals, buyers close deals.

This sales truth was impeccably documented by Neil Rackham, author of the 1988 classic *SPIN Selling*. The role of the seller is to guide the buyer to a close with the right discovery questions—questions that surface a prospect's pain and turn it into potential value.

Rackham's insight is more true today than it was in the 1980s. Today's buyers are saturated with an almost overwhelming amount of information from websites, peer review sites, and social media sites. They come to meetings with you and your team deeply informed, with a strong sense of their goals and a lot less time for sellers. They do not want more information on your product or company. What they do want is your help cutting through information overload to understand quickly if you can help achieve a critical business goal.

The heart of an authentic buyer journey lies in guided buyer discovery. I often say to go-to-market teams, "Our buyers will build the target and the bull's-eye for exactly what they will purchase if we just ask the right question." The reality, however, is that good buyer discovery is a broken skill.

More often than not, the discovery phase is "shallow discovery," as discussed in chapter 2. It is a set of high-level questions about a buyer's goals, pain, and priorities that do

Good buyer discovery takes the guesswork out of acquiring new customers and upselling existing customers. It lets customers tell you exactly what they care about most and what will motivate them to purchase.

not really lead to meaningful information about what would motivate a buyer to action. Shallow buyer discovery is often the prelude to a product pitch. You may see this pattern with your sales and go-to-market team members: they ask a few questions, thank the buyer for sharing more about their goals and priorities, and then proceed to give a canned product discussion or demonstration without referencing anything they learned from the buyer.

You may also have seen one of the go-to-market teams that have in recent years started to de-emphasize buyer discovery altogether in favor of leading with "buyer insights." Sales methodologies like challenger selling, disruptive selling, and insight selling focus on delivering insight about an unknown problem or unconsidered need to motivate buyer engagement. The idea behind this approach is that if the buyer does not even know their needs, there is little value in buyer discovery.

Both shallow discovery and insight-based sales methodologies that diminish discovery lead to a less authentic buyer journey and cause your buyers to disengage. They anchor your buyer interactions not on what the buyer values the most or on the buyer's critical goals, but on your company's product, expertise, or insights. Many go-to-market teams that have a strong focus on sharing buyer insights do not recognize that, from a buyer point of view, an "insight pitch" is not less alienating than a "product pitch." Until the buyer is ready to hear your insight, it is unlikely to have much of an impact.

Three Levels of Value Discovery

As we saw in the story of Credly, good buyer discovery is not an open-ended or random set of questions; it is a *guided* set of questions. It is focused on leading the buyer toward a business goal and specific impact that your company and product can help address. The Credly example also shows how good discovery happens at three levels.

THREE LEVELS OF VALUE DISCOVERY

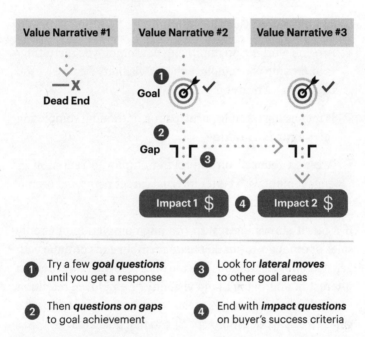

| Value Narrative #1 | Value Narrative #2 | Value Narrative #3 |

1. Try a few **goal questions** until you get a response

2. Then **questions on gaps** to goal achievement

3. Look for **lateral moves** to other goal areas

4. End with **impact questions** on buyer's success criteria

Level 1 discovery focuses on *goal questions* that help identify your buyer's goals, priorities, or initiatives. This is where shallow discovery typically stops. Level 2 discovery focuses on *gap questions* that probe on capability or organizational gaps that are keeping your buyer from achieving their goal. Gap questioning offers a powerful opportunity to lead a buyer to a capability or insight, but it is done through a question rather than a statement. Level 3 discovery focuses on *impact questions* that highlight a financial, organizational, or emotional impact of value to your buyer. The impact questions get the buyer to define a successful outcome and connect fixing a current gap to this successful outcome.

For Credly, potential discovery questions at each level could include things like these:

Level 1 Discovery: Goal Questions

- Are you working on improving new employee recruiting? Is improving your employer brand visibility for passive job candidates a priority?

- Is increasing training participation or training completion rates a current priority?

- Are you focused on improving employee retention or engagement with better internal career paths and promotion opportunities?

If a buyer shows interest in training completion, a Credly sales or other go-to-market team member can continue with gap and impact questions like the ones below. If they show an interest in improving brand visibility or employee retention, similarly, the go-to-market team member can continue with gap and impact questions specific to that goal area.

Level 2 Discovery: Gap Questions for Training Completion Goal

- What is your current training completion rate for different courses? Are there specific courses with a big gap between your current state and target ideal state?

- What have you already tried in order to increase training completion? What has worked or not worked?

- Do you think badging multiple skills in a training course could increase motivation to finish?

- Could badging make a stronger connection between training completion and job promotion?

Level 3 Discovery: Impact Questions for Training Completion Goal

- Have you set a goal for improving training completion? What is that goal?

- Who would be excited about improving training completion rates? You? Your team? Your VP?

- Would higher-training completion help with managing training resources, scheduling, or costs?

The value narrative playbook introduced in chapter 2 makes good value discovery at these three levels repeatable across a go-to-market team. It helps all team members lead buyer conversation around their key organizational goals, which might include things like improving revenue, reducing costs, managing budgets, increasing staff impact, and changing a user experience or an employee behavior. It gives a guided set of questions for each goal area to further explore buyer goals, gaps, and potential impacts. The example above gives gap and impact questions only for the training completion goal area; in full value narrative playbooks, there are gap and impact questions for each buyer goal area.

Without a known gap and specific impact, a buyer conversation is likely to remain superficial rather than substantive. It is the gap to achieving a key goal and the belief that a vendor's product or solution may be able to close the gap that marks the beginning of a true sales conversation. Buyers

Good discovery goes beyond high-level questions on goals and priorities. It uses several levels of questions to help you and your buyer identify a specific impact that could motivate a purchase.

without this known gap or meaningful impact that comes from fixing that gap may continue talking, but they are more likely to be "tire kickers," with limited urgency to get into a meaningful buying conversation.

Getting a buyer to powerful, recognized—or unrecognized—insights is a key goal of the value narrative playbook. However, rather than leading a conversation with buyer insights, the value narrative playbook focuses on using guided questioning to lead the buyer to their own insights. The best term I have heard for this is "education with questions." Proactively sharing an insight with a buyer and telling them why it is important is really just a different kind of product pitch; it is a lot less powerful than the buyer getting an insight on their own. The process of being guided with questions leads the buyer to be open to hearing and internalizing the insight—and feeling that it is *their* insight.

Broad Value Discovery and Identifying Buyer Impacts

Moving from shallow discovery, or insight pitching, to deep value discovery on what your buyer cares about the most is one key element of an authentic buyer journey. The other is broad value discovery across multiple different buyer goal areas.

Expanding discovery to a range of goal areas is good for the buyer and for the go-to-market team trying to engage that buyer. The Credly team, in our example above, talks about presenting the buyer with a "buffet menu" of goal areas in order to get a response. Presenting the buyer with a range of potential goals and asking for a response shifts the energy in the conversation. It is no longer about trying to sell the buyer something, but rather exploring fit or alignment between the buyer's goals and your company's capabilities.

Broad value discovery also makes it easier for you to find the buyer goal area with the highest urgency and strongest return on investment related to a specific buyer impact. Finding a higher-urgency goal increases the likelihood of your buyer conversation ending in a successful result with a closed-won opportunity. It also tends to lead to less price pushback and less discounting around your won opportunities.

As we will see in chapter 7, expanding discovery to a range of goal areas also improves account management and customer success. It sets up the idea of a "platform sale" that points toward your company and product being able to help a buyer solve multiple different challenges or advance multiple goal areas. It makes it a lot easier for your account managers or customer success managers to leverage a range of buyer goal areas to deepen an existing customer relationship, with a broader set of internal users and potential champions.

Broad discovery in the sales process can also shorten the time between an initial sale and an upsell opportunity. Broad discovery helps all of your go-to-market team members continue to focus on buyer goals, gaps, or impacts that might motivate a purchase.

A value narrative playbook is a key support not only for deep discovery in a single buyer goal area, but also for broad discovery across a range of goals. It continually reminds your go-to-market team about new goal areas to explore and the follow-on gap and impact questions that can be used to build buying energy.

There is always a considerable amount of inertia around buying any new product or service. Agreeing to purchase means the buyer must commit to moving out of their comfort zone by introducing a new system, software, process, or way of doing things. They are also going to have to pay for this privilege. To get your buyers to pay to move out their comfort zone, there has to be a very strong perceived impact.

Whisps Breaks Through Inertia with Buyer Impacts

To understand how important it is to use broad goal discovery to identify buyer impact and build engagement, let's look at the example of Whisps, a fast-growing natural food company.

"We do not have any problem figuring out our buyers' goals," Ilana Fischer, CEO of Whisps, told me at the start of our conversation. "All the food retailers we sell to want to make more money from their shelf space. Our challenge is to discover the business impact that will lead a retailer to take a current product off the shelf in order to make space for our product."

I had reconnected for a video call with Ilana after almost fifteen years. She and I had worked together at Eduventures, the higher education benchmarking research company I described in chapter 1, where I had my first true revenue leader role. I remembered Ilana as a whip-smart analyst. After Eduventures, she got her MBA from the Stern School of Business at NYU and then worked with consultancy Bain & Company, helping Fortune 500 companies build business strategies. She was good at thinking about customers and business growth. I reached out to reconnect because I was curious about how she was applying those skills at a natural food company.

Whisps's mission is to put real cheese back into snacking. The company has achieved fast growth in the natural food market with cheese crisps snacks that combine three things many natural food consumers are looking for: great taste from award-winning cheeses, 100 percent natural ingredients, and low carbs and low calories.

I held up my hand. "Step back for a second. I know the food retail market is incredibly competitive. Even with a great product, how do you get your buyers' attention in the first place?"

"Well, that's exactly it," she said. "Most natural food products are sold around the concept of product quality. When they talk to a retailer, they say, 'We have an amazing oatmeal cookie! We make our own oats! We have only organic ingredients! We bake them with love and care!' To the retailer, it sounds like 'blah, blah, blah.' They hear it all the time."

I was starting to connect the dots on why an uber-smart analyst-turned-CEO was in the natural food business. She sensed a business opportunity in building a different buyer journey in a market sector where competitors focused on their product.

"We flip the switch," she continued. "We do not start with our product; we start with their business goals. We ask, 'Can we talk about how many more dollars we can move for you from the same shelf space?' It not only disrupts the pattern they are used to, but focuses on a key pain area."

Whisps's clever approach to impact buyers' attention by focusing on earning more dollars from the same shelf space, along with the quality of its product, supported quick growth. The company achieved more than $10 million in revenue in just a few short years after launch. I was talking to Ilana at a time when she was looking to increase new sales by over $10 million every single year and was actively looking for strategies to support this next level of growth.

"Okay, so that's a clever way to get your buyers' attention," I said. "Where do things get more difficult? Is it engaging the right buyer or navigating the decision-making process?"

"It's a little of both," Ilana said. "We know exactly who the buyer is for our product. Whether it's at a supermarket like Stop & Shop or a retailer like Target with a big grocery section or a drugstore like CVS with very limited food items, our purchaser is going to be the senior buyer for groceries. These are really busy people. The challenge comes first in getting their attention, and then, more importantly, getting them and their bosses interested in changing up their product mix."

The real goal of buyer discovery is to identify a specific buyer impact— financial, organizational, or emotional—that will motivate the buyer to invest the time, internal political capital, and funding to do something new.

"I assume there's a natural inertia," I said. "The 'if it's not broken, don't fix it' kind of thing that puts the burden on your team to make a very strong case for doing something different."

"Yes. We need to very quickly engage them with something compelling, as you say, or we lose their attention." Ilana paused, leaned back, and looked directly into the camera. "Are there tips you have for a situation like that?"

"Well, tell me this. What is your sales team's goal for their first meeting?" I asked. "Are they focusing on getting the buyer to share what success would be for increasing revenue from their shelf space? Are they looking to get a specific impact statement?"

"Can you say more about an impact statement?" Ilana said. "How would that work for us?"

"It would build on this idea of more revenue from the same shelf space, but be specific on the gap that is keeping them from that goal, and the impact that would get them or their boss or team excited about continuing the conversation," I said. "I can imagine asking your team to finish and follow up on each meeting with a statement like, 'I understand your team is looking for an average increase of five percent in shelf revenue from natural foods products this year. You shared that thirty percent of your current SKUs are underperforming this goal, and that you are particularly interested in finding high revenue, natural foods snacks like Whisps.'"

"Now I get it," said Ilana as she leaned forward. "It takes what we know is the buyer's goal and looks for what you called a 'gap' that is keeping them from that goal, and also highlights what you called an 'impact' that would motivate them to purchase. That requires good discovery work."

"Yes," I said. "Just as important, it requires being very intentional in thinking about the goal for each meeting. Certainly, we will spend time in a meeting building rapport, doing discovery, and sharing our product, but a good meeting is one in which we have strong enough discovery to recap a specific impact statement at the end."

"I can see how if we commit to that type of discovery and specific financial impact, it could help take us to the next level of growth," Ilana concluded.

Impact Statements and Buyer Personas

As the Whisps example shows, your real goal in all value discovery is to get a strong impact statement. A strong impact statement captures, in two to three sentences, a key goal, a known gap that hinders goal achievement, and a specific impact that would support investing in closing that gap to advance the goal.

Buyer impacts can be emotional, organizational, or financial. An impact statement can focus on one or more of these buyer impacts, depending on the priorities of the buyer organization and the individual buyer's style. To go back to our Credly story from earlier in the chapter, there could be a different impact statement for a VP of learning and development who signs off on the budget than for a director of learning design who is interested in learner experience and outcomes.

For example, the impact statement for the VP who signs off on the budget might look like this:

> I understand that you would like to see a 10 percent increase in training completion rates, and you believe digital badging would help by showing a direct connection to job promotion. You also shared that each 1 percent impact in training completion leads to tens of thousands of dollars in savings in additional training seats you do not have to offer.

The impact statement for the director whose main concern is learner experience might look like this:

I understand your VP has set the goal of a 10 percent increase in training completion rates, and you believe digital badging would help. You shared it could help employees directly connect training to job promotion, showcase their skills to discover new career opportunities, and support learning narratives for career growth.

As the Credly example shows, one key strength of the value narratives framework is that it can help you bring many different buyer personas into alignment as a go-to-market team works on engaging new buyers or expanding accounts with existing buyers. While there can be dozens of buyer personas at a target company, there are probably only three or four really important business problems that any product or service can help achieve. Getting to an impact statement for each buyer persona on the same goal areas can be a very powerful way to bring your stakeholder or decision group at your buyer organization into alignment when discussing a partnership opportunity.

GETTING TO AN IMPACT STATEMENT

 Organizational goal related to revenue, cost, process improvement, or user experience

 Identified barrier that creates a gap between the current state and an ideal state

 Targeted improvement with a financial, emotional, or organizational impact

Impact Statements and Deal Momentum

Asking yourself or your team members if you are getting to an impact statement in each buyer conversation is the best way to check whether you are leading buyers through an authentic, personalized journey. An impact statement is specific to an individual buyer. The reality is that until you are able to recap an impact statement specific to your buyer, your product discussions will still be product pitching. You will likely be sharing product features and functionality in the hope that "something sticks" rather than sharing your product in a way that is directly aligned with your buyer's goals and target impact.

The impact statement has to be developed in collaboration with the buyer and is often an iterative process. The best impact statements are written to include the buyer's own words and language. Getting to the right impact statement may involve a back-and-forth discovery, further discovery, and confirmation through a couple of conversations as the buyer helps define what success would really look like for them.

A good impact statement anchors the entire arc of the conversation with a new potential buyer or with an existing customer interested in adding a new product or capability. It is the most important "sell through" tool, giving an internal champion for a product or service a crisp way to present a case for a conversation and bring in other decision-makers. An impact statement should be recapped at the end of an initial discovery call, reconfirmed in each prospect call, and included at the beginning of a follow-up email as a way to keep focus on the goal for a potential partnership.

Discovery on buyer impacts, Level 3 of value discovery, is the most critical. It is the buyer impact captured in an impact statement that can be shared and socialized within a buyer's organization and creates the urgency for a buyer to invest the time, effort, internal political capital, and, eventually, financial resources in doing something new.

Given the importance of an impact statement to buying urgency, every go-to-market team should build into their

The highest momentum in your buyer and customer conversations comes from connecting all buyer personas to the same goal area while offering impact statements tailored to what each persona values most.

playbooks a set of impact questions that capture potential emotional, organizational, and financial impacts. Here are examples that can be customized to be more specific to a company's buyer and product:

Emotional Impacts

- Which of the areas we discussed could remove the biggest pain from your workday?

- Which of the areas we discussed fill a gap that you really need to fill to do your job?

- How could introducing the capabilities we discussed make you a hero to your team?

Organizational Impacts

- How could introducing the capabilities we discussed make you a hero to your team?

- What outcome or improvement would get your VPs, CEOs, or leadership's attention?

- Is the critical goal a named business goal or road map issue for this year?

Financial Impacts

- Could we build an ROI case together? What is a 1–2 percent improvement or your targeted goal worth in terms of increased revenue or decreased cost?

- If you do nothing at all about the challenge and pains we've discussed, is that a sustainable outcome? If not, what's the potential business risk or cost?

Value Discovery Across
the Buyer and Customer Journey

Good value discovery is not isolated to sales, but happens across the buyer and customer journey in each interaction. One of the key strengths of the value narrative playbook is that it builds consistency across sales, marketing, and customer success. This consistency in goals, gaps to goals, and impact questions educate a buyer a lot more quickly on how to best leverage a new vendor or how to deepen their relationship with an existing vendor.

We will explore how value discovery fits each phase of the buyer journey in more depth in chapters 6 through 9 as we look at team-level playbooks that leverage the value narrative playbooks, but here is a short overview.

In marketing and prospecting campaigns, good value discovery means using email, phone, and social outreach to lead with questions around a buyer's unfulfilled goals as well as targeted improvement areas to invite a value-added conversation. Target goal and gap questions in prospecting campaigns can be used to figure out which elements of a company's offering have the highest buying motivation for different buyer personas and different target market segments.

In sales, good value discovery means spending the first five to ten minutes of every sales conversation on discovery or rediscovery of a buyer's critical business goals and the gaps to achieving those goals, as well as potential impacts. Good value discovery leads to much higher buyer engagement with a product or service capability by focusing product discussions and demonstrations on those elements of the offering that are most relevant to the buyer's goals.

In account management and customer success, similarly, good value discovery means reconfirming the buyer's goals and targeted impacts before jumping into implementing a product or service, so you focus implementation and training on the areas most aligned to a buyer's success criteria. Good value discovery for customer success and account managers also means connecting an initial buyer goal area to expansion goal areas that can deepen the customer relationship.

It is putting together goals, gap to goals, and impact discovery throughout the entire buyer journey that creates the opportunities for the fastest revenue growth.

CeriFi Leverages Continual Value Discovery to Grow Faster

Let's look at how CeriFi has used good value discovery throughout the buyer journey to achieve significant growth in the commodity market for financial licensing exams.

I was introduced to Adam Ellingson, executive VP of sales at CeriFi, by a mutual colleague who had worked with Adam at Kaplan. This colleague told me that there was no one better than Adam at driving sales growth. I knew CeriFi sold into top banks and other financial service firms. So, when I joined our scheduled video call, I anticipated a fast-talking, slightly arrogant business driver type. Adam was not what I expected. He showed up wearing a baseball cap and had a mellow, intentional Midwestern style. As soon as Adam started to speak, it became clear that his success as a business leader came from the quality of his thought about the buyer journey, not from an overtly hard-driving style.

"We focus the entire buyer journey on two questions," Adam said to start the conversation. "First, 'What is your success rate today?' Then, 'How could this success rate be higher?'" He was describing the crux of his team's successful approach. "The whole buyer and customer journey needs to be about getting the buyer to continually rethink their goal and deepen their understanding of the key gaps that may be keeping them from that goal."

CeriFi is part of a large but highly competitive market focused on the Series 6, Series 7, and certified financial planner (CFP) licensures, which allow employees in financial services firms to manage other people's stocks, bonds, and investment portfolios. To obtain these licenses, employees must successfully complete regulatory-approved licensing exams issued by the Financial Industry Regulatory Authority (FINRA). That's where CeriFi comes in.

The population of financial advisors is not growing, and they have many program options. There are more than three hundred board-registered programs available to complete the CFP education requirement and a similarly large number of programs for Series 6 and Series 7 licensing. While financial planners can seek out this education individually, larger financial services firms that need staff with these licenses typically set up education programs for their advisor employees and manage participation.

Growth in this market requires a different way of thinking about uncovering buyer value.

Adam finished his coffee and told me more about his team's approach to leading buyers toward CeriFi's unique market position. "CeriFi has brought together a unique set of capabilities to move away from being perceived as an undifferentiated, commodity offering. For us, the real question we need our buyers to answer is, 'What is not happening today in your financial licensure training that is keeping you from raising your test pass rate? What is your current gap? Is it the quality of content, the ability to personalize learning, or using analytics to see the principal barriers to higher success pass rates?'"

Many revenue leaders think of "buyer discovery" as a sales activity, but **top-performing companies do continual discovery on buyer value across sales, marketing, and customer success.**

CeriFi was not an organically grown company. It emerged from the acquisition of many companies, including Dalton Education, Money Education, Keir Financial Education, the Association of Certified Financial Crime Specialists (ACFCS), the Committee on Payments and Market Infrastructures (CPMI), Bionic Turtle, and Pass Perfect. Collectively, the merged companies provided a range of different high-quality content for Series 6, Series 7, and certified financial planner education. They also brought together a banner list of financial service clients including companies such as Ameriprise, Wells Fargo, Merrill Lynch (now Merrill), Fidelity, and UBS. CeriFi has a small business line that focuses on selling financial services training directly to individual financial managers, but the vast majority of its revenue comes from B2B relationships, with a company providing certification training for its employees.

"Most acquirers would be content to just cross-sell high-quality content." Adam was now speaking quickly. "We have brought together all of these assets to be able to focus on re-educating buyers on what is possible. And we want this process of re-education to happen across the entire buyer journey, starting with how we engage new buyers and continuing through to how we start new partnerships and how we look at deepening existing accounts."

Many companies think of discovery around a buyer's goals, pains, and impacts as happening in early discovery, as part of the first introductory sales calls. Adam and his team at CeriFi have built their growth trajectory on the understanding that discovery of a buyer's goals and targeted impacts happens continually through the buyer journey.

"The process of educating buyers on improving Series 6, Series 7, and CFP exam pass rates starts in marketing with a series of self-service buyer journeys," Adam explained. Many go-to-market leaders talk about creating a connected buyer and customer journey, but Adam described how his team had actually done it. "We have content playbooks that automate the early discovery with videos, blog posts, and tools that help explore why someone might want a certificate, the right course for them, and the steps they need to take to get it."

For CeriFi, the value discovery process continues into the sales conversation with a focus on the level of exam pass rate performance that would lead to excitement and the process of getting there.

"Once we have the buyer engaged, we start to qualify toward a pilot program to show the impact of our solution on their exam pass rates," Adam continued. "Often, we try to focus the path on using our three pillars of high-quality content, personalized learning, and learning analytics to improve pass rates. For example, one large brokerage firm that hires thousands of employees each year partnered with CeriFi to increase pass rates by fifteen percent while decreasing time-to-production by twenty-five percent. That success translated to over a million dollars in cost savings."

For CeriFi, the consistency of its value discovery process from the self-service buyer journey to pre-pilot sales calls makes it easier for account managers to push for the close in a way that still feels authentic to the buyer.

"If it looks like we have a fit," Adam concluded, "we will simply say, 'We have talked about the value of a specific rate of improvement in our exam pass rate. Can you give us four weeks to show the impact we can have for your learners?'" There was no mistaking his confidence in the quality of CeriFi's approach.

For CeriFi, the consistency of buyer discovery also makes it easier for account managers to look for opportunities to deepen existing relationships. It is the same set of discovery questions regarding current success rates, desired success rates, and the path to improvements that can be used to identify new employee groups to target for deepening the number of courses.

"With existing partners, the discovery process focuses on their success rate today and their target success rate," Adam said. "However, now we have a chance to plan different types of pilot outcomes and explore both qualitative and quantitative improvements in exam performance. The ultimate aim of a course is to show a quantitative improvement in test scores, but the path is often through more qualitative elements related to a better learner experience."

Value Discovery at the Heart of the Authentic Buyer Journey

As we have seen with the examples of Credly, Whisps, and CeriFi, strong value discovery is at the heart of an authentic buyer journey. In good buyer discovery, you can use guided questioning to have the buyer lead to an impact statement with a specific goal and target improvement that could motivate a purchase.

Impact statements are specific to each individual buyer, and you can use them just as effectively in an initial sale to a new buyer as an expansion sale to one of your current customers. Good value discovery is not specific to just sales and should happen at each phase of the buyer journey, from marketing and prospecting to sales and customer success.

Good value discovery makes it possible to thrill and delight each individual customer by sharing only the product and company information most relevant to the customer's goal. In chapter 4, we will connect good value discovery to deeper buyer engagement and personalization by using a value narrative playbook to identify the capability talk tracks, success stories, impact statements, and other content that maps directly to our buyer goal.

YOUR NEXT STEPS ON VALUE DISCOVERY

- **Value discovery strategy:** What are your top questions to get your buyers to talk about their goals? What about sharing the gaps keeping them from goal achievement? Or the type of impacts that they see as a success?

- **Buyer personas and impact statements:** What financial, organizational, or emotional impacts motivate each of your buyers? What are the similarities or differences between your C-, VP, and director-level target buyers as well as user buyers?

Access supplemental content at winalytics.com/theplays to help you walk through your next steps on building value discovery and impact statement plays as an individual contributor or team.

4

Value Mapping and Value Confirmation

"**M**Y TEAM has access to great content," Rachael Hawkey, True Fit's area VP of sales, East region, told me over a video call. "They have case studies with very clear ROI outcomes, compelling thought leadership white papers, and value-added industry benchmarks. But I'm not sure how well they are really using this content in their buyer conversations."

Rachael is one of those rare sales leaders who is just as good at helping her team drive sales deals and pipelines as she is at coaching on the key skills her team needs to be more effective. I was speaking to her as part of our client work with True Fit. She was sitting in her home office, and behind her on the bookshelf were a number of business and sales books, as well as several pictures of two adorable school-age daughters. For me, this perfectly captured the blend Rachael had of being both a strong sales driver and a nurturing coach. It was because of this blend that I would ask her to evaluate possible directions in the True Fit partnership.

"Is it that they aren't using the content at all, or aren't using it as effectively as you think they could?" I asked. "In my work with go-to-market teams, I've seen that either can be a challenge."

Rachael paused to reflect. "You know, each of my team members definitely has a couple of case studies and data benchmarks that they use consistently, but it feels like they use the same ones over and over. Sometimes it lands, sometimes it seems to distract from the business case we are trying to make to the customer. "

"That's pretty common," I said. I wanted Rachael to know that we were talking about a coachable skill area and that there was a path to improvement. "The product demonstrations and discussions offered by sales teams are often far too generic. The team member presents a standard run-through of the product or case study rather than mapping the product back to a buyer's specific goals and targeted impacts."

True Fit offers an AI-driven retail platform that personalizes every step of a consumer's retail journey, helping shoppers find the right products, styles, and sizes. True Fit's buyers are footwear, apparel, and retail companies that want to leverage personalization to improve the overall consumer experience. Those companies use True Fit technology primarily on their customer-facing websites to aid buying decisions and drive loyalty.

Through its retail company clients, True Fit serves almost two hundred million retail consumers who use the True Fit recommendation engine to guide their shopping experience. In turn, True Fit uses data from this large group of retail consumers to continuously expand and evolve its industry-leading fashion genome, which combines this data with data on more than seventeen thousand brands to drive its unique recommendation engine. The size of consumer data is impressive. However, the data set begins to generate business value for an individual retailer only when it can be directly linked to that retailer's goals for revenue growth and cost reduction.

True Fit Links Value Discovery and Value Mapping

Rachael paused, reflected, and took some notes. "Now that I think about it, the way we use product materials and case studies may not be serving us well," she said. "Our product demos and content assets are often presented as stand-alones not well linked to buyer goals. We have access to this large group of retail consumers to build an amazing data set and generate rich and detailed content marketing for our sales team. Those product discussions, our case studies, and other content assets really need to link to specific revenue goals for each buyer."

"You nailed it," I said. "You have a very experienced sales team, skilled at facilitating leadership-level conversations across multiple departments at buyer companies. They could probably benefit a lot from building a set of True Fit value narratives that make it easier to tell a story for each buyer. The rubber hits the road in that story specific to each buyer, connecting retail personalization to revenue achievement."

Rachael leaned forward slightly. "That sounds interesting. Can you say more about how value narratives work?"

"A value narrative is a framework to link each buyer's specific goals to True Fit's most aligned capabilities and client success stories," I said. "There is a set of discovery questions that guide a conversation in each goal area. With clarity on a buyer's specific goal and targeted impact, the value narrative then connects capability talk tracks and client success stories that present evidence on how True Fit helps with goal achievement."

Buyers tune out when your product presentation is not linked to their specific goals. **If you don't know their specific goals and targeted impacts, it's probably too early to talk about your product.**

"I see," Rachael said. "It's a way of really understanding what each buyer wants out of conversation with us, so we can then share the right product capabilities, content assets, success stories, and so on."

"That's right," I said. "A value narrative leads to much quicker buyer engagement because it makes mapping products and company capabilities to a buyer's specific goals more structured and repeatable."

"I'm wondering if you find that senior salespeople push back on using value narratives," Rachel said, furrowing her brow slightly. "Do they feel like they are being scripted?"

"I actually think it's the opposite," I said. "We call it a 'value narrative playbook,' not a 'value narrative script.' It does include a set of discovery questions and capability talk tracks by buyer goal area, but each individual salesperson needs to find their own voice and language. The structure helps senior sellers refine their own art of selling. It frees up a lot of mental energy, which supports more individual creativity on building buyer engagement and deal strategy."

Rachael took action on our conversation. She, her two other area sales VP colleagues, and the marketing team began collaborating to build out four value narratives around the ways the True Fit retail personalization platform created value for its company buyers. The four areas of value they focused on were:

1 Driving more web traffic through personalized real time targeting or retargeting of buyers with footwear and apparel offers most aligned to each consumer's preferences.

2 Converting more web browsers to buyers by improving the number of direct product matches appearing in those first three items on the webpage, which accounted for 64 percent of click-throughs.

3   Reducing returns by an average of 20 percent or more by getting more consumers' size and style preferences right the first time they purchased.

4   Increasing the lifetime value of retail customers by 3–10 percent with lifecycle personalization, which aligns marketing outreach and product offers to engage the most profitable customers.

The sales and marketing leadership team also developed a set of value discovery questions to educate buyers on areas of potential goal and impact alignment. It included topics like the following:

* Frictionless personalization: How do you match consumers to clothes they are most likely to buy?

* Purchase confidence: How are you using personalization on style and category to drive customer conversions? Or increase consumer confidence in a purchase?

* Size-related returns: Do you have an approach to size and fit recommendations that can help reduce fit as the most significant category of returns?

* Holistic view and loyalty: How do you use a holistic customer view and their personal information to increase the relevance of product offers and drive loyalty?

The discovery questions for each value narrative were also mapped to product talk tracks to specific goal areas. These talk tracks are typically a discussion of capability and also evidence on the revenue impact for the buyer's organization:

* Frictionless personalization: True Fit matches people to clothes they are statistically most likely to buy and least

likely to return. We help you surprise and delight your customers.

- Purchase confidence: True Fit provides personal fit ratings and size recommendations that deliver 4–8 percent incremental net revenue gains by increasing purchasing confidence and increasing the number of browsers that become buyers.

- Size-related returns: True Fit has helped several of its retail partners reduce returns by 20 percent or more by curating products for each buyer with fit details to eliminate size guesswork, and recommending more items or replacements for out-of-stock items.

- Holistic view and loyalty: True Fit's dashboards support hyper-personalization for each buyer with a holistic view of other brands bought alongside yours in online and in-store purchases. Our partners, who are putting this holistic view into practice, have each increased lifetime value from 3.3 percent to 9.7 percent.

A few weeks after the value narratives project was complete, I was on a call with Rachael again.

"How's it going with using the four value narratives identified by the sales and marketing leadership team?" I asked. "Are you having each of your team members identify specific discovery questions, capability talk tracks, and content assets from the value narratives?"

Rachael smiled and retrieved a piece of paper from her desk. It was a one-page sheet of discovery questions. She showed me a bunch of yellow highlights. "I asked each of my account executives to print out the same document and highlight in yellow their top discovery questions by buyer goal area. I wanted them to take ownership. Then I asked them to prep these questions for each prospect conversation and that I wanted to hear those questions in our next call with the prospect."

"That's great that you're asking them to take ownership of the discovery questions," I replied. "And is coming up with their own questions by value narrative also helping to pick the most relevant content examples?"

Rachael had a look of satisfaction with the work she and her team had done to up their game. "Overall, I'm finding my team using content assets that are much better aligned to goals in each buyer discussion. They are consciously using the value narrative to drive content choices. They refine the slides they pick for their sales deck, and they tailor assets they send with their follow-up emails directly to each buyer conversation."

"And did the senior sales people find that this framework felt too scripted?" I asked.

"As you suggested, it was the opposite," Rachael said. "I think they saw really quickly that the framework made it easier to prepare and follow up on their buyer meetings with the right questions and content. It freed up time and mental space to focus on the strategy for each call."

Value Mapping and Product Discussions

In chapter 3, we walked through how a good value narrative starts with strong discovery on a buyer's goals and targeted improvements. Good value discovery takes the guesswork out of marketing and sales work on acquiring new customers and customer success or account management work on upselling existing customers. It begins the authentic buyer journey by letting your buyers tell you exactly what they care about most and are most likely to purchase.

Value narratives map buyer and customer goals to your product in a consistent way, which frees up your team's mental energy to hear and respond to each buyer in a personalized and creative way.

Once you have a clear understanding of a buyer's goal and targeted impacts, your focus then shifts to value mapping. Value mapping means providing evidence that a company can help advance a buyer's goal. It links a company's capabilities to buyer goals, showing how those capabilities can resolve current gaps, and it provides evidence that those capabilities will lead to buyer impact or payoff.

The transition from value discovery to value mapping should start with confirming an understanding of the buyer's goal. A verbal recap of the buyer's goal builds trust and rapport. It demonstrates active listening and understanding. It keeps the focus on engaging the buyer by sharing only product and company information most relevant to their goal. You can recap both organizational and individual goal areas with phrases such as:

- I heard you say that X and Y are top company priorities. Did I hear that correctly?

- My takeaway is that your organization is prioritizing X, Y, and Z. Is that correct?

- You mentioned X, Y, and Z goals. Which of those is most important to your role? Which keep you up at night or are the most difficult for you to accomplish?

- You mentioned X, Y, and Z goals. Which are on this year's product or business road map? Which are most important to your VP or CEO?

Once you confirm a buyer's goal, you can focus next on the product capabilities that help advance it. Product capabilities are best expressed in short two- or three-sentence capability talk tracks that give a brief overview of key functionality, address a gap area for a buyer, and explain how this will move that buyer from their current, less-than-ideal state toward a state closer to their goal.

After presenting one or more capability talk tracks aligned to a buyer's goal, the next step in value mapping is presenting direct evidence of how you can help the buyer's goal achievement. It is not enough just to claim impact; a buyer wants to see it demonstrated. By far, the most effective type of evidence is a success story about another customer you have already helped to achieve the desired results. The closer the alignment in the success case to the buyer's goal area, buyer role, and market segment, the better.

VALUE MAPPING AND
VALUE CONFIRMATION PLAY

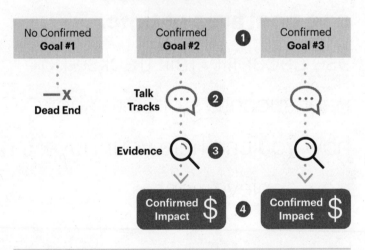

1. **Recap and confirm goal(s)** before presenting product

2. Share **capability talk** tracks aligned to goal

3. Share **success/impact stories** showing goal achievement

4. Ask buyer to **confirm value** with first and top impact(s)

The best product discussions are organized into short presentations, one goal area at time. They use capability talk tracks and peer success stories to show how you can help your buyer's goal achievement.

Let's go back to True Fit to look at how value mapping might work using the company's value narrative for reducing returns:

> I understand that your COO is looking to reduce returns by as much as 15 percent over the next year. You shared that your outdoor clothing lines are the biggest problem for returns. You also shared that you currently give fit guidelines to your web shoppers but do not have any personalization technology.
>
> True Fit's platform reduces returns by curating products for each of your web shoppers with fit details to eliminate size guesswork. The platform recommends more items or replacement items to increase the likelihood of the right fit on the first purchase.
>
> True Fit's platform also helps you proactively remove high-return items by analyzing trends from return types. It uses artificial intelligence and comparative data across our more than 17,000 supported brands to identify size sampling and sequential size sampling behaviors.
>
> Like you, our customer Moosejaw sells a lot of outdoor apparel, and they were also struggling with returns. When they implemented True Fit's platform, they were able to target size sampling at its source and reduce returns by 24 percent.
>
> As one of my follow-ups to this conversation, I will share that case study. I will also share our recent "State of Returns" report, which offers a step-by-step guide on how retailers like you can reduce returns by up to 35 percent.

In addition to this value narrative on reducing product returns, True Fit's value narrative playbook also has suggested product capability talk tracks, success stories, and content assets for its three other key value narratives: using personalization to increase website traffic, converting a higher percentage of web browsers to buyers, and increasing lifetime customer value.

This example from True Fit demonstrates two key ways a value narrative playbook helps product information and marketing content come alive in a buyer conversation. It helps a sales, customer success, or account management team member anchor in a buyer's goals and share peer examples most relevant to that buyer.

The value narrative is designed to align exactly with how buyers want to consume content. Rather than the product pitch that drones on and on for twenty, thirty, or forty minutes without any substantive conversation about what the buyer cares about, value narratives encourage "micro-presentation" style. The micro-presentation involves five to seven minutes on product capabilities that focuses on a specific buyer goal, followed by peer client success stories or other outcome metrics as evidence of impact. The sales or technical sales team should then stop to get feedback.

The purpose in stopping to get feedback is to let the buyer continue to shape the exact impact or payoff that would get them most excited. Unfortunately, almost all questions I hear sellers ask in product demonstrations add little or no value to the conversation. The pause is usually used to ask something generic, like, "Any questions?" or "What did you think?" or "Isn't that cool?" Instead, use that pause to have your buyer tell you about impact: "How would what I just shared help you?" or "Where is the first place you would think to apply this?"

The purpose of the product discussion is not to show the product; rather, it is to get the buyer to tell you if they see how your product could help them in a meaningful way. So, you need to stop and ask that directly.

Don't think of content as individual content assets. Organize it into content pathways that align with specific goals and can lead step-by-step through each phase of the buyer or customer journey toward a purchase decision.

Value Mapping and Content Strategy Across the Buyer Journey

Value mapping, just like value discovery, also needs to happen at each step of the buyer journey. One of the biggest disconnects for many buyers is that when they transition from marketing to sales to customer success, the company language changes. Each team often has a different way of talking about product capabilities, draws on different content, and shares different client stories. If your different go-to-market teams have different languages, it's disorienting for the buyer and causes friction that can hurt both your new sales and your upsell opportunities.

A key strength of the value narrative playbook is that it can help you and your go-to-market team create consistency across your marketing, sales, and customer success departments with regard to capabilities messaging, content, and client success stories. A value narrative playbook makes it easier for you to maintain an authentic buyer journey as the buyer transitions across go-to-market teams.

However, content marketing can support an authentic buyer journey and value mapping in each buyer interaction only if there is a clear content strategy. Content marketing comes in a wide variety of formats, including case studies, white papers, blogs, webinars, research-based buyer insights, videos, press releases, social media feeds, sell sheets, sales decks, content-rich website use cases, and targeted lists of peer clients by market segment. Each type of content can provide evidence of how a company helps a buyer achieve their goals.

Many companies make two mistakes in their content strategy. Content is often developed as individual content assets focused on a company's products and services and not directly linked to specific buyer goals and priorities. Content is also often not organized in a step-by-step way to align with each phase of the buyer journey. While content is important across the entire buyer journey, a buyer's willingness to engage with product information or spend time reviewing capabilities and evidence varies significantly as they move through the buying process. If you want to make your content marketing really land, then you need to align your content strategy with each of your buyer value narratives.

CONTENT AS INDIVIDUAL ASSETS

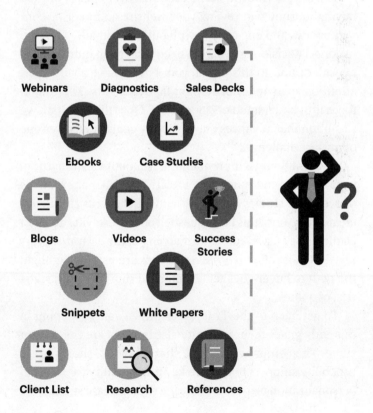

Webinars   Diagnostics   Sales Decks

Ebooks   Case Studies

Blogs   Videos   Success Stories

Snippets   White Papers

Client List   Research   References

To have a strong content strategy playbook, focus on mapping your content to a buyer's specific goal areas and share specific stories of peer success for each goal area. According to the 2019 Demand Gen survey, 92 percent of B2B buyers give the most credence to peer reviews and feedback, 68 percent are more likely to engage with content categorized this way, and 58 percent are more likely to engage with content organized by industry vertical. A strong content strategy also aligns content delivery with the phase of the buyer journey to build a content pathway that can lead a buyer step-by-step toward a purchase.

The buyers who are in the early discovery phase of their buying journey will review your website and peer or competitor sites and engage you with outreach emails. They are making a decision on whether to commit to an initial discovery call or not. In this phase, your buyers have a very short attention span and mostly want quick insights. Their main focus is to understand one question: "Does this vendor have a solution that advances one of my key goals or resolves one of my key challenges?"

Details about your product, the competitive strengths of your features and function set relative to other alternatives, or even case studies of success with other clients can all just create noise until this basic question about resolving a goal or challenge is answered. Value mapping in the early discovery phase is most effective when websites are used to highlight the path to buyer goal achievement in short phrases, statistics, or quotes.

To get back to the True Fit example, value mapping in this early phase focuses on bite-size bits that are easy to consume. The company's website shares bolded, short-phrase capability snippets to capture key functionality for its retail personalization platform. There are detailed case studies, but each has a quick callout box with a couple of bullet points naming specific impacts related to increasing buyer conversion rates, reducing product returns, or increasing lifetime value. Company logos on the home and partner pages make it easy to see peer clients.

CONTENT LINKED TO VALUE NARRATIVES

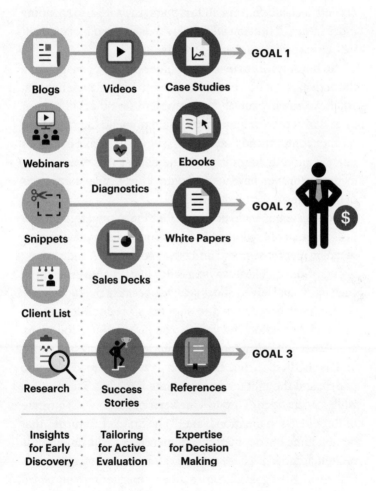

Blogs · Videos · Case Studies → GOAL 1

Webinars · Diagnostics · Ebooks

Snippets · · White Papers → GOAL 2

Client List · Sales Decks

Research · Success Stories · References → GOAL 3

| Insights for Early Discovery | Tailoring for Active Evaluation | Expertise for Decision Making |

As your buyers move from early discovery to active evaluation, they start to believe a vendor can help them with a key business goal or challenge. In active evaluation, their main focus is now to understand, "Why is this company the best partner to help solve my challenge and advance my goal?"

Your buyers in active evaluation are moving on from an initial discovery call and into follow-up conversations that may include a product demonstration and other stakeholders and decision-makers. At this point, they are also spending more in-depth time on websites, reviewing product capabilities, case studies, and white papers.

No buyer wants to feel like a guinea pig. Value mapping in the active evaluation phase involves providing evidence that you have already solved their problem for others like them. Buyers in active evaluation are going to spend the most time on your content, and they want to see very specific use cases tailored directly to their goals and needs. They want to see evidence that you have worked with other, similar companies or others in similar buying roles.

For those buyers in active evaluation, True Fit is using a best practice of having a library of success story slides organized by market segment and buyer goal area. A slide library is one of the quickest ways to tailor a sales conversation to each individual buyer. Slides selected because they are a most-similar peer can be used to support a product demonstration and discussion and can also be included in a follow-up email that will be shared with other decision-makers.

It is also in the active evaluation phase that True Fit's white papers and thought leadership come into play. True Fit has white papers titled "One-to-One Personalization," "The State of Retail Personalization," and "The State of Returns" that demonstrate the depth of their expertise and the uniqueness of their approach. These are powerful ways to engage buyers with an aligned goal who are actively considering a purchase.

When your buyer moves from active evaluation to a decision-making phase, they are choosing between a company's solution, an alternative solution, or doing nothing at all. They believe a vendor can solve their problem, and their main focus is now to understand, "What are my risks in selecting this vendor, and do the benefits outweigh the risks?"

When a buyer gets to the point of considering a proposal from a vendor, the purchasing process changes in two ways. First, the sales process expands and starts to include new decision-makers, such as a chief financial officer or vice president in a related department, who may not join the sales discussions directly. Second, there is a much higher focus on vendor risk and a desire to feel very good about the probability that if they invest time, money, and effort into this partnership, it will bear the fruit of the promised business outcomes.

Buyers in a decision-making phase typically use content to de-risk a vendor decision and build confidence and trust in a broader decision-making group. Value mapping in the decision-making phase needs to demonstrate expertise and to de-risk, for all decision-makers, the choice to move forward into a partnership.

It is during this phase that True Fit's detailed, written case studies, white papers, and ebooks become good ways to demonstrate expertise, particularly to individuals not directly involved in the purchasing conversations. Providing a list of peer customers and an opportunity for references to direct peers is another way to de-risk the decision; it allows all potential buyers to hear directly from a client about the before-and-after case for their organization.

Finally, the other great thing about True Fit's value narrative playbooks and the high-quality, aligned content in each buyer goal area is that it accelerates the account expansion motion. Buyers were deeply educated about True Fit's product capabilities, outcomes, and client success stories in the

Accelerate collaboration between marketing, sales, and customer success by **mapping your content and product capability to specific buyer goals and phases of the buyer journey.**

first sales cycle, which makes it easier to reintroduce them to address another potential goal area to expand the partnership within the first six to twelve months of the working relationship.

IMPACT Stays Focused on Value Mapping Across Teams

Let's turn now to look at IMPACT, a digital sales and marketing agency, for another example of how value mapping and strong content at each phase of the buyer journey helps drive business growth. IMPACT has experienced dramatic growth with the core philosophy, "They ask, you answer." The IMPACT team describes this as an approach to communication, company culture, and the way a company sells to their buyers that rejects the typical self-focused way of doing business and wholly embraces an obsession with understanding what buyers are really thinking, searching for, asking, and feeling.

I was introduced to Bob Ruffolo, CEO and cofounder of IMPACT, as well as his partner and cofounder, Marcus Sheridan, by a mutual colleague, a marketing guru and bestselling author of a number of books on marketing strategy. This colleague said, "If you are going to talk about content strategy, then you need to talk to Bob and Marcus at IMPACT. They are the best there is when it comes to content in sales and marketing."

I set up a video call with Bob and Marcus. One of the first things Bob said was, "Content can have a dramatic impact on a business, but a salesperson needs to know how to align with a buyer's goals before, during, and after each sales conversation."

"Buyers are not dumb," Marcus added. "They are going to get the information they need someplace." Marcus is a world-famous keynote speaker, as brilliant as he is direct in sharing what he knows to be true in engaging buyers and customers. "Good content gets ahead of the buyer's questions and creates the feeling that 'they have been reading my thoughts.' In today's marketplace, the idea of 'seeing is believing' has never been more true. You cannot just claim to help buyers achieve a goal. You need to demonstrate it with content and evidence throughout the marketing and sales process."

Bob, Marcus, and the IMPACT team believe that in an "age of transparency," where buyers are going to find answers to their questions somehow, companies do better when every buyer question gets an honest and transparent answer. This core commitment informs all of IMPACT's offerings across its work on marketing strategy, web design, inbound and content marketing, and video projects, as well as paid and social search marketing.

"Like any company, we have tension between sales and marketing," Marcus said, the intensity in his voice increasing. "A key element of our success is committing to getting beyond sales and marketing. At most companies, ninety percent of marketing-created content never gets used by the sales team. Our sales people talk with potential customers all day long, so they are going to know better the business-use cases that sell. Having the sales team co-develop our capabilities messaging and content helps us align directly with buyer's goals and keeps our messaging consistent across sales and marketing."

IMPACT has implemented a key best practice in making positioning language and content development a cross-functional activity. Too many companies have their marketing department develop a positioning strategy for their product or service, along with aligned content assets, and then hand it off to their sales and customer success teams, who—as Marcus said—mostly don't use it. That changes when the people who will use it are involved in creating it.

"Another element of our success is content at different levels of depth for different parts of the buyer journey," Marcus continued, getting into a rhythm and outlining what he and IMPACT have learned are critical elements of effective content strategy. "Early in buyer discovery, we have interactive web elements and short, personal videos from every one of our experts to create a quick connection to buyers. We also have a ton of blogs and video blogs that can be used after an initial sales conversation to speak to a buyer's specific goals. We use detailed case studies that highlight our very strong results and can be easily circulated within a buyer organization to support the decision-making phase."

You will have seen in both the IMPACT and True Fit stories that a key strength of the value narratives framework is that it accelerates cross-functional collaboration to optimize content for each phase of the buyer journey. Once capability talk tracks and content assets are linked to specific buyer goal areas, sales and customer success teams can share targeted feedback with the marketing team on what is working and not working to build engagement with buyers and customers.

"We also train our sales team on how to use content," Bob said, putting his CEO hat on and walking through key elements of organizational enablement around content. "Training on mapping content to a buyer's goals is part of the onboarding process for any new sales or marketing team member. We review content needs and best practices in using content in our weekly sales and marketing team meetings. Those meetings are really important to capture direct feedback from our buyers and customers to understand the content that is really landing."

Bob continued with another easily implemented best practice being used by IMPACT: using content to get the buyer to confirm if and how they are seeing value in the sales conversation. "We expect our sales team to actively use content in qualifying their deals. We train them to wrap up sales calls by saying something like, 'Before our next meeting, I need you to watch this video and read this information to see if you can confirm a fit with your goals.' And then we ask them to follow up with prospects before the call to see if they had a chance to read the information, and if not, to consider rescheduling. We use content to educate but also to qualify where we spend our time." He sat back in his chair, raised an eyebrow, and smiled.

For the IMPACT team, well-designed content that helps map capabilities and success cases to specific buyer goals at each phase of the buyer journey has helped accelerate growth. It has helped the team by anticipating and neutralizing buyer questions. It has helped qualify buyers by offering content aligned with goals and providing a way for sales team members to see if prospects engage with it in ways that deepen the conversation.

Value Confirmation and Qualifying Buyers

So far we have discussed how you can use a value narrative framework with several levels of good discovery questions, capability talk tracks, client success cases, and other key content for each buyer goal area. As you saw in the True Fit and IMPACT examples earlier in the chapter, the structure of the value narrative builds quicker and deeper buyer engagement. It creates an authentic buyer journey by shifting sales and customer success conversations from generic product discussion to product discussion aligned with each buyer's specific goals and the problems they most want to solve.

The shortest but most important phase of value mapping comes at the very end: value confirmation. Your sales or customer success team members can execute perfectly in recapping goals, discussing or demonstrating exactly the

At the end of each buyer or customer upsell conversation, you need to intentionally pause and let the buyer confirm where they see value in your partnership. Only then does it make sense to take any steps toward closing.

right capabilities, and sharing a strong peer success case, and then forget to stop and see if they even moved the needle with the buyer. You need to create a specific, intentional pause to see if the buyer confirms that they believe a proposed product or service can move them forward.

The purpose of value confirmation is to bring the buyer right back to an impact statement they helped construct. Through a good value discovery process, the buyer has shared their goal and targeted impacts or payoff with you. Now, the questions are, first, do they see how your capabilities will close a gap to move them toward that goal achievement, and, second, do they believe your success with peer customers will translate into success with them?

Going back to the True Fit story, we looked at how a sales team member might map capabilities and success cases to a buyer goal of reducing product returns. However, in many sales conversations, multiple buyer goal areas may have surfaced. So, an example of how a True Fit sales team member might structure value confirmation could be something like the following:

> I understand from our conversation today that your COO is looking to reduce returns by as much as 15 percent over the next year. I also understand that your CMO is looking to increase the rate at which your website visitors turn into buyers by 3–4 percent.
>
> You shared that you currently do not have a personalization technology, and that achieving both reduced returns and increased browser-to-buyer conversion would be worth millions to your business.
>
> Do you see how the True Fit capabilities I just shared would build that personalization and move you toward one or both of those goals?
>
> Do you think it would be most helpful with one goal area or the other?

Were there elements of the Moosejaw success case I shared that resonated with your situation?

Value confirmation is a key step before you spend any time and effort trying to work a deal to a close. The stronger the buyer value confirmation, the more likely the deal is to close. In my client companies, before they invested in developing strong value confirmation skills, I saw sales and account management teams waste up to 35 percent of their time chasing unqualified deals with little or no likelihood of closing.

Research Solutions Confirms Value by Asking, "Should We Continue?"

Let's now look at how Research Solutions has used disciplined value mapping and value confirmation to grow quickly and renew customers at an extremely high rate. Research Solutions is a market leader in providing journal content to corporate, government, and university clients.

I was connected with Rogier van Erkel, chief commercial officer at Research Solutions, by an executive at another company in the same market, who said, "These guys have some of the highest new-customer conversion rates and current-customer renewal rates I have ever seen. You should talk to them." I had a video call with Rogier, who was sitting in Research Solutions's European headquarters in Amsterdam.

Rogier has decades of experience leading marketing, sales, and account management teams, and he had a cool confidence about his go-to-market strategy. "Our philosophy," he explained, "is to check at the end of every buyer interaction to see if both sides see a reason to continue. We will just ask directly during a buyer conversation or in an email, 'Is it worthwhile to continue?'" He smiled a bit mischievously. "Some people say this is crazy. They ask, 'Why would you

If your sales and account management teams do not consistently ask buyers to confirm perceived value, they will waste a lot of time chasing unqualified deals. **Don't focus on closing before you have direct confirmation on fit.**

give a prospect a reason to say no?' But"—he leaned forward slightly—"our experience is that by focusing on the customers most motivated to work with us, we close deals more quickly, sell more to each account, and renew at higher rates."

Research Solutions's flagship product is called Article Galaxy. It provides researchers one-click access to scientific papers from any comprehensive literature search, and then manages the content and references in terms of the researchers' personal preferences. The company helps its buyer focus on reducing the time researchers spend finding and managing articles, reducing the costs of sourcing this research, and increasing organization-wide insights around research use.

Rogier continued to walk me through his approach, speaking in fluent English with just the slightest Dutch accent. "We let buyers confirm value and self-qualify right from the prospecting phase. Our most effective way to source new discovery meetings is to use regular marketing emails on key uses to see what engages a new buyer. Heads of research departments or librarians are our most important users. We 'drip' emails to these groups"—he emphasized this with a small gesture—"that focus on ease of accessing, storing, and collaborating on research. Heads of IT or chief science officers are our most likely funders, and they want to see the financial case to purchase."

In prospecting work, there is no direct way to ask a buyer what they value most or to confirm interest in considering a product or solution. Regular drip marketing around proven use cases and buyer value narratives is a great way to let new buyers confirm they are interested in a conversation. Research Solutions uses regular drip marketing to then focus its outbound prospecting on already-engaged buyers.

"We see which new buyers interact with our drip emails in some way," Rogier continued, walking through the power of letting buyers self-qualify around the things they care about most. "Then every Tuesday morning, each member of our prospecting team gets a list of qualified prospects who have engaged with our nurture outreach to contact for initial discovery meetings. This focus on letting new buyers confirm their interest has contributed to an eighty percent conversion rate from an initial discovery call to a group meeting."

Several years ago, I saw a sobering webinar presentation by Aberdeen Strategy & Research that said, as I recall, only 37 percent of first meetings had any kind of follow-on meetings. Our client work at Winalytics suggests that best-in-class organizations achieve 60 percent conversion from a first discovery meeting to a second meeting, so Research Solutions's 80 percent conversion rate from a first meeting to a group meeting is truly world-class.

"We get a very high conversion rate from a first discovery call to a group meeting for two reasons," Rogier said nonchalantly, as if the team's impressive first-meeting conversion rates were totally normal. "The first, as I just shared, is that we use our prospecting to effectively qualify buyers who are already a good fit. The second is that we use the discovery meeting to get the buyer to lean into the conversation and confirm where to focus. We clarify buyer goals, present our capabilities that align, and then ask them directly to identify both a personal win and a business win that would come from implementing our platform. We basically ask them: 'Do you see value in continuing?'"

Rogier and his team have perfected using buyer value confirmation to qualify and progress the right deals. What the team understands well is that sales team members really cannot "close" deals. Only buyers can close deals—when they are motivated enough by goal, gap, and impact. The role of the seller is to use good questions to educate their buyer on why they need to do something different, and then to direct this buying energy to partnering on building organizational readiness to purchase.

"The focus of our next conversation with a group is to turn the person from the first call into our champion and internal sales person," Rogier continued. "Before the group call, we ask the champion for insight. Whom do we want to bring into the group conversation? Why this group? Will this group see the same areas of value that you see? During the call, we confirm the group's goal areas, show how we advance these goals, and then ask the group, 'Shall we continue to a trial? Do we agree on trial goals?'"

For buyers in early discovery and active evaluation, Research Solutions uses value mapping and value confirmation to build agreement that its capabilities can help with the buyer's goal achievement. As the buyer moves through active evaluation into decision-making mode, the focus of value mapping and value confirmation shifts to building agreement on the type of impact that would differentiate Research Solutions from other options and justify a budget investment. The purpose of the trial is then to produce evidence and show a path to this agreed-on impact.

"When a buyer group has confirmed that they see how we can help with their goals, and also confirmed the value of continuing, we then focus on scoping the right trial," Rogier said. "A pilot lasts only two weeks and never has more than ten people, so it needs to align directly with their goals. Does the buyer think in terms of time savings with three fewer researchers a good outcome? Or cost savings with a $10,000 reduction in article costs a good outcome? If we map to their goal area, then we can close right after the trial. If we don't map to their goal area"—he shook his head slowly—"then it's like they are speaking English and we are speaking Chinese."

For Research Solutions, this focus on introducing use cases around specific buyer goals and then asking the buyer, "Shall we continue?" starts with marketing and sales, but it continues into customer success. Account renewal and expansion activities are all anchored in confirming where the customer is experiencing the most value.

"Customer success is in a different organization from sales and marketing in our company," Rogier continued. "However, they have the same buyer value areas, use cases, and processes to deepen accounts. They use data in our platform to see which use cases are most important at each account, and then reach out to share new functionality information and offer educational opportunities related to those areas of interest. So, if a person is annotating a lot, the customer success team may focus outreach on new workflows for personal management of research. Or, if a person is using the insights and reporting features a lot, our team will reach out about new administrative features that might be helpful."

Research Solutions's focus on letting customers continue to confirm where they see fit and value has led to an impressive 99 percent renewal rate and made renewals and upsells a key driver of this growth. Research Solutions has grown to $32 million in revenue with more than three million users at over 1,400 corporate, government, and university customers.

Value Mapping and Value Confirmation Deepen an Authentic Buyer Journey

In this chapter, we have seen in the True Fit and IMPACT examples how you can use strong value discovery to set up deeper buyer engagement in an authentic buyer journey and to align your product and capability discussions directly with each buyer's individual goals. The Research Solutions example shows that the last and most important phase of value mapping is stopping for value confirmation: you need to let your buyer or customer confirm directly where they see the most value.

Next, in chapter 5, we will look at the example of Aginity, a company that provides a collaborative analytics platform, to see how a value narratives framework connects to individual playbooks for each go-to-market team. While a value narrative playbook creates an overall philosophy of buyer value across a revenue organization, it is in playbooks used by sales, marketing, and customer success teams that an authentic buyer journey comes alive in all buyer interactions.

YOUR NEXT STEPS ON VALUE MAPPING

- **Developing your content pathways:** Can you align content assets, like webinars, white papers, blogs, success stories, etc., to individual buyer goals? Build a one- or two-page content pathway to bring together these assets for each goal area.

- **Building your value mapping sheets:** For each buyer goal or buyer persona, build a one-page document with your top product talk tracks, success stories, and other content assets that provide evidence on how those product capabilities advance a specific buyer goal.

Access supplemental resources and questions at winalytics .com/theplays to help you build plays for a value-mapping strategy as an individual contributor or team.

5

A Value Playbook and Team-Level Playbooks

"WE HAVE signed up some of the world's top insurers, e-commerce players, biotech companies, and hospitals almost by brute force, by selling on product features," Rick Hall, CEO of Aginity, told his team. "To grow to ten million dollars, and then to a hundred million dollars, we need to fully engage our buyers with how exactly we increase the efficiency and impact of analytics to create business value across the enterprise."

Rick was on a videoconference call one late February day with his VP of customer development, Chris Coad, and the sales, marketing, and customer success team members who reported to Chris. The focus was on revising and updating customer-facing processes to anchor them on Aginity's unique value proposition and create a faster growth trajectory. I had the opportunity to support the team in building the next phase of Aginity's revenue growth strategy.

Aginity started the market for collaborative analytics. For most businesses, data and data analytics have become essential input to marketing, pricing, supply chain, operational, and other key types of decision-making. The importance of data has led to an "analytics everywhere" business environment. It is not just business analysts and analytic engineers in a central corporate department that need the ability to quickly respond to data and business insight needs; all business units and departments do. Both Rick and Chris had early-career experience as data analysts, and Rick had experience on midsize-to-large analytic teams. Both brought a passion and sense of mission to their work on collaborative analytics.

The goal of Aginity's collaborative analytics approach was to make it possible for data operations to be decentralized in individual departments and units while still connecting across the entire enterprise analytics ecosystem. The first versions of Aginity analytic solutions were offered for free, which created an install base of 30,000 users across more than 1,000 enterprise accounts. Large groups of customers were in a wide variety of market sectors, including financial services, insurance, retail, biotech, and health care providers.

"We did a great job last year converting one hundred accounts from free to paid by finding users who were really motivated to not lose access to Aginity," Rick said. "We now need to accelerate growth this year and next year by positioning the importance of democratizing analytic processes and operations across larger analytics teams—and the value Aginity can bring by making that possible."

That meeting began an intensive process to update all of Aginity's go-to-market processes so they led with buyer value. The process of implementing the ideas of value narratives across the entire buyer journey typically takes twelve to eighteen months. Aginity completed the process in less than six months.

Aginity Writes Down Its Value Narratives

"What is Aginity's overall value to your buyers and then specific areas of value for different individuals within your buyer organization?" I asked the group.

Chris responded immediately and showed why his early-career work as a data analyst had made him so passionate about Aginity's mission. "Data scientists and data engineers spend a ton of time cleaning, organizing, and transforming data into a usable format as well as writing code to run analytics on this data. They typically have no way to reuse their best work or share code and data across broader analyst teams. We solve that problem by reusing and sharing work to help teams reduce the time needed to complete data and analytic projects by up to forty percent."

"That's powerful," I said. "And how does that translate into specific improvements for different roles within the analytics organization? It's often not the overall value but specific value narratives, those that speak to goals and impacts for specific buyer roles, that are most powerful."

"There are four buyer personas we help," Chris responded, sharing his screen so that we could all have a visual as he walked through the buyer personas. "There are specific benefits for individual business analysts and analytic engineers, and for the analytic managers who oversee these teams. There is also value for the analytic leaders (C-level) of organizations responsible for the enterprise data analytics strategy and business insights. Finally, there is value for the license managers in the IT department who are responsible for managing, supporting, and deploying technology platforms."

Chris proceeded to describe the benefits to each of those groups in what became Aginity's key value narratives. After some additional dialogue with the go-to-market team in the meeting that day, they identified four key value narratives:

1 Individual ease for SQL analysts and engineers by reducing the amount of time cleaning, organizing, and transforming data or having to rewrite code.

2 Team productivity gains from easy-to-use workflows for searching, sharing, and modularizing code across analytics teams.

3 Time-to-business insight on key pricing, positioning, and operational supply chain decision-making, by increasing consistency of data operations and analytic output across analysts and engineers.

4 Reducing IT deployment, support, and maintenance costs with a shift to one analytics platform.

In a later conversation, I followed up with Chris. "Now that you've built out your value narratives, you can start to build them into team-level playbooks for sales, marketing, and customer success. There's no right order to do this, but often it helps to prioritize around your most important revenue outcomes."

Chris paused for a minute to collect his thoughts and then said, "Well, right now we need to renew an important group of customers in Q1, find new buyers, and expand our paid customer accounts. So, we really need to move all of these revenue outcomes forward at the same time."

"Okay," I said. "Let's start with your overall value narrative playbook. Then we can work on team-level playbooks for prospecting, content strategy, sales, and customer success."

A key focus was on converting the more than 1,000 enterprise accounts and 30,000 users of the free version to paid accounts. When Aginity initiated this process, its marketing and sales messaging focused first on the opportunity to move from the free version of its product to a paid version with greater functionality. Then, a second round of messaging was added to tell customers that the free version was being sunsetted, and that to stay "in compliance," users would need to migrate to the paid version.

This was the "brute force approach" Rick Hall had mentioned. It helped the company convert around a hundred accounts, many of them large enterprises with big analytics teams. However, the next phase of growth was targeting a doubling or tripling of revenue each year. That would require a value-driven approach to acquire and expand customer accounts.

In this chapter, I will use the Aginity example to show how go-to-market teams can build overall value playbooks that align value narratives with specific buyer personas, and then translate into team-specific playbooks. The Aginity example of building team-level playbooks and individual plays can help you begin to understand how to implement these in your business as well. The next four chapters of this book each take a deep dive into one of the four team-level playbooks covered in this chapter.

Value Narratives and Buyer Personas

As you know by now, value narratives are high-level buyer goals and outcomes. A value narrative playbook includes the three levels of value discovery questions we discussed in chapter 3 as well as the product talk track, client success stories, and impact stories used during the value mapping phase of each buyer interaction that we discussed in chapter 4.

If you create your value narrative playbook before your individual team-level playbooks, it makes an authentic buyer journey more consistent and repeatable. It builds consistency in how each go-to-market team engages with buyers and customers, and in communicating a company's unique impacts on buyer goals. It also reduces friction for buyers and customers as they move between go-to-market teams.

In a follow-up meeting with Chris, we worked on mapping this out. "So, we have defined Aginity's overall value narrative," I said. "What are your top discovery questions to invite a buyer or customer into a conversation about each value area?"

We were videoconferencing that day. Chris paused to open up a couple of different documents on his computer for reference and then said, "There's a long list and probably three or four for each value narrative. But there are probably a top five or six that get buyers most interested."

Chris then proceeded to share a list of his top buyer discovery questions. They included:

- Are you doing the same analysis over and over again?

- Would you like to reduce time organizing, ingesting, or merging data?

- How do analysts and engineer teams currently search, share, and manage code?

- How easily can teams reuse and repurpose their code?

- How do you currently review, understand, and compare data through descriptive statistics to test for quality and get to business insight quicker?

- How do you manage data governance and data access?

"The questions you just shared are all great," I told him. "They sound like they could be used in an email outreach to a new buyer, on a sales call, or during a customer success call focused on exploring new goal areas. Is that right?"

You can use value narratives to engage your buyer personas in a consistent way across marketing outreach, sales, and customer success conversations.

"Yes, definitely," Chris said. "Those are good ways to lead either a buyer or a customer to understand the different ways we can provide value."

"So, they are great questions to include in the overall value narrative playbook that can be used to build individual team-level playbooks," I said. "Next would be the capability talk tracks that align to those goal areas, as well as client success stories and impact data that provide evidence to support those talk tracks."

"Well, starting with the impact data," Chris said, "our clients tell us that we can increase their team productivity and time-to-business insight by thirty to forty percent by increasing individual efficiency as well as team collaboration."

He paused briefly as he pulled out a list. "There are lots of product talk tracks that we share based on the buyer's top data analytics goals, but there are a handful of talk tracks that are most important and cut across our value narrative."

Chris then shared what he considered the five most important product talk tracks:

1 Manage and reuse your code with an active analytics catalog that allows you to add a searchable title and description so you and others know what the code is trying to accomplish.

2 Use a shared code catalog to update code in one spot as well as share and reuse code across analytics teams with five or five thousand.

3 Get multiple database support, choose your database connection, and use database specific objects, code dialects, and capabilities.

4 Gain quick data insight through descriptive statistics, aggregations, charting, and grid functionality before putting it into production.

5 Have the ability to govern SQL code using permission-level access with multiple user types (editors, viewers, admins) to balance access and security.

"Okay, so now we have an approach to messaging our capabilities," I said. "How do you provide evidence that the capabilities actually work and have meaningful client impact? Do you have good client success stories for your major segments in financial services, biotech, and hospitals?"

Chris stood up and stretched his back slightly as he responded. "We do have good success stories with companies like Suncorp, Aetna, Amazon, Eli Lilly, and Magellan Health. Right now, we're thinking less about segment-specific stories and more about examples of how we have helped large analytics teams move from fragmented data operations to connected operations with the ability to collaborate, share, and reuse code across multiple database types."

"I assume that different parts of those stories appeal to different buyer personas in those larger analytics teams?" I said.

"As we expand accounts, we definitely create new versions of the stories to appeal to different buyers," Chris said. "We often start with individual users and focus on the individual efficiency of their SQL work. Then we move to analytics managers to focus on how team efficiency and time-to-business insights can increase with deeper team collaboration. We speak to analytics leaders, as well as IT teams who manage software deployments, about the value of one data platform across the entire enterprise team."

The Aginity example shows how value narrative playbooks reduce buyer friction by helping manage and align multiple buyer personas across the buyer journey. While your marketing may happen at the individual buyer persona level, your sales and customer success teams need to align multiple buyer personas with a new sale or an upsell decision. For Aginity, there may be a dozen different buyer personas that come into a sales or customer success conversation, but those buyer personas can be aligned with two, or maybe three, value narratives to help structure a sales or upsell conversation.

AGINITY'S EXAMPLE:
VALUE NARRATIVE–BUYER PERSONA MAPPING

Value Narrative	Buyer Persona	Value Narrative Description
Individual Ease	SQL Analysts SQL Engineers	Increase individual ease for SQL analysts and engineers by reducing the amount of time of cleaning, organizing, and transforming data as well as having to rewrite code
Team Productivity	Analytic Managers	Build team productivity gains from easy-to-use workflows for searching, sharing, and modularizing code access across analytics teams
Time-to-Business Insight	Analytic Leaders	Increase time-to-business insight on key pricing, positioning, supply chain, and operational decision-making through increased consistency of data operations and outputs
One Platform	CDO CIO IT License Manager	Connect multiple on-premise or cloud-based databases with shared data governance while reducing IT deployment, support, and maintenance costs

Team-Level Playbooks and Revenue Outcomes

As the Aginity example shows, a value narrative playbook creates an overall approach to buyer value. However, those value narratives need to be integrated into team-level play-books that guide sales, marketing, and customer success interactions and bring an authentic buyer journey into action consistently across a go-to-market team. It is developing and optimizing the team-level playbooks that accelerates individual revenue outcomes.

Team-level playbooks capture "plays" run by market-facing teams. Each individual play suggests a set of individual or coordinated actions to respond to a specific buyer situation. Your individual revenue teams in sales, marketing, and customer success likely have developed their own playbooks to support team execution. However, it is only when each of your team-level playbooks is connected to a shared value narrative that they can help build an authentic buyer journey. If your team-level playbooks are developed independently of a shared value narrative, they end up with different language capability talk tracks and ways of presenting buyer value and impacts. All of this creates confusion and friction for the buyer.

One way to illustrate the relationship between value narratives and team-level playbooks is to use the analogy of an American football team. Each football team is really a combination of five different, more specialized teams: the offense that tries to score points; the defense that tries to prevent the opponent from scoring points; the "red zone" offense that runs a specific set of offensive plays to score within 20 yards of the opponent's goal line; the "red zone" defense that runs a set of defensive plays to prevent the opponent from scoring within 20 yards of their own goal line; and specials that manage transitions in possession with punts, kickoffs, and extra points.

A value narrative playbook supports an authentic buyer journey across go-to-market teams. It creates consistency in messaging buyer goals, discovery questions, product talk tracks, and client success stories.

Each of these five teams has its own playbook and set of plays, but they are unified as a cohesive team by a coaching philosophy. If each specialized group ran its own plays without any attention to, or coordination with, the plays of the other groups, you wouldn't expect the team to win many games.

TEAM-LEVEL PLAYBOOKS AND REVENUE OUTCOMES

Value Playbooks

Value narratives and buyer personas

Value discovery strategy

Value mapping and confirmation

Revenue outcomes strategy

Team-Level Playbooks

Content strategy

Prospecting

Sales and deal velocity

Closing and expansion

Renewal and customer success

Revenue Outcomes

More new opps

More won opps

Higher account value

Deeper segment growth

Bill Belichick is the legendary head coach for the New England Patriots. His team has won seventeen consecutive division titles and made nine appearances in Super Bowl championships, with a record six Super Bowl wins. His coaching philosophy is "Do your job, own your performance, and embrace the clarity that comes with that focus." Bill Walsh, by contrast, another legendary American football head coach, who is third on the list of winningest coaches with three Super Bowl wins, had a coaching philosophy based on "preparing for contingencies." He trained his team to work for the best outcome but prepare for the worst by practicing for contingencies.

I recommend that a go-to-market team have five specific team-level playbooks linked to their overall value narrative playbook:

1 **A content strategy playbook** to help the marketing team connect individual content assets to specific buyer goals and value narratives, so content is consistently deployed across prospecting, sales, account management, and customer success activities.

2 **A prospecting playbook** to leverage value narratives and associated content for a focus on sourcing more new opportunities by inviting buyers into value-added discovery conversations on their critical goals and targeted impacts.

3 **A sales and deal velocity playbook** to build greater consistency in managing sales conversation around buyer goals first, product second and resisting the pull back to product pitching, in order to increase the rate at which new opportunities move to closed won.

4 **A closing and expansion playbook** to connect and anchor sales, account management, and customer success team

activities on buyer value to increase deal values on initial closed deals and speed the time frame to expansion sales.

5   **A renewal and customer success playbook** to carry the narratives through to customer conversations aimed at achieving higher renewal rates, higher account values, and deeper segment growth.

Well-developed team-level playbooks have a number of advantages for your go-to-market team. A good playbook captures and socializes best practices for every buyer or customer situation. The playbooks support practice and repetition to build skills outside of direct buyer interactions. They offer suggested questions, talk tracks, and qualifying strategies that can be reviewed and discussed in your team calls, used for role-plays, or used to directly evaluate recorded buyer or customer conversations. Good playbooks also provide flexibility and options for each of your team members to find their own voice. Each team member has their own style. They will ask discovery questions in a slightly different way, will have their own client stories, and may describe your product capabilities in their own language. The playbooks create a shared framework with rules of the road, so each team member can have their own style but still maintain consistency.

In total, there are more than twenty-five team-level plays in our revenue acceleration playbook that a go-to-market team can put in place to deepen an authentic buyer and customer journey. The most dramatic growth gains come when a go-to-market team commits to building set value playbooks and then, step-by-step, integrates these value playbooks across its team. In chapter 2, we saw the example of how Mursion did exactly this to unlock the full growth potential of a transformational immersive VR training platform. Mursion committed to building the plays to put buyer goals first

There are more than twenty-five team-level plays in a fully developed revenue acceleration playbook. However, **the good news is that every single play you put in place will have a positive impact on your revenue outcomes.**

and product second across its content marketing, prospecting, sales, and account management, and it led to a growth run with several consecutive years of more than 250 percent revenue growth.

Building an entire revenue acceleration playbook usually takes time. Aginity accomplished it in just a few months, but they are an exception. However, here is the good news: every single play you put in place that encourages your go-to-market team to put buyer goals first and your product second will have a positive impact on your revenue outcomes. You can, like Mursion or Aginity, commit to building value narratives and team-level playbooks across your entire go-to-market team. You can build just one play at time or just one team-level playbook at time. In the chapters to come, we will see several examples of companies that focused on implementing a single team-level playbook like prospecting, sales, and deal velocity, or closing and expansion.

Content Strategy Playbook

The first of your team-level playbooks connected to the overall value narrative structure is the content strategy playbook. As discussed in chapter 4, the content strategy playbook helps marketing teams shift from thinking about individual content assets to aligning content with specific buyer goals and phases of the buyer journey. Marketing content is key to value mapping at every phase of buyer interaction, from prospecting to sales to customer success. It anchors the discussion of product capabilities; provides evidence of impact in the form of success stories, testimonials, and cases; and offers expertise and insight in the form of blogs, research, and white papers.

However, as mentioned earlier, the majority of marketing content is never used. If you use a content strategy playbook, this will change, and your content will become easier to bring into sales and success conversations. A content strategy playbook means that every individual content asset is tagged to one or more specific value narratives, market segments, and buyer personas. You can also tag content to broad phases of the buyer journey. Some content is effective in providing insights for early discovery; other content helps in tailoring to specific buyer goals in active evaluation; and then there is content that demonstrates expertise to persuade a broader decision-making group in a closing process.

Content organized around value narratives and phases of the buyer journey then becomes a "picklist" of assets. This picklist allows your content to be more easily integrated into specific sales, account management, and customer success plays and playbooks. Content becomes more actionable for other go-to-market teams because they know exactly which content assets to pick for each type of buyer interaction. Content also has a higher impact for the buyer because it is better aligned with what the buyer cares about.

A well-designed content strategy playbook supports more authentic interactions at each phase of the buyer journey. It helps your go-to-market teams move away from generic buyer interactions to targeted buyer interactions. Your prospecting campaigns can be designed to include discovery questions, research snippets, success stories, client testimonials, and product talk tracks to a specific buyer goal or specific buyer persona in a market segment. The content strategy playbook also makes it easier to use discovery during a sales call as a tool to map product talk tracks and success stories to specific buyer goals. This, in turn, leads to fewer generic product demonstrations in favor of product discussions that tell a story about how a company can solve a specific buyer problem.

Aginity framed its overall content strategy with a single organizing theme of "collaborative analytics" that captured all four of its key value narratives: individual ease, team productivity, time-to-business insight, and one analytics platform.

For Aginity, blog posts and white papers became a core part of the content strategy playbook. The blog posts target the individual business analyst or analytic engineers, inviting potential Aginity users to "stop rewriting, copying, and pasting SQL code." The posts targeting analytic managers show how collaborative sharing of data and code supports ongoing knowledge transfer within teams that are at the core of the "future of analytics." Other blog posts and white papers highlight a single data architecture as key to the success of the artificial intelligence and machine-learning models that have become so crucial to business insight. Inconsistent data and structures make it hard to leverage artificial intelligence and machine-learning models without a considerable amount of time and effort.

A clever and innovative part of Aginity's content strategy is to offer free courses for data engineers and business analysts. The courses are not Aginity-specific but help contribute skill sets and data processes that would make the person a better Aginity user. For data engineers, the courses are on things like Redshift Utilities, which is a key data platform connection for potential Aginity users. Other lessons for data engineers cover vital data processes that Aginity can facilitate, things like "Generating SQL to Profile Table Data" or "Building a Random Number Generator to Create an Image." For business analysts, similarly, the lessons focus on common business calculations such as "Calculating an Internal Rate of Return," used in evaluating investment returns, or "Creating a Recency, Frequency, and Monetary Analysis," used in a common marketing model for behavior-based segmentation. Like a lot of strong content marketing, Aginity's courses create value for a potential buyer by sharing knowledge and skills while also building familiarity with the company and increasing the likelihood of a purchase.

As a final element of Aginity's content marketing playbook, the company put together a series of thought leadership webinars. Some of these webinars were targeted at potential end users and analytics managers and focused on new forms of collaboration that could build team productivity. Other webinars targeted a wider audience, including chief data officers, chief analytics officers, vice presidents of analytics, and other senior-level decision-makers. These webinars feature Aginity's CEO and third-party experts, as well as clients, to position Aginity as the market leader in collaborative analytics, "a new approach to using data in a rapidly changing world."

Prospecting Playbook

Your prospecting playbook should connect marketing and sales teams to demand generation and new-opportunity creation. The prospecting playbook makes use of value narratives and associated content with a focus on sourcing more new opportunities by inviting buyers into value-added discovery conversations. Your prospecting playbook should cover prospecting both to completely new buyers and to existing clients for expansion opportunities.

In chapter 6, we take a more detailed look at how anchoring a prospecting playbook to an authentic buyer journey leads to faster new-opportunity production. Aginity's prospecting playbook made it possible to engage the four key

You can use a content strategy playbook to align marketing content with buyer goal areas and buyer personas. This makes content more valuable for your buyers and more actionable for your go-to-market teams.

buying personas most important for initial sales, as well as for expansion opportunities.

"Our situation for prospecting campaigns is different from other business-to-business sales teams," said Chris Coad during a video call focused on Aginity's prospecting playbook. You will remember that Chris is Aginity's VP of customer development.

He paused to open up a PowerPoint presentation that highlighted the Aginity customer segmentation model. "Our growth opportunity this year, and probably into the next, will be driven by prospecting into accounts that already use Aginity. You will see from this chart that we have started conversations with a thousand of our top target accounts, but there are at least another seven hundred to go. We will focus on converting existing free customers to paying accounts, then expanding these enterprise accounts. We'll work totally new accounts when they come to us."

"That makes sense," I said. "I assume in those existing accounts there is still a lot of buyer education to be done and different buyer roles that need to be engaged to turn them from free accounts into paying customers?"

"Yes. There are three different groups of buyers that we can engage in prospecting campaigns to secure an initial sale," Chris said. "There are the individual users who value Aginity because it helps them manage and repurpose code and be more efficient in their work. There are the analytic managers of these users who want to see knowledge sharing, code sharing, great collaboration, and faster results across their teams. Then there are user license managers, usually in IT, who want to be able to effectively manage licenses and deployments of the Aginity user groups in a single location and platform."

"Are these the same groups that you would target for the expansion opportunities?" I asked.

Before replying, Chris held up his phone to indicate he needed to take a quick call. He spoke for about a minute and then returned to our call, smiled, and said, "Speaking of expansion opportunities, that was Aetna wanting to add licenses in a new user group. On your question about expansion opportunities, we definitely want to move horizontally across different analytics groups and managers, and encourage analytics managers to introduce us to their internal peers. However, we will also directly target analytics leaders in a director or vice president role who may oversee multiple groups, as well as analytics leaders in the corporate offices responsible for overall analytics strategy."

"So, it is really four key buyer personas you are targeting," I said. "And for three of your four buyer personas, there is a key value narrative. Individual users would see individual efficiency messages, analytics managers would engage with team collaboration and time-to-insight messages, and user license managers would engage with the one-platform message. But for the analytics leaders, it is probably all four value narratives that matter."

"You are correct about that," Chris said. "The analytics leaders care about all the value narratives."

"Are all four of those personas potential purchasers?" I asked. "Or are you building a coalition of support with a buying group, trying to get one of those personas to make a purchase?"

"Three of four can typically make a purchase," Chris said. "Everyone except the individual user. But the coalition of support ideas is still right. We want to invite each of these individuals into a conversation that focuses on how Aginity can add value to their role. Some of these buyers are more important to the initial sale, but all are going to be an important part of the buying group on expansion opportunities that can help us fully tap into the account potential."

The most successful prospecting playbooks invite buyers into an authentic, value-added conversation. They also connect buyer personas to shared goals to set up a stronger sales conversation.

To support its shift from product-led growth to growth related to authentic buyer journeys, Aginity developed a series of prospecting campaigns for each of these four target buyer personas. There are several key plays in Aginity's prospecting playbook, including:

- Campaigns that involve proactive outreach by the sales team with six to eight outbound touches, including email, call, voicemail, and social touches.

- Passive marketing email campaigns that use a constant "drip" of twelve to fifteen emails over a sixty-day period to remind potential buyers of Aginity's value and opportunities to engage.

- Alignment with the content strategy playbook to link each campaign to specific themes, questions, and capability statements from Aginity's value narrative playbook and appropriate content.

By anchoring its prospecting playbook to a connected set of value narratives, Aginity was able to build an authentic buying journey for the individual buying personas most important to an initial landing deal, as well as for a buying group that would support expansion and build account value. Each prospecting campaign focused on one or two value narratives and the buyer goals most important to an individual buyer persona. Narrowing the focus to goals specific to each buyer but linking them to larger value themes created continuity and consistency across the whole buyer journey.

Sales and Deal Velocity Playbook

Your sales and deal velocity playbook should also be organized around value narratives, to help your sales and technical sales teams anchor their conversations on buyer goals and resist the pull to product pitching. Your most important sales plays are those that support initial discovery calls, discovery call follow-up, stakeholder calls with decision-making groups, and product demonstration calls. Each of these calls needs to be used to re-anchor to and prioritize buyer goals in ways that enhance an authentic buyer journey.

Chapter 7 will focus on how deal velocity plays, aligned with an authentic buyer journey, lead to a higher percentage of new opportunities converting to closed-won deals. This was especially important for Aginity, which wanted its sales and deal velocity playbook to help a newly formed sales team find the sales tactics that would build momentum from one sales conversation to the next.

"With a more technical product, the first buyer goal is always to solve a technical problem," said Rick Hall, whom you will recall is Aginity's CEO.

I was speaking to Rick from his home office in Steamboat, Colorado. He had just come back to work after a couple of days spent skiing with his daughter, and he had a healthy, tanned glow to show for it. "In most of our sales calls, we are going to be talking to a direct user or the leader of an analytics team. They are going to want to know how Aginity helps them efficiently acquire, prepare, and analyze data."

"Is solving that technical problem important enough to motivate an initial purchase?" I asked. I have seen so many products fail to produce consistent sales because they get an end user motivated, but do not connect to something that a more senior buyer with a budget cares about.

"It can be, but your instinct is right; the technical problem will likely only lead to a smaller sale," Rick said. Then he showed the breadth of knowledge he had gained from his experiences directing large analytics teams at Nielsen Media

Research, Acosta, and elsewhere. "To get to bigger sales and support expansion opportunities, we need to connect to the value the analytics group is driving for a business function. This could be marketing or sales supporting revenue generation, operations or supply chain driving out cost, or customer service improving a customer experience."

"So, I understand it is a technical product," I said, "but it sounds pretty typical of many software products. You can get smaller sales to individual users or groups of users, but to get the bigger sale, you need to find an economic buyer who is interested in solving a bigger business problem and has a budget."

"Yes, I'd say that's fair," Rick said. He leaned back to listen to how I would respond.

"There are a couple of challenges in getting that type of sale closed consistently," I said. "One is the need to have good discovery on both individual user problems and the bigger business problem. The other challenge is keeping those conversations connected, so that the sales team members can build the right picture of buyer value across both groups."

"I have certainly seen that happen," Rick said. "We have a good call, the energy is high around our solution, and there are follow-up action items, so everything seems like it's going right. And then we don't get to the next right step quick enough, and the deal stalls or dies. One of the best sales leaders I had the chance to see in action used to say, 'Sales is all about momentum.' So, how do we build momentum consistently?"

"You've already done one big part of it in the work Chris and the team have done on the value narratives," I said. "The discovery strategy and questions and the product talk tracks around each value narrative are great to guide each of your four key buyer personas toward finding the right unique

Aginity value for individual users, teams, and the business as a whole."

"So, that may help build momentum directly in the call," Rick said, "but that doesn't necessarily lead to momentum into the next step with a decision-making group."

"Yes, deal velocity starts with a good discovery meeting," I said. "Ultimately, though, what is most important is what the buyer agrees to and how that buyer-seller agreement is communicated from one sales interaction to the next."

"So, how does that happen?" Rick asked, shifting his weight forward.

"It sounds simple, but if the team just thinks differently about their sales follow-up emails and sales presentation decks, it can make a ton of difference," I said. "The traditional follow-up email or sales presentation is nearly a hundred percent focused on sharing product and company information. If you just shift that so you always start with a recap of how the buyer defines value and then end with the actions they will take to secure that value, it changes everything."

"I see," Rick said, his tanned faced now breaking into a satisfied smile. "The communication back to the buyer confirms that we have correctly heard their goals and that they are willing to take action to move forward with us. It is sort of an audit on the quality of sales conversation that you ask the buyer to validate."

"Yes. You started the conversation focusing on the importance of buyer goals for individual users as well as the business," I said. "Products are only valuable to the extent that they help a buyer accomplish a goal and the buyer perceives enough impact and high enough value that they are willing to take action."

Rick and I were talking about good discovery and deal velocity strategies that could help the sales team. But it was under Chris Coad's leadership that Aginity completed its sales and deal velocity playbook with its value narratives, to support more consistent deal momentum and velocity from the initial sales call to a closed-won deal. A few key plays at the core of Aginity's sales playbook were:

- A three-part sales meeting structure that starts with discovery about a buyer's technical and business goals, continues with product discussion or demonstration aligned with those goals, and ends by qualifying buyers toward next steps.

- A discovery call checklist that encourages sales team members to follow the three-part structure when running their discovery meetings.

- A set of templated discovery call follow-up emails that encourage a structured report to the buyer on key areas of goal alignment and next steps.

- An updated product demonstration deck that leads with confirmation on buyer goals prior to a demo and ends, post-demo, with a discussion of a mutual plan to confirm technical fit and product rollout.

Closing and Expansion Playbook

Your closing and expansion playbook should use your value narratives to keep sales, account management, and customer success teams focused on connecting initial sales to future expansion upsells. Achieving higher account values comes from broad discovery on a range of buyer goal areas, but broad goal discovery needs to balance an immediate focus on the buyer goal areas that can lead to an initial partnership.

In this closing and expansion playbook, mutual success plans and account plans are the plays that guide the transition from your sales team closing an initial deal to your account management or a customer success team managing expansion opportunities. In chapter 8, we will see how closing and expansion plays can increase account values by increasing the likelihood of product bundling, as well as by shortening the time to upsell expansion.

"For Aginity, account growth is all about turning an initial analytics user group into paying customers and then expanding horizontally," Chris Coad said. We were speaking again by videoconference, continuing our process of moving through one team-level playbook after another to build an end-to-end authentic buyer and customer journey.

"So, your team needs to be really good at mapping out the analytics organization and capturing goals at different levels," I said.

"Well, for us the key is starting bottom-up and getting proof at the individual and team levels and then moving sideways into new departments," Chris said. "That's a lot more important to enterprise-wide adoption for us than going directly to senior analytics leadership at the top of the overall analytics organization."

"We've seen teams use mutual success plans in this situation to help document and prioritize a range of goals for different buyers within the same organization," I said. "It improves focus on the immediate Phase I goal as well as on goals for Phase II, Phase III, and beyond. Is that how you're approaching horizontal expansion?"

"We call it a rollout plan, but the idea is the same," Chris said. "The goal, as you say, is to have a clearer view of what groups are first, second, and so on, in the expansion path. This mapping of the analytics organization is definitely one of the toughest parts of the expansion process. We're still working on tactics to more quickly understand the different groups or teams and how they connect to leadership."

The best sales playbooks focus not on your product, but on the process of continually confirming and refining the buyer goals and target impacts. **Deal velocity is at its highest when a buyer co-develops a specific success statement.**

"So, what have you put in place, and what are you working to put in place?" I asked.

"There are two main things that are helping on the expansion side," Chris said. He counted them off with his fingers as he named them, "The first is building an account plan for each enterprise potential account. The second is building out an account expansion pipeline that is different from the sales pipeline. The account plan is really about the high-level view of key analytics initiatives, the analytics organization, and key decision-making roles, as well as the technical and competitive environment. The account expansion pipeline helps identify those next groups or teams we want to sell to after the first team."

"An account expansion pipeline of your target accounts is a great idea," I said. "It's definitely a best practice we are seeing. It helps make a higher account value actionable by breaking it down into a series of individual deals that might be connected to a new unit or new decision-maker with funding authority."

"Yes, that's how I was thinking about it," Chris said. "Along those lines, I ask my team to think about the 'north star' for each account, meaning the total potential account value based on the head count of analytics engineers and business analysts. Then, I want them to use their expansion pipeline to fill in the opportunities with individual teams that can get them there. Obviously, the more they can connect team goals to overarching analytics initiatives for the company, the more likely they are to be successful in expanding faster."

Aginity's closing and expansion playbook helped build a path to moving more deliberately from value narratives focused on individual efficiency and team collaboration to enterprise-wide goals of a faster time to business insight and one platform for data operations. The core plays in their expansion playbook included:

- A rollout plan (or mutual success plan) to prioritize team-by-team expansion opportunities.

- An account plan with strategic information on analytics priorities, organization, and key decision-makers to develop a strategy toward realizing the "north star," or overall enterprise potential, of an account.

- An expansion opportunity pipeline, outside the sales pipeline, to build a step-by-step road map toward that overall potential.

Renewal and Customer Success Playbook

Your renewal and customer success playbook should focus on building a customer success cycle oriented around buyer goals to support higher renewal rates, higher account values, and deeper segment growth. The renewal and customer success playbook helps customer success teams work toward and manage higher renewal rates and faster account expansions by using the core principle of the authentic buyer journey—buyer goals first, product second. A customer success playbook also helps the customer success team do more strategic work on identifying the buyer voice in each target market segment. Documenting a buyer voice by segment can help customer success team members be more effective in supporting customer use of products and services, and help sales team members more effectively sell to other, new peer customers.

In chapter 9, we will look at how the customer success playbook helps balance tactical renewal and strategic growth activities to fully unlock the potential of customer success as a third revenue team along with marketing and sales. For Aginity, the renewal and customer success playbook focuses on securing a high revenue renewal rate, internal referrals from happy customers that can be turned into a pipeline of account expansion opportunities, and external referrals that can support the development of a pipeline in new accounts.

"We are just building out our renewal and customer success process," Chris explained. "We have a lot of good data on the user base and usage, so we need to start there to work with each account on securing the renewal."

"Have you developed a set of customer success and renewal metrics?" I asked. "Then connected these metrics to a series of customer success plays to manage the health of each account?"

"We definitely have a set of metrics," Chris said. "They include the size of the active user base, the level of usage, and the individual and total number of data platforms being connected to Aginity. We also have metrics looking at individual net promoter scores to see how likely customers are to refer Aginity to new groups or new customers."

"And in looking at those metrics, have you seen patterns emerge around different buyer personas?" I asked.

"I would say there are three broad groups," Chris said. He placed three invisible boxes in the air with his hands as he said, "There are accounts that are in what I would call a 'promoter' mode—very happy, likely to renew with multiple internal advocates. There are accounts in a 'utilization' mode— some good experiences and usage, but a mix of internal promoters and detractors that suggests we should proactively manage the renewal. Finally, there are accounts in a 'detractor' mode—not actively using the service, or dissatisfied, with no really strong internal promoters."

"Let's take those one at a time," I said. "I assume the goal with the promoters is to look for expansion opportunities as well as internal and external referrals?"

"Yes, correct. First we want to hear where they are experiencing the most value and use that to confirm the renewal," Chris said. "Then we want to see if they are open to referrals and references, but we would also like to invite them into a thought leadership conversation. If we can get some of our strongest supporters to write blogs, give video testimonials, or participate in webinars, that will obviously carry a lot of weight with their peers."

"Okay, and how are you thinking about the second group, the accounts in need of higher utilization?"

"Well, with this group, we want to take them back to their original goals for purchasing and also revisit the rollout plan," Chris said. "We need to figure out if there are technical or usability issues that have kept them from the level of expected utilization. We also want to reprioritize the analytics users or groups who might use Aginity. Sometimes there are role or business transitions that cause a gap in usage."

"Okay, that makes sense," I said. "Usually with the folks in a detractor mode, there's little to be done other than just having a very honest conversation about how things have not worked as expected and exploring the reason behind this gap."

"In this case, I would like our customer success team to just 'fall on their sword,' so to speak," Chris said. "I want them to ask if there were any specific functionality limitations, gaps in training or implementation, or challenges in user deployment. If we see openness to troubleshooting these past challenges together, then we would go back to their initial goals for a purchase and see if they're open to hearing what has helped other, similar accounts with utilization."

"So, you are looking for a bit of a reset," I said. "And to see if that reset might restart a conversation about the buyer's past goals or about a new set of goals that point toward a path forward."

Top customer success teams use a handful of metrics to measure renewal and expansion potential. These metrics help segment customers into promoter, utilization, and detractor accounts.

"A reset conversation is a good way to think about it," Chris said.

"So, you have pretty well-built-out customer success plays to support renewals and account expansions," I said. "Are you also having your account team work on customer success stories that can build a customer voice by segment? This can really help create deeper growth in target market sectors."

Chris nodded. "That's definitely on our road map, but still a little ways off, as we really need to refine the renewals and expansion plays you noted."

In building out its renewal and customer success playbook, Aginity incorporated key plays but also had a road map for evolving the playbook down the road. As the company prioritized what to work on, the first version included all of the key plays that can turn customer success into a revenue driver, including:

- A customer success renewal dashboard to manage individual account health.

- A set of renewal plays that includes promoter plays to support account expansions, as well as utilization and detractor plays to manage at-risk renewals.

- Midterm plans to get the customer success team involved in developing both success stories and "a customer voice by market segment" to support faster growth in target market verticals.

Team-Level Playbooks
Support Authentic Conversations

The Aginity example shows how building five aligned team-level playbooks to guide and connect buyer-facing interactions can bring value narratives into action for sales, marketing, and customer success teams. In Part II of this book, we will focus on how value narratives embedded in team-level playbooks can accelerate revenue outcomes for individual go-to-market teams. Chapter 6 focuses on leveraging the value narratives framework and building out prospecting playbooks that increase new opportunity production. Chapter 7 looks at building sales and deal velocity playbooks that begin and end every sales conversation with buyer goals that support sales teams in producing more closed-won opportunities. Chapter 8 looks at the handoff between sales, account management, and customer success and specifically explores how deeper discovery by all of these teams can raise account values by reducing both price discounting and the time from a first sale to expansion sales. Chapter 9 looks at how the customer success team can leverage value narratives to manage a goal-oriented customer success process in ways that drive higher renewal rates while also building out the "voice of the customer by segment" to drive faster growth in target market segments.

YOUR NEXT STEPS ON TEAM-LEVEL PLAYBOOKS

- **Go-to-market playbook audits:** Review content marketing, marketing campaigns, and playbooks for sales, account management, and customer success. How aligned are they with your value narratives, value discovery questions, and key capability talk tracks?

- **Revenue outcomes strategy:** Where should you focus first in developing or deepening team-level playbooks? To make quick progress on one or two key revenue outcomes, pick your top outcomes for improvement, then select playbooks to develop.

Get supplemental content at winalytics.com/theplays on moving from your value narratives to team-level playbooks focused on your most important revenue outcomes.

PART II

An Authentic Buyer Journey and Revenue Outcomes

6

Prospecting as a Trusted Advisor

"**I** AM ON the hook for really big growth in our direct sales," Torchlight's incoming VP of sales—let's call her Mary—told me. "Our CEO is basically looking for a record number in my first year in the role, and we don't yet know the best strategy for getting new prospects into our pipeline."

I was sitting with Mary in Torchlight's main conference room. It was a beautiful spring morning in New England, and sunlight was streaming through the east-facing floor-to-ceiling glass wall. I was at one end of a long conference table; Mary was at the other end, and on the wall above her head was Torchlight's tagline, "Caring Is Everyone's Business," in large print. Torchlight is the provider of a digital caregiver platform sold to human resources departments as an employee benefit. The platform helps employee caregivers better manage their work–life balance.

"Before I arrived, the strategy relied on high-volume email campaigns that pitched features of the Torchlight platform," Mary continued. "It got some meetings early on, but then meetings dried up and it sort of alienated the market. I've been to conferences where the running joke when I walked in the room was, 'Hey, have you heard from Torchlight lately?'"

She winced slightly, and she sounded a bit disheartened as she continued, "As someone caring for an elderly parent with Alzheimer's, it was really challenging to think that the market might be stepping back from a high-quality product backed by deep medical expertise like Torchlight."

With Torchlight, companies can provide employees like Mary, who have family caregiving responsibilities, with resources to help care for a parent with Alzheimer's or a parent with a physical disability who finds it difficult to live alone. Employees with a dependent child who has a learning disability, attention deficit disorder, video game addiction, or some other challenge can also use Torchlight to find support. The platform creates a one-stop place for a caregiver to find resources and experts, schedule and manage appointments, and even petition for government or school supplemental support.

"Before I arrived, Torchlight struggled with its direct sales effort," Mary explained. "Growth all came through channel partnerships. Those channel sales brought in revenue from almost a hundred large companies, but there was no access to the channel partner's sales and marketing data to generate insight on how to grow sales faster. The good news is that just before I arrived, the company went through a positioning exercise to identify three key value narratives for our existing customers. Each of these value areas was well documented with data directly from our platform."

The first of the documented value narratives Mary described was increasing employee engagement: 86 percent of employees who used the Torchlight platform said they felt more positive about their employers. The second value driver was increasing employee productivity: platform users saved an average of 2.35 hours per week, or 115 hours per year, on caregiver tasks. The third was reducing benefits costs specifically for employee child caregiving, with an average savings per child dependent of nearly $3,500 in costs that could be moved from corporate benefits to a local school district service.

Torchlight Uses Value Narratives to Accelerate Prospecting

"With the new value narratives and data, we quickly started to do two things very differently in our prospecting," Mary said. It was clear she was a true believer in Torchlight and had directly experienced the importance of its resources. "First, we started to lead with insights on supporting employee caregivers rather than our product. We shared insights from our client success stories, as well as short research snippets from industry research studies. We wanted our potential buyers to understand we had a ton of expertise to share."

Mary is describing the shift from a more traditional "spray and pray," high-volume outreach to a focus on what I call prospecting as a trusted advisor. At the heart of the shift is a focus on buyer empathy and leading not with your company's product or history, but by inviting your buyers into a value-added conversation about their goals, challenges, and the things keeping them up at night.

"Second, we also stopped the high-volume email blasts," Mary continued. "We moved to smaller prospecting campaigns of eighty to a hundred emails with tailored messages for different levels of human resource leadership in different market sectors. We also started using mixed-touch cadences with email, call, and voicemail outreach, so our prospects know there is a human on the other end. Over a six-month period, we reached out to around one thousand ideal buyers in the financial services, life sciences, professional services, manufacturing, and energy sectors as well as to Employer of Choice award winners."

Empathizing with your buyer becomes more powerful when you personalize outreach with a human voice over the phone and through voicemail, video, or social media outreach. Prospecting as a trusted advisor around a buyer's goals and with more personalized engagement leaves prospects with a much more positive impression of a company. Typically, 90-95 percent of your prospects will not take a meeting on a first round of outreach, but if the communication is empathetic and personalized, they are more likely to keep information on your company, join a webinar, download a white paper, or respond positively to the next outreach.

"The new approach dramatically increased our prospecting productivity," Mary finished, with a twinkle in her eye and just the slightest fist pump. "The number of new discovery calls per month increased by sixty-one percent and stayed elevated for the next twelve months. The shift away from product pitching to sharing buyer insights increased not only the quantity of discovery calls, but the quality as well. As a result, the percentage of initial discovery calls that progressed to a second call with a decision-making group increased by about twenty percent."

The new prospecting approach helped Mary hit that aggressive direct sales number set by her CEO. It made her inaugural year as the VP of sales the first time in five years that the company had achieved its direct sales target.

Your buyers are much more likely to commit to a first call if they believe they will learn something of value about their goals and challenges. **The last thing your buyers want is to sit through a product pitch.**

Prospecting as a Trusted Advisor

Sales and marketing teams often make two big mistakes in their prospecting work. First, in their messaging, they rely too heavily on their product pitching, content, and attention grabbers, which leads to an information blur and causes prospects to check out. Second, in their outreach approach, they default to high-volume email sequences, forgetting that often the quickest path to getting a prospect to take a meeting is more traditional phone outreach, one-to-one social media engagement, targeted video, or mailings that can personalize interactions.

PROSPECTING AS A TRUSTED ADVISOR

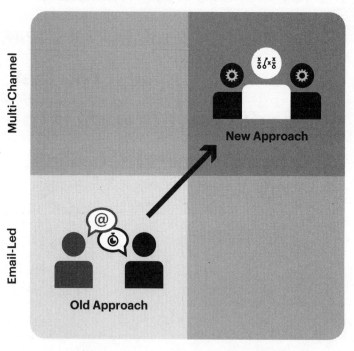

In my work with Winalytics clients, I have seen teams that shift to prospecting as trusted advisors increase their average prospecting productivity dramatically, typically with a 40–45 percent gain in the number of discovery calls yielded from the same pool of buyer contacts.

If your team prospects with a focus on the product, the buyer knows that if they commit to a discovery call, the meeting is going to be all about the product. And as I've said, no one wants to sit through a product pitch. By contrast, when your team commits to prospecting with buying insights, you are saying to the buyer, "We are going to provide you with a ton of value in early discovery, even if you do not decide to work with us." This makes a buyer more interested in taking part in a discovery call.

When prospecting as a trusted advisor, it's also critical to personalize outreach. This means picking up the phone to catch buyers at their desks, leaving voicemails, tailoring follow-up emails, connecting on LinkedIn, or sending a targeted video. All of these alternatives to generic email show your potential buyer that there is a human being on the other side of the email outreach. They also say to your buyer, "I am interested in engaging with you through the communication channel of your choice." However, teams too often struggle to stay motivated with more personalized phone, voicemail, print, or video outreach and revert to "spray and pray" email blasts.

A study by Salesforce found that phone-led outreach was 274 times more effective than email-led outreach. It involves what Ken Krogue, a XANT (formerly InsideSales) cofounder, calls "pleasant persistence." However, XANT's own research shows that while maximum yield to first meetings happens with six call attempts to the same contact, the average seller makes just 1.4 outreach attempts. SalesLoft has shown that including a video in an email outreach increases responses

Authentic prospecting campaigns tell a story about buyer goal achievement. The first touches describe a common buyer goal or challenge. Later, touches share proof you can help with that goal and then invite a conversation.

rates by 26 percent, and HubSpot has shown how opportunities sourced from emails that included a video convert at a much higher rate.

As we discussed in chapter 5, a value narrative playbook identifies a specific route to buyer value that can be used by your entire go-to-market organization, from marketing to sales to customer success. It is then team-specific playbooks that bring the value narratives to life and make each step of the buyer journey authentic. Within each team playbook is a series of individual "plays" that suggest a set of individual or coordinated actions to guide that team's buyer-facing interactions.

A prospecting playbook guides the activities of prospecting teams, often called either business development representative (BDR) teams or sales development representative (SDR) teams. It can also guide the activities of account executives who are responsible for sourcing new opportunities as well as working on advancing and closing those opportunities. The prospecting playbook has three foundational plays that all need to be put in place together to move the needle on prospecting outcomes. The three key plays in the prospecting playbook are:

1 An authentic campaign narrative
2 A prospecting block schedule
3 An authentic commercial (or call pickup script)

Prospecting Playbook: Authentic Campaign Narrative

The first and most foundational play is the authentic campaign narrative, which tells a story about value creation for a specific buyer role in a target market segment.

Marketers and prospecting teams often think of campaigns as a "touch" cadence or a series of sequential email or phone outreaches to a potential buyer. Most marketing campaigns share too much information about a company, its product, and its content marketing. The difference between a traditional campaign touch sequence and an authentic campaign narrative is that the authentic narrative uses the touches intentionally to build a story about achieving a buyer's goals.

An authentic narrative typically includes five to eight touches paced over three to four weeks. The touch sequence starts with describing a common buyer problem, continues with proof that you can solve that problem, and then outlines goals for a short intro call that includes benefits on both sides.

A strong authentic campaign narrative gets the buyer journey off to a good start by drawing on key elements of the value narrative playbook, including:

- Value discovery questions in email and call outreach that invite a prospect into a value-added conversation about their goal and challenges.

- Capability talk tracks and research snippets with buyer insights mapped to specific buyer goal areas and opportunities for buyer value.

- Client success story snippets, testimonials, and client lists to provide direct evidence of helping with their goal achievement.

At Torchlight, they developed authentic narratives focused on employee engagement, employee productivity, and benefits cost savings. Before building campaign narratives to support prospecting outreach, the Torchlight team's outreach, like most prospecting, was essentially asking for the product order in its email outreach. By putting value narratives into their campaigns, the team's new approach started conversations that were valuable to the buyer.

AUTHENTIC PROSPECTING NARRATIVE

Touch Types	
Email Call Voicemail LinkedIn Embedded Video 1–3 Content Assets	**Touch 1: Invite** Email | Content #1
	4 DAYS
	Touch 2/3: Offer Evidence Call/VM | 2nd Email
	7 DAYS
	Touch 4/5: Reinforce Call/VM | 3rd Email | Content #2 & #3
	7 DAYS
	Touch 6/7: Expand Call/VM | 4th Email | Social Touch
	7 DAYS
	Touch 8+: Next Time Goodbye | VM/Email

Torchlight's new campaign narratives use value discovery questions to encourage a prospect to think about how solving the caregiver challenge could help with key human resource goals:

- What can you do for your employees who struggle with work-life balance due to family caregiving responsibilities?

- How can you retain and career track more high potential women leaders who also need to manage caregiving responsibilities?

- Have you considered that school-based programming could not only lead to a better outcome for child learning challenges but also reduce your benefits cost?

Torchlight's agile campaigns also include research snippets, which make any follow-up phone outreach feel more value-added and intended to help educate a human resource leader or benefits manager on caregiver challenges. The emails include phrases with article links, such as:

- I write to share this SHRM article, "More Workers Than You Realize Are Caregivers," which highlights how 56 percent of caregivers never disclose their responsibility.

- You may have read the AARP guide titled "Supporting Caregivers in the Workplace," which details the broad set of responsibilities and activities that can distract employee caregivers from their work.

Later emails in the Torchlight narrative shift to providing evidence of how Torchlight can help with a business goal area, with statements like:

- Torchlight complements rather than replaces other wellness benefit choices, like your Employee Assistance Program, but is specifically designed to manage caregiving challenges.

- On a call, we can include examples of our work with other leading employers, such as Dell EMC, Tripadvisor, and Discover Financial Services, to increase employee caregiver engagement and retention.

- On a call, we can share how we helped more than 3,100 caregivers at Johnson & Johnson and supported the transfer of $2.9 million in health care costs to public and school resources.

Prospecting with a focus on your buyer's goal achievement makes it more likely that an individual buyer will not only engage, but also be willing to include their boss and colleagues.

Getting more prospects to take an initial meeting is not the only benefit of shifting to prospecting as a trusted advisor. It also increases the likelihood that a buyer who did not take a meeting the first time they were contacted will take a meeting the next time. It leaves a good impression. As important, the shift also makes it a lot easier for your buyer to introduce their boss and colleagues to a new vendor. Rather than the internal conversation being focused on getting them to "come learn about this product," it can be: "Let's see how this might help us solve that challenge we've been talking about recently."

Prospecting Playbook: Prospecting Blocks

The second key play in the prospecting playbook is a schedule of individual prospecting blocks for each member of the sales or prospecting team.

The prospecting block schedule builds a commitment to consistent execution of the campaign narratives by guiding the pacing and timing of each prospect outreach. The prospecting block schedule outlines two-to-three-hour prospecting blocks that focus on nothing but call and email outreach to prospects. Each prospecting block is assigned to a specific set of touches in a specific campaign narrative.

If presented the wrong way, the idea of prospecting block schedules could come across as either micromanaging or treating working professionals as juveniles. So, in our work at Winalytics, we emphasize three reasons this play is so important to prospecting success.

The first reason that prospecting blocks are so important is that the majority of BDR and SDR team members doing prospecting work are very early in their careers. There are some "old dog" sales representatives who just really enjoy the hunt of continually finding new buyers and choose to specialize in prospecting rather than work a full sales pipeline. However, about 80–90 percent of BDR and SDR teams are made up of recent college graduates or early-career professionals who are exploring sales as a career. For these people, the prospecting schedule becomes a very clear step-by-step road map to being successful in their role.

PROSPECTING BLOCK SCHEDULE

	MON	TUE	WED	THU	FRI
8 am					
9 am					
10 am		Campaign 2 Call/VM 2		Campaign 2 Social Touch	Campaign 1/2 Outstanding
11 am					
12 pm					
1 pm					
2 pm	Campaign 1 Email 2		Campaign 2 Email 3		
3 pm					
4 pm					
5 pm					

In addition, prospecting teams are typically juggling multiple campaigns and campaign narratives involving hundreds of contacts at any one time. The prospecting block schedule makes sure they are hitting each of their campaigns enough times and at the right time. For more seasoned sales professionals who are running an end-to-end sales pipeline and are

The best prospecting playbooks treat each prospecting campaign as an opportunity for persona-message testing. Each campaign provides evidence on the areas of highest value by buyer persona.

responsible for prospecting new deals, as well as progressing and closing those deals, a prospecting block can ensure they are spending enough time at the front of the funnel and not all of their time closing deals.

Finally, the prospecting block schedule ensures a higher level of discipline and commitment. It helps insulate a team from the many distractions that can discourage prospecting outreach. It helps those involved in prospecting stretch themselves from the common 1.4 touches per contact noted earlier to something closer to eight touches per contact.

Prospecting Playbook: Authentic Commercial

The third foundational play in the prospecting playbook, following the campaign narrative and the prospecting block schedule, is the authentic commercial. The authentic commercial is a short introduction to your company on the goals and problems you help a buyer solve. It is authentic because rather than being one-directional, it is designed to be interactive. Like the authentic campaign, you can use the authentic commercial to invite a buyer into a value-added conversation about your unique approach to a buyer goal or pain. It can be used when a prospect picks up the phone or in a voicemail or video script. When your team runs a prospecting campaign, their phone outreach will result in either a call pickup, meaning reaching the prospect directly by phone, or an opportunity to leave a voicemail if the prospect does not pick up their phone.

In my work with Winalytics clients, I have seen that call pickups and voicemails can generate 40-50 percent of initial discovery calls from prospecting campaigns. The call pickup gives a prospector the chance to directly make their case for why a first call will be valuable. The voicemail can also be used to make the case and put a human at the other end of the email.

I have also seen that a well-executed call pickup is really difficult. To be successful, you have to resist the temptation to immediately pitch your product or sale and instead feel the buyer out on what might make them receptive to agreeing to a discovery call. Call pickups are most likely to lead to a longer discovery call when the potential buyer feels there will be a ton of value from joining that call.

It is often nervousness about the call pickup that will keep SDRs or sales executives from picking up the phone in the first place. So, building and practicing a call pickup script can be critical to prospecting success. The authentic commercial, like the other elements of the prospecting playbook, needs to be rooted in the company's value narratives.

The authentic commercial used by Torchlight draws on all the same value discovery questions, value mapping talk tracks, and success cases as the prospecting emails, but now they are shared verbally. Torchlight's call pickup script follows an ideal structure and includes the following guidelines:

- **Be transparent:** Share your name and that you work for Torchlight.

- **Demonstrate empathy:** Highlight your focus on supporting employee caregivers.

- **Invite a conversation:** Use value discovery questions to probe about initiatives in supporting employee caregivers to increase engagement or retention while reducing benefits costs.

- **Set up the discovery call:** Map to buyer goal areas with evidence of success and unique value that could include capability talk track, peer reference companies, or success case snippets.

- **Let the prospect confirm value:** Directly ask if they are willing to schedule a meeting and discuss their top areas of focus for that meeting.

The authentic campaign narrative, prospecting block schedule, and authentic commercial are three key plays that set the foundation for prospecting as a trusted advisor. The next level of prospecting productivity comes from building a library of campaign narratives and running agile market tests to identify the fastest path to more high-quality first meetings. Your best prospecting is going to rely on micro-messaging with the language in your campaign narratives tailored to individual buyer personas for each of your target market segments. If you structure each of your campaigns as a market test, you can directly collect the market data on the specific value messaging and language, by buyer persona and market segment, that drives the most first meetings and new opportunities.

I call these "persona-messaging tests," and they are designed to provide feedback and updates directly to the campaign narrative messaging and structure. The tests help a company double down on prospecting as a trusted advisor by identifying how to add the most value in early discovery for each buying role and market segment.

Persona-messaging tests also help optimize prospecting investments. In prospecting work, unlike sales or customer success conversations at other parts of the buyer journey, there is no direct way to ask a buyer to confirm what they value most. Structured comparison of campaign outcomes— that is, which campaign narratives, by segment and buyer role, lead to the most first meetings and new opportunities— is the best way to directly observe what buyers value most.

Companies that build their prospecting productivity the quickest think of each prospecting campaign as a market test.

Let's look now at how AdmitHub combined the shift to prospecting as a trusted advisor with persona-message testing on different campaign narratives to drive prospecting productivity and support rapid growth.

PERSONA–MESSAGING TESTS
ON OPTIMAL PERSONA MESSAGING

Prospecting Tests	Messaging / Persona Test #1	Messaging / Persona Test #2	Messaging / Persona Test #3
Value Narrative	Value Message #1	Value Message #2	Value Message #3
Persona in Target Segment	Persona #1 Target Segment #1	Persona #1 Target Segment #1	Persona #1 Target Segment #2
Evidence and Social Proof	Peer client lists Success story snippets Client testimonials Company blogs Research snippets		
Personalization Strategies	Peer references Direct experiences Personal video Print mailing		

AdmitHub Develops Persona-Messaging Tests

"We are getting a great volume of inbound leads," Brian Ruhlmann, AdmitHub's director of sales and marketing, told me, "but almost all are from director- or manager-level staff in the enrollment management, admissions, or marketing offices." Brian and I were meeting on a December morning in the kitchen of Harvard Innovation Labs with a cold-brew coffee, strategizing about building out AdmitHub's prospecting playbooks. Brian was moonlighting as an extra in a historical film set in Ireland during the mid-nineteenth century, so he had grown his hair long for weekend film shoots, which gave a visual impression that contrasted with his acute business smarts.

"It's nice that these mid-level managers are interested in us," he continued, "but it takes a long time for them to get the attention of the higher-ups who control the purse strings. We really have to figure out the prospecting strategies that get us to campus leaders and decision-makers quicker."

AdmitHub was at the beginning of its run to become the premier AI-based conversational messaging platform that helps colleges and universities achieve their enrollment goals. AdmitHub's platform uses AI and two-way testing to have individual conversations with thousands of students at one time in a way that would never be possible for human advisors alone. The company's college and university clients use AdmitHub to boost enrollments from their applicant pools and to increase the number of enrolling students into their second year of college and beyond.

"We are launching a set of marketing campaigns we call the 'Big Cheese' campaigns," Brian told me. "We are going to develop a very different set of prospecting campaigns for senior leaders. We've been using product- and capability-related concepts and phrases like 'hire AI,' 'scaling support,' and 'FAQ automation' for mid-level managers. For senior leaders, we're going to focus on economic impact. I want to find out what appeals most to these senior leaders: increasing enrollments, reducing student dropouts, or reducing the cost of student support."

Brian had just described his plan to shift from a more traditional high-volume campaign to a set of agile campaigns that would be new in their playbook. He realized that to engage more senior leaders they needed to lead not with product but with a more authentic, personalized buyer experience focused on the enrollment goals that were most important to senior academic leaders.

"Also, rather than just sequences of email outreaches, we're going to use mixed-touch cadences." Brian got up and continued talking as he walked a few steps over to the coffee bar to refill his cold brew. "We plan to combine email with phone and voicemail outreach to senior decision-makers and their administrators. We are also going to mail out a copy of our cofounder's book with handwritten notes to these senior leaders. The call outreach and the book mailing are both designed to set the tone of having a higher-level strategic conversation."

He continued, describing the plan used for active market campaign testing to figure out the buying goals, buyer roles, and market segments that led to the highest prospecting productivity. Part of that testing was figuring out the types of prospecting touches that resonated the most with senior buyers, and where it was worth investing in the higher-cost touch of the book mailing.

"We don't know yet whether it is a provost, CIO [chief information officer], VP of enrollment management, or VP of student affairs who will be a most effective executive sponsor." Brian paused, thinking. Then he explained, "We are

Your persona-messaging tests can focus on identifying the messages and touch types with the highest impact by persona. Or, alternatively, you can test for highest impact messages by buyer personas in different market segments.

going to run messaging tests for each. We'll focus on enrollment gains with the VP of enrollment management, retention gains with the VP of student affairs, staff efficiency gains with the CIO, and test all three messages with the provosts."

"I have identified just over thirty-five hundred contacts with those roles and titles at institutions in our target markets." Brian leaned forward, put both hands on his cold brew, and smiled broadly. "That list was a really big lift but worth the effort. It includes large public universities with more than ten thousand students, two-year community colleges, and top doctoral research universities. We've been careful to build around good reference accounts that can support targeted outreach."

AdmitHub Uses Market Learnings to Grow Faster

Brian's Big Cheese campaigns ran through the winter and into early spring. AdmitHub was trying to get ahead of the admissions season, with the bulk of admissions decisions going out in April and then several months of work to yield admitted students to land the next year's class. About six months after our initial meeting on prospecting campaigns, Brian and I met to debrief on the Big Cheese initiative.

"Revising our prospecting playbook with outbound campaign narratives took our first meeting setting to a whole new level," Brian said. "At the start of these campaigns, just one in six new prospect meetings came from outbound prospecting. Six months later, our outbound meetings have doubled to thirty percent of new prospect calls. Almost all of that increase in new meetings is with senior buyers either in the enrollment management group, reporting to the VP of enrollment, or in academic leadership groups, reporting to the provost."

Brian and the AdmitHub team also learned that the role of the buyer who took part in the first meeting had a dramatic impact on their sales productivity. When their first discovery call was at an associate VP level or better, they closed the deal 22 percent of the time, compared to just 7 percent of the time when first discovery calls were with a director-level staff member or below.

The focus on active market testing also confirmed large public universities to be AdmitHub's top target market segment. For its large public university clients like Georgia State, Cal State Northridge, and West Texas A&M, AdmitHub was a unique platform that could help in all phases of "lifecycle student engagement," from attracting student interest, to getting them to enroll, to retaining them through the first year.

"I remember our very first call with Kent State," Brian shared. "They were impressed with how we'd had great success in other large public university settings, but the conversation also showed that taking time to personalize outreach with our book mailing really paid off. The provost started the call saying, 'We have the president and the leadership team here. We've all read your book and have bought in. Can we tell you what's going on at Kent State and how we might partner?'" Brian paused and smiled broadly. "We got a verbal commitment for an eighty-thousand-dollar-a-year contract about eight weeks later."

Prospecting Playbook:
Three More Value-Based Campaign Plays

Most teams do not immediately arrive at their best messaging in prospecting campaign narratives by buyer persona or market segment. For a growth company like AdmitHub, it can take four to six months of active market testing to find the right mix of message, buyer, and segment. For enterprise companies, it often takes even longer and requires more effective leadership. In enterprise teams, responsibility for marketing messages and content typically sits with the marketing organization, while execution of prospecting touch cadences sits with a sales development or sales team.

Once a team has a good sense of the right campaign narratives for positioning value for each buyer role and market segment, there are three subsequent plays that can continue to build prospecting velocity while also enhancing the approach of prospecting around a buyer's goals as a trusted advisor:

1 Smart blast campaigns
2 Peer referral campaigns
3 Expansion campaigns

FOUR VALUE-BASED CAMPAIGNS

Campaigns	Campaign Description
Authentic campaign narrative	Tell a story about buyer value creation with a mix of email, call, and social touches
Smart blast campaigns	Use value-added emails to qualify prospects into more personal touches
Peer referral campaigns	Tell a story about peer value creation with quotes, stories, and customer lists
Account expansion campaigns	Target new buyers at existing customers by highlighting value already created

The first new play is what we call a *smart blast campaign*. It involves targeted outreach around a proven campaign narrative to a larger list of between two hundred and four hundred contacts for the same buyer personas or same buyer roles. In the smart blast, a campaign starts with three value-added emails in a row before any calling begins. The emails lead with discovery questions about buyer goals, research snippets from studies that share insights on the buyer problem, and client success case snippets.

The smart blast campaign is a good way to help focus time, follow-up calls, and emails with the most engaged prospects. Those contacts you place on the list for follow-up call and email outreach are the ones who opened emails, clicked on links, downloaded content assets from the web, or registered for webinars. From my work with Winalytics clients, I've seen that a well-designed smart blast campaign typically has a 30–35 percent engagement rate, so two hundred to four hundred contacts in the initial smart blast sequence might yield between seventy and one hundred forty most engaged contacts for direct calling.

A second new campaign play is the *peer referral campaign*. Peer referral campaigns draw on the same discovery questions, research snippets, and capabilities statements as the typical value-based campaign narrative, but rely more heavily on the use of peer referencing. Each email or voicemail includes a reference to a list of peer client names and/or a peer client success case snippet. We saw how AdmitHub used its work with Georgia State, as well as Cal State Northridge and West Texas A&M, to build reference value for large public universities wrestling with "lifecycle student engagement," from attracting student interest, to getting them to enroll, to retaining them through and beyond the first year.

Similarly, one of Torchlight's most successful peer referral campaigns was about a "best of employers" prospect list. The list was put together from top employer lists in magazine publications, including AARP *The Magazine*, *Fortune*, and *Working Mother*. The companies were recognized as top employers with strong business growth while also being family-friendly. Torchlight's outreach focused on its work helping the "best of employers" engage and retain top employee talent. Their reference campaigns shared examples of work with the "best of employers" in a broad set of sectors, including Accenture in consulting, BioGen in biotech, Dell in computers, and Johnson & Johnson in consumer goods.

The final new prospecting play is the *expansion campaign*. Expansion campaigns are also commonly referred to as white space campaigns. These campaigns focus on the existing customer base and look for opportunities to increase upsell and cross-sell activity by prospecting into the "white" or open space where there is no business relationship. Many companies run expansion campaigns that focus on pitching products that a client has not currently purchased.

Expansion campaigns, however, work best when they focus on a new buyer goal area. In the strongest expansion campaigns, there is synergy between the initial and the expansion goal areas.

The strongest expansion campaigns use a value narratives framework to connect buyer goal achievement in one area to the opportunity to partner on new goal areas. As we will see in our next company example, with Augmedix, one of the strengths of the value narratives framework is that it makes it possible to directly link engaging a buyer for a new product purchase to the value they derived from the first product purchase.

Augmedix Prospects Around Landing and Expanding

"I joined Augmedix at a really exciting time of new product innovation but also of very aggressive growth expectations," shared Jon Hawkins, CRO at Augmedix. "To hit our growth targets, we were going to need to be very efficient in using our prospecting capacity to focus on the campaigns with the highest returns across new customer acquisition and current account expansion."

I had been introduced to Jon through a Stanford connection. Our connection noted that he was a bright and talented revenue leader with an undergraduate degree from Stanford, an MBA from Harvard, and deep experience working with venture capital and private equity–backed companies. Going into the call, I wondered if I was going to experience the barrage of acronyms and revenue metrics—CAC ratios for customer acquisition costs, NRR for net revenue retention, time to payback, etc.—that were common in conversations with revenue leaders who had that kind of pedigree.

Jon sat in his home office for our videoconference. The call was a pleasant surprise. His grasp of growth metrics was certainly strong, but the quality of his training came through the most in his focus on go-to-market excellence with a clever approach to connecting product, positioning, and sales strategy.

Augmedix is a tech-enabled virtual medical documentation service that removes the heavy burden of capturing medical notes during the doctor-patient interaction. Anyone who has been to the doctor's office has witnessed the issue doctors face splitting their mind between their patients and taking accurate notes. This is the problem Augmedix solves.

The burden of note-taking has increased in recent years with growing state and federal electronic health record requirements. The company's Augmedix Live solution offers a live virtual assistant that takes notes, puts in referrals, and offers doctor reminders. The Augmedix Notes solution is a tech-enabled service that captures and records notes in the background via smartphones or Google Glass, which the doctor then reviews and signs off on.

Most teams significantly underuse peer referral and expansion campaigns. Both types of campaigns leverage success with a known buyer to make it easier to get a new buyer.

"The good news is that when I joined Augmedix, I was able to immediately identify a new and higher-value buyer goal area to engage CFOs and other executive-level buyers." Jon immediately demonstrated his instinct to deepen go-to-market excellence by building one success upon another. "For years, the company had positioned itself as helping with physician burnout by removing the burden of note-taking. However, that goes only so far with CFOs or senior executives. To engage these buyers, we had to show a financial return measured in revenue units to invest in a third-party documentation solution."

Jon developed his revenue growth strategy around an idea that many revenue leaders neglect. Upselling and cross-selling work best when they're focused on new buyer goal areas and new business impacts. Without connecting the first and second investment, the upsell ask can be perceived as a vendor-centric "ask for more budget" rather than a buyer-centric investment in deepening goal achievement.

Jon showed his knack for leveraging data not for its own sake but to tighten the link between product outcomes and positioning value to buyers. "Just after I joined, we completed a large-scale study on doctor productivity with one of the health system clients. That study identified a direct correlation between doctor productivity and time spent on electronic health records. Doctors were spending up to half their day taking notes manually. If Augmedix took away that note-taking responsibility, the doctors could save two to three hours a day and see more patients. Every clinical department can put financial worth on that."

The addition of clinician productivity gave Augmedix the right mix of buyer goals and impacts to accelerate growth. Augmedix's initial impacts were emotional and organizational. Freeing doctors from note-taking increases physician quality of life, builds higher clinic morale, and reduces physician burnout. By directly linking its technology to higher physician productivity, Augmedix added a very clear financial payoff to these existing emotional and organizational impacts.

"That very clear ROI payoff," Jon continued, "gave us a crisp message to directly prospect high-level executive champions in new health systems as well as engage CFOs and other executive sponsors at existing health system clients for upselling into more practice areas and departments."

Augmedix works with nearly one thousand doctors at fifteen large health systems, like Sutter Health, Dignity Health, CommonSpirit Health, and US Oncology. It has an addressable market of several hundred large health systems that are not currently clients. The new focus on physician ROI provided a fresh opportunity to launch a series of prospecting campaigns to grow within existing as well as new hospital systems.

"In this new phase of growth, we needed to get very disciplined in figuring out how we could win faster," Jon said. He shifted forward in his chair and began to walk through a plan for measuring investments while building new sales opportunities. "We started to do structured comparisons across all of our inbound and outbound campaigns. We began to measure the total number of leads and meetings associated with each campaign to get to a 'conversion to meeting' metric and figure out what messages were working. We also started to collect qualitative information on the quality of those meetings."

From my experience working with companies of all sizes and sectors, I recognized that Jon's plan easily fit into the "top 10 percent" bucket. Most revenue leaders do not have a plan to measure across all of their prospecting approaches or to track both the quality and quantity of new opportunities generated. Jon's approach also helped Augmedix build a new "land and expand" strategy for account growth.

"We learned quickly that primary care had one of the highest needs but lowest ROIs, and often not the discretionary budget to invest in our platform," Jon said. "We could get primary care engaged in reducing physician burnout, but to convert a larger deal, we would get a 'wealthier' practice area like orthopedics to pay for primary care, and use both areas to build the ROI case with the CFO. If we could get even ten to twenty doctors in any clinical area to use our platform, within six months we would have the ROI data we need to go to the CFO."

Augmedix's focus on growing into the "white space" and their disciplined testing to identify key impacts and ROI opportunities by buyer role helped the company grow from about $11 million in revenue—when it began to fully integrate the physician productivity ROI case—to just under $17 million in annualized revenue two years later.

Prospecting as a Trusted Advisor Builds Faster Engagement

In this chapter, we have learned from the Torchlight, Admit-Hub, and Augmedix examples how if you embed buyer value narratives in a prospecting playbook, you can drive a faster pace of new first meetings and high-quality opportunities. Prospecting as a trusted advisor with a focus on buyer goal achievement is as effective with new buyers as it is for existing customers. Your buyers and customers who are approached in this way are more likely to engage. They know, even if they do not decide to do business (or more business) with your company, that they are taking away learnings and insights that will help with their day-to-day work. Focusing prospecting campaigns on buyer goals, research insights, and success with peers also leaves a much stronger brand impression with those buyers who opt against taking a meeting after the first outreach attempts.

In chapter 7, we will turn to linking buyer value narratives from prospecting to sales. The chapter focuses on developing a sales and deal velocity playbook that increases the number of closed-won deals by starting and ending each sales call with a focus on what each buyer cares most about.

YOUR NEXT STEPS ON PROSPECTING AS A TRUSTED ADVISOR

- **Authentic campaign strategy:** Review your main prospecting campaigns to see how effectively you're inviting buyers into a value-added conversation rather than leading with your product. What discovery questions, content assets, personalization options, and peer references invite a conversation?

- **Authentic commercial:** Review your strategy for quickly positioning unique value. How effectively do you use call pickups, voicemails, video, or social touches to convey that message of unique value?

Get more resources to build plays that support authentic prospecting at winalytics.com/theplays. You can revise your prospecting strategy on your own with marketing content available to you. You can also work with marketing and sales to advocate for new content.

7

Selling into Buyer-Defined Value

"IF WE'RE competing on price, that's no one's fault but our own," declared a VP-level sales leader for Avis Budget Group's corporate business—let's call her Sharon. "Our buyers may think they're making a commodity purchase. It's our job to show them that if they're thinking only about price, they are dramatically underestimating the value of their employees' time."

I was speaking to Sharon in her home office via videoconference. I quickly learned that while she is a senior sales leader, she could just as easily be a senior marketing leader. Her sales strategy starts with buyer personas, positioning, product, and pricing considerations rather than just a focus on blocking and tackling sales execution. In fact, she teaches business school courses on sales strategy that are cross-listed in the marketing department.

Avis Budget's corporate sales team sells car rental programs for employee travelers to a range of businesses, governments, and associations. One team is responsible for large global companies, like Boeing, Apple, and Microsoft. Another team is responsible for governmental organizations, like the Federal Emergency Management Agency and the State of Florida, and associations, like Red Cross. There are also teams responsible for mid-market and small businesses.

"We have maintained a leadership position in the corporate rental market by encouraging our buyers to think first not about renting a car but about travel-time efficiency and the quality of the travel experience," Sharon continued. For her, buyer engagement starts with a focus on positioning value and differentiation. "We are not always the cheapest option, but those looking for the cheapest option probably give no thought to the value of their road warriors' time."

Through internal investments and acquisitions, Avis Budget has invested in product innovations and technologies that add a service layer and the ability to customize travel options to its car rentals. The company's ability to differentiate stems from focusing its corporate buyers on the opportunity for time saving, cost saving, and conveniences for its traveling employees.

Another key element of Sharon's sales strategy focused on positioning value to both the buyer personas using and buying Avis Budget's car rental services. "Our buyers are usually in operations or human resources," she said. "They have mostly traveled for leisure and have no experience of back-to-back business travel days or weeks. We need to use good questions to help them understand the value of travel efficiency."

Avis Budget has a profile-driven reservation system that selects a car and creates a digital wallet for the rental and travel documents. For a business traveler in the preferred program, this means no reservations, no counters, no wait lines, and no paperwork. They can show up at the airport, be picked

Asking buyers to directly confirm and define value from your product or service is key to a successful sales effort. Asking them to take specific action to secure that value is even better.

up by the shuttle bus, and be driven right to their car. They show their license at the exit and are on their way. Additionally, with the bill-splitting workflow, business travelers can have both their business and personal credit cards in the system and can quickly flag any items that should be billed to them personally.

"What is all that time saving before and during a travel experience worth? That's the question we want our buyers to focus on," Sharon added. Her instinct was clear and good: to have her team position sales conversations around clear, verifiable product outcomes. "We also want them to think about how a bill-splitting workflow saves a ton of time for the traveler and for finance departments post-travel. How often have you seen sales team members delay submitting reimbursements by weeks or even months because of the hassle of line-item reconciliations? We want them to be mentally counting the days."

Avis Budget Focuses on Buyers Co-Defining Value

The approach Sharon takes with her team at Avis Budget demonstrates the power of a value narrative playbook even in an established commodity market, where price-driven competition can easily take hold. Like that of many of the successful companies discussed in this book, the Avis Budget sales approach is to focus on buyer goals first, getting the buyer to anchor on the financial, organizational, or emotional impact that might motivate a purchase.

"We do really good discovery on how much our buyer cares about their employees' travel efficiency and experience," Sharon continued. "We get them to confirm each of the aspects of our rental program that would be valuable to their employees. Before we talk about the amazing travel experience we've developed, we want to know what they care about most. Is it ease of reservations? Cost savings from repeat reservations? Time savings in the on-site experience? Flexibility in billing workflows? We want to know this before we go any further." She tapped her desk to emphasize her point.

Sharon's team is winning in the commodity market by starting with good value discovery on what each buyer cares about most and then focusing on strong value mapping and value confirmation. They let the buyer share what goal they are most focused on—time savings, traveler convenience, or cost savings—before sharing the technology-based workflows that can map to that goal. They then ask the buyer to build their own ROI case to verify that they see value in the capability.

"After we have gotten our buyer to confirm the workflows that would be most valuable to their business travelers, we then ask them to do their own worksheet on the number of minutes saved for each of the workflows. We want them to think about the total time savings across their employees. Then we want them to tell us who else will care about the ROI case."

This last step used by Sharon's team is a best practice that can also be used by your sales teams. Asking a buyer to verbally confirm that they see value and a potential impact from a product or service is good. Asking them to take an action toward securing that impact is even better.

"We find that those buyers who are willing to take action, especially early on in our relationship, to show they value travel efficiency are a lot more likely to buy from us," Sharon concluded. "This action should include putting time into building the ROI case and identifying who needs to be in the next meetings to discuss the ROI case. If they are not willing to do these things, it probably isn't worth our team members spending a lot more time."

Teams that build the tools and skills to effectively run authentic, three-part meetings typically have **a qualified-opportunity-to-closed-won conversion rate that is 40 percent higher compared with teams without these skills.**

The Avis Budget example shows how sales teams are most successful when they structure each buyer interaction around value discovery first, then move to value mapping and value confirmation. This is why I coach sales teams to adopt the three-part meeting as a critical foundation for sales success.

The Authentic, Three-Part Meeting as a Sales Foundation

All go-to-market teams achieve greater success by focusing on buyer value first and product second. This is, however, most difficult to pull off in the sales phase of the buyer and customer journey. Even friendly sales calls can feel like "hand-to-hand verbal combat" as a sales team member manages the balance of listening and speaking, staying on message, managing technologies, and responding to multiple buyer personas and interests. Adding to the complexity, many of these interactions are with new buyers, where there is often no existing personal relationship, limited buyer knowledge about a company and its product, and buyer skepticism about "being sold to."

Sales teams need to be uniquely skilled at building an authentic experience during a thirty-to-sixty-minute sales call that involves direct interaction. If you want to give your sales team a leg up in running effective sales calls, have them build the skills to run an authentic, three-part sales meeting. An authentic sales meeting should be run in three parts:

- Part 1 should focus on value discovery on what goals and impacts the buyer cares about most.

- Part 2 should focus on value mapping and linking the product and company discussion to these buyer goals.

- Part 3 should focus on value confirmation and building the decision road map with next steps on both sides to move the conversation forward.

The three-part meeting seems most obvious in a scheduled in-person or video sales call, but is just as important in a short conversation on a tradeshow floor, for example. Establishing at the outset the buyer's goals and how the buyer defines value makes it possible to spend the available time with the buyer—whether that is ten, thirty, or sixty minutes— to have maximum impact.

AUTHENTIC, THREE-PART MEETING

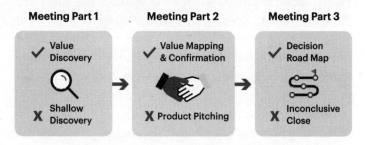

In my work with sales teams, I have seen teams that effectively implement three-part sales meetings achieve dramatic improvements in deal velocity or deal conversion rates from a new qualified sales opportunity to a closed-won deal. Gains of 40 percent or more in deal velocity are possible for teams that really commit to building three-part meeting skills.

A three-part meeting results in more high-quality opportunities for a number of reasons. It engages and excites buyers by focusing conversations on their specific goals and potential impacts. It moves away from generic product pitching. It also helps sellers focus their time and energy on the sales conversations with the highest likelihood of resulting in business, because the seller can tell when a buyer's perceived value and impacts are high enough to motivate them to action. Lastly, it leads to a lot less time and effort spent chasing around buyers to figure out what to do with them next, because each meeting concludes with intentional agreement on next actions.

Part 1 of an Authentic Meeting: Value Discovery

Part 1 of an authentic sales meeting should start with *value discovery*. This means three levels of discovery, with goal, gap, and impact questions, in every sales interaction. In a first meeting with a new buyer, your sales team member will be conducting discovery on a buyer's goals and targeted impacts. In a second or third sales conversation, they need to revisit these same questions to do further discovery, rediscovery, or confirmation. This phase of the conversation needs to focus on getting a deeper and deeper understanding of these questions:

- What is the buyer trying to accomplish?
- Why did they agree to this conversation?
- What type of impact or improvement would make them excited?
- How would the buyer define success in a partnership with your team?
- What will keep them interested in continuing the conversation?

Good value discovery, as discussed in chapter 3, is broad. Good discovery involves using a first discovery call with a champion to explore buyer goals across several value narratives. It continues with a second discovery call with a champion, or a stakeholder call with a decision group, to continue exploring goals areas, identifying specific impacts of each goal, and then prioritizing across the goal areas. As we will see in the next two chapters, broad value discovery early in the sales process is a key element in deal closing and account expansion. Broad goal discovery makes it easier to identify a higher-priority, high-ROI goal area with less price pushback. It also decreases the time between landing an initial sale around a top-priority goal and expanding the account value around other, secondary goal areas.

We see this commitment to broad and deep value discovery in the Avis Budget example. The sales team focuses on exploring the mix of goals a corporate buyer has for their employee travelers and the value they place on travel efficiency, convenience, and cost reduction. Discovery starts with these goal questions and then goes on to gap questions regarding current employee travel processes. In this case, they want to find out: What are the biggest obstacles to the buyer's goals related to travel planning? To the on-site experience in the airport? Or to travel documents and billing?

After identifying gaps, the Avis sales team members use impact questions to guide the buyers to think about cost and time savings that could be achieved by closing their current gaps. The Avis Budget discovery process follows two key best practices around discovery questioning. First, it does not stop at one buyer goal area, but instead explores multiple related goal areas. If a buyer opens up about a first goal area, the selling team tries to connect to a second and third goal area and then get the buyer to prioritize. Second, it goes beyond shallow goal discovery with second-level gap questions and third-level impact questions that also educate the buyer on why they need to do something differently.

One question I get all the time from sales leaders and team members is, "How do I respond if the buyer says something like, 'Just tell me about the product' or 'I want to see a demo'?" My answer is always, "Stay committed to your discovery."

Ask your team to start every sales conversation with discovery, further discovery, or confirmation on a buyer's goal and target impacts. **Things change, new goals emerge, additional buyer personas need to be engaged.**

You can do it in a buyer-centric way by coming up with your own version of this talk track:

> Before we get to our product, let's start by spending a few minutes on your goals and current priorities. There are dozens of things I can show, and I want to make sure we spend time on the product elements most aligned to your goals.

> Or

> That's a great question about our product. I am eager to get to a product discussion as well. Let me just ask a couple more questions, so I can use your time well and focus on the right aspects of our product.

Part 2 of an Authentic Meeting: Value Mapping and Value Confirmation

Part 2 of an authentic sales meeting should focus on *value mapping* and *value confirmation*. Your team will build the most buyer engagement and excitement when they share only the product and company information directly relevant to the buyer's goals, gaps, and targeted impacts.

The value mapping phase of the sales conversation needs to focus on confirming things like:

- Does the buyer see how your product or service capabilities will help them advance their goal?

- Do they have a clear sense of your business impact in moving them from their current state to a target ideal state?

- Can they share the first place they see your product or service having an impact on their business goals?

Many product discussions and demonstrations are really just generic product pitches. They are a standard set of talking points about the company and the product that are not aligned to the buyer's specific situation. The whole purpose of your value discovery is to identify the things a buyer values most so that your product discussion is directly aligned to areas of highest value. I often say to sales and technical sales teams that a good product discussion or demonstration needs to include at least two or three active understanding phrases statements. These phrases could sound something like:

- You shared X as one of your top goal areas, and Y gap in your current capabilities. Let me show you how our product closes that gap.

- I wanted to share this product feature with you because I believe it maps directly to the goal and target improvement you shared for Z.

Active understanding phrases show a buyer that a sales team member is listening and focused on solving the buyer's problem, not on pitching a product. If a sales team member is not able to make these value mapping statements, it is often a sign that the quality of their discovery is not good enough.

Mapping a product or capabilities discussion back to the buyer's goals also naturally sets up value confirmation. After discussing or demonstrating a product, the sales team member can then engage the buyer by asking questions such as:

- Do you see how our capabilities will move you toward the goal you shared?

- Which capabilities would be most helpful in closing the gap or achieving the impact we discussed earlier?

- Where is the first place you might use the capabilities I just shared?

In the Avis Budget case, value mapping and value confirmation means connecting Avis Budget's technology platform back to the buyer's goals. Just talking about the platform features themselves—digital wallets for travel documents, profile-driven reservations, bill splitting workflows—can sound technical or jargony. Starting with strong value discovery allows this product features discussion to come alive by being directly aligned with the buyer's goals. It allows the team to say things like:

> I understand you want to reduce time for your travelers at the airport. Our profile-driven reservations mean that a preselected vehicle can be assigned to a traveler without any paperwork. Our digital wallet for all of their travel documents means the traveler can be picked up curbside, dropped at their car, and be out of the airport without any lines or counter conversations. Do you see how a profile-driven reservation or a digital wallet could reduce traveler time at the airport?

> Or

> I understand you want to save your traveling employees and finance team time on reconciling bills between different business accounts, as well personal versus business travel items. Our bill splitting workflow does exactly that with a simple user interface. Do you see how this workflow would simplify and reduce time on travel expense reconciliation?

Value confirmation in the Avis Budget case means getting the buyer to confirm which of these capabilities would be most valuable to their goals for travel efficiency and travel convenience. They then take it a step further by having the buyer build an ROI case toward achieving a specific impact on their stated goals.

Part 3 of an Authentic Meeting:
Building the Decision Road Map

Value confirmation also sets up Part 3 of an authentic sales meeting, which is building the *decision road map*. The third part of the meeting should be used by the seller to gauge the buyer's readiness to take steps that build organizational support to purchase. This phase of the sales conversation needs to focus on confirming questions like:

- Will the buyer take action and engage their colleagues to make a partnership possible?

- Is there an impact or payoff big enough to get them excited enough to take next steps?

- Are they a true advocate or kicking the tires on your product?

Too many sales meetings have an inconclusive close. A very common meeting pattern is to let the buyer continue to ask product questions or to continue product demos right until the allotted time is over, and then end with, "Good meeting. Thanks for your time! I will email you next week to follow up." Inconclusive meetings kill sales productivity because they leave a seller guessing about which sales conversations are of the highest quality and most likely to turn into closed-won deals and partnerships.

When your buyer directly confirms where they see value and an impact in a partnership, the deal will be more qualified. The more action a buyer is willing to take to secure this value, the more qualified the deal. Those buyer actions might include things like: choosing top goals or priorities from a list of potential priorities, bringing in other decision-makers, exploring funding and timeline options, or building a business impact or ROI case to justify a budget investment. It is

The best sales meetings leave five to ten minutes at the end to **ask the buyer to confirm where they see the most value in a partnership and what action they plan to take next to secure that value.**

the "hard questions" on the buyer's next actions that usually do not receive enough air time in a sales meeting but are the most important in qualifying the deal.

Sellers often miss the opportunity to use the last five to ten minutes of every meeting, with the buyer right in front of them, to confirm the buyer's level of perceived value and what they are willing to do about it. Adopting the three-part meeting structure reminds sellers to reserve the last part of every sales meeting to do this.

What should the seller ask in Part 3 of the meeting? That's more complicated than it sounds. There are more than fifteen different sales methodologies, and each has different recommendations on the right types and sequencing of questions. My personal preference is a modified version of the BANT (budget, authority, need, timeline) where "need" is updated to focus on impacts and timeline is updated to focus on urgency.

My advice to sales team members is to write down your own version of these questions in the five decision road map areas and use them as a checklist at the end of every sales conversation:

- Could you tell me where you see the top areas of fit or impact in partnering with us?

- What part of our conversation are you most excited about?

- Who are other decision-makers who would also evaluate a partnership opportunity? And can we meet with them together to discuss a potential partnership?

- How are solutions or projects like this typically funded? Is funding available? Who is the ultimate funder or final decider?

- Do you have an ideal timeline for the project we are considering? What would lead to consider starting sooner? How does urgency on this initiative compare to others?

- What are the right next steps to continue our conversation?

As you get these qualifying questions down, you can also work on some advanced qualification questions that focus on understanding the broader decision environment:

- What internal or external alternatives are being considered? What do you see as our strengths or gaps relative to these alternatives?

- What would get your boss, VP, and/or leadership team most excited about our conversation? What goals or impacts would they care about most?

- Are there strategic priorities or is there a road map that aligns with our conversation? What organizational initiatives are the most strongly aligned?

One way to make sure you do not run out of time on the decision road map question is to build a habit of verbally transitioning to a meeting wrap-up with ten to fifteen minutes left. For example, you might say something like:

> I want to be aware of our time. We have another fifteen minutes today. We've talked about your goals and our product, so now let's explore areas where you see a fit with us, and talk about the right next steps to continue the conversation.

It will often take a couple of attempts to get the meeting participants into the mode of discussing fit and impacts, decision-makers, funding, timeline, and agreement on the next scheduled call. If you start this process with ten to fifteen minutes left and then continue to nudge the meeting participants, you will have a much better chance of getting critical deal qualifiers. Then, as we will discuss later in our section on deal velocity strategies, it is best to recap buyer-defined goals and impacts as well as their committed next steps in follow-up emails.

Sales Playbook: Authentic, Three-Part Meeting Plays

Authentic, three-part meetings are the foundation for sales success because they drive increased revenue and sales efficiency outcomes. Building team skills around running three-part meetings, however, requires continual reinforcement. There are three key foundational plays a sales team should develop: the *value discovery cheat sheet*, the *decision road map cheat sheet*, the *three-part meeting transitions cheat sheet*, and the *authentic follow-up email.*

The first foundational play in every sales playbook includes the *value discovery cheat sheet.* Best tweaked by each seller to reflect their own version, this is for the purpose of identifying and confirming buyer value.

Sales team members should start by referencing the overall team-wide value narrative playbook, including the discovery questions about buyer goal areas and the value confirmation questions that confirm buyer actions to secure an identified goal or targeted impact. Beginning the development of their cheat sheet from the team-wide framework means there will be consistency in the team-wide approach and language. At the same time, having each sales member write down their version of the value narrative playbook makes it more actionable and genuine, as it helps each seller put the value narrative elements into their own voice. It also creates accountability to bring the value discovery questions, talk tracks, and success cases directly into their sales conversations.

Rachael Hawkey, area VP of True Fit, mentioned in chapter 4, went through exactly this process with her team. True Fit is the retail personalization platform that draws on data from more than two hundred million retail consumers to help retail partners guide the shopping experience with personalization and fit recommendations. As we described earlier, True Fit's marketing and sales leadership developed an initial set of value narratives around key buyer goals, including using personalization to increase website traffic, converting a higher percentage of web browsers to buyers, reducing product returns, and increasing lifetime customer value. They developed an initial set of discovery questions, capability talk tracks, and content assets for each area.

Rachael asked each of her team members to take ownership of these value narratives and develop a one-page sheet of discovery questions as well as a one-page sheet of content assets and success cases. Her goal was to make it easier for her team to put the value narratives into their own words while also creating accountability to use this team-wide messaging framework. She communicated the expectation that she would hear these questions and success case references directly in buyer calls.

One key element of the value discovery cheat sheet is sales team members' approach to starting each meeting with a goal-oriented agenda and authentic commercial. The best meetings start with a clear focus on finding fit or alignment with buyer value and highlighting the three parts of the upcoming meeting. It could be presented like this:

Is there one thing I can help you get out of today's meeting?
Do you have a top goal for our time together?

Okay, thanks for sharing that goal. Here's what I'd like to cover in our call:

- I'll start with a quick overview on us and our work on [value narratives].
- Next, I'd like to explore your goals related to [value narratives].
- My aim for today is to identify where [seller's company] might fit in advancing your goals and, if we find a fit, agree on next steps.

How does that sound? Anything you would add?

I scheduled us for [agreed upon time frame]. Does that timing still work?

The opening agenda can then be followed by the authentic commercial we discussed in the last chapter—giving a new, quick sense of the problem your company solves, what is unique about your solution, and the specific buyer goal areas you help advance. Opening with the authentic commercial is a great way to immediately build a "menu" of buyer goals that link to your company's value narratives. It helps accelerate the process of getting to specific buyer goals and target impacts, and gets the conversation immediately focused on value discovery.

The second three-part meeting play is the *decision road map cheat sheet*. Just like the value discovery cheat sheet, the purpose of the decision road map cheat sheet is for each team member to personalize and take ownership of the questions they use to bring a sales meeting to an effective close. Earlier, in Part 3 of an Authentic Meeting, we discussed five types of questions that should be used at the end of every sales meeting. These questions help confirm where the buyer sees the most value, who else needs to be involved in decision-making, potential funding and timeline options, as well as the right next steps. Just as with the value narratives, it is helpful to develop a teamwide set of decision road map questions and then allow each team member to revise these questions in their own voice.

Another play to support running effective meetings is using a *three-part meeting transitions cheat sheet*. As we moved through the elements of the three-part meeting earlier in the chapter, I offered a series of verbal prompts and cues that can help with meeting transitions. There are five types of verbal prompts and transitions that help run an authentic sales meeting:

- Opening with an agenda and sixty-second commercial

- Committing to value discovery

- Mapping product discussions to your understanding of buyer goals

- Stopping to confirm where buyers see value in your product

- Transitioning in the last ten to fifteen minutes to the decision road map and buyer qualification

As with the discovery and decision road map cheat sheets, the three-part meeting transitions cheat sheet allows each of your team members to start with teamwide language on verbal transitions and then version these verbal transitions into their own language.

The final three-part meeting play is the authentic follow-up email, to be sent twenty-four to forty-eight hours after a prospect call, with particular importance given to following up on the initial discovery call. The follow-up email uses a similar structure to the three-part meeting checklist. It begins

Your team's skills to run three-part meetings will develop faster if **each team member creates their own cheat sheet of questions, has planned verbal transitions across all three parts, and sends follow-up emails recapping each meeting section.**

with an impact statement that recaps key business goals and potential impacts. It continues with sharing the specific capabilities that can address current gaps in the buyer organization to advancing the identified goals. It ends by recapping agreed-on items from the decision road map discussion (remember, this is the third part of the three-part meeting) and confirming the target date or time frame to check back on actions taken on each person's homework list.

In work with sales teams, I do a lot of coaching around follow-up emails and encourage sales leaders to do the same. A review of the follow-up email is a very quick way to see if a seller hit all parts of the three-part meeting. It can answer the question of whether a they did strong enough value discovery to identify an impact aligned with a specific goal, gap, and impact expressed by the buyer. It will show if the sales team member is mapping follow-up product talk tracks and resources to that goal and impact or just positioning them generically.

The Temptation to Fall Back on Product Pitching

Building a set of sales plays to support running three-part meetings is the foundation, but it is not sufficient to keep your sales team focused on an authentic buyer journey. Your team also needs to build a set of deal velocity plays that continually re-anchor each sale conversation to the buyer goal and target impacts. Without these deal velocity plays, sales conversations have a tendency to drift back to product pitches, which results in fewer active sales opportunities turning into closed-won deals.

Below, I outline the key deal velocity plays. However, before doing that, I want to share an example of the drift back to product pitching, to illustrate why this is so common.

I worked with a top sales representative at ThirdChannel. ThirdChannel helps product companies that sell through big-box retailers manage the in-store experience to build brand loyalty and increase sales. Its customers are mostly food, apparel, and eyewear brands, like Kashi, Nature Valley, Clif Bar, Keds, Speedo, Kering Eyewear, Oakley, and Ray-Ban.

ThirdChannel has a mix of service and software offerings that help product companies identify and recruit "brand aligned" in-store agents. The in-store agents act as dedicated brand evangelists who answer questions and support in-store promotion. The company also offers field management tools and in-store data to optimize the impact of brand displays, in-store offerings, and brand evangelists.

Let's call this top sales representative Ryan. Ryan was sharing a recent prospect call with me. "The Asics call was great," he told me. "They were impressed with our ability to recruit brand ambassadors. They were wowed that they could have deep detail on the in-store shopper experience and merge it with their point-of-sale data to give insight into how different display options or promotions performed."

"That's good news that they found the product impressive," I responded. "I remember in your very first discovery call, you did a great job of surfacing their concerns about the large variability of in-store brand engagement and sales across their network of retail outlets. You shared they were looking to capture best practices for in-store displays and merchandising from the high-performing stores that could be rolled out to lower-performing stores. Did you have a chance to learn more about their specific store goals? Or how much revenue gain would come from raising the performance of the lower performers?"

He grew quiet. "Shoot!" he blurted out. "I totally forgot to revisit those goals and potential impacts, as we had discussed. They were just excited about the platform and kept

The pull back to product pitching is strong throughout the sales process. To stay focused on an authentic buyer journey, revise your email templates, sales presentations, and proposals to anchor on buyer goals and committed buyer actions.

asking to see more workflows and data pulls, and I lost track of time. Before we knew it, we were at the end of our time. I'll follow up by email to see if I can confirm their specific store and revenue goals."

Ryan's experience with Asics is typical and demonstrates the constant challenge of staying focused on buyer goals and impacts throughout the sales process. It's difficult, even for top sales reps, to resist drifting back into product pitching. Strong business growth, however, comes from business value delivered by a product, not from the product itself.

The drift back toward product pitching has a number of causes. Buyers are often quick to ask for more details on a product or to insist that they need a product demonstration. Sellers are often most comfortable when discussing their product. They have their standard talk tracks on all the key features and benefits worked out and know exactly what to say. Conversations on buyer goals, by contrast, are fluid and can be unpredictable.

Sales Playbook: Deal Velocity Plays

I always recommend to sales teams that they start with building tools and skills around the three-part sales meeting. The heart of an authentic buyer journey lies in guided buyer discovery; you continually deepen an understanding of what the buyer values most, and then you map product capabilities and success stories directly to those areas of value to build excitement and commitment to purchasing.

However, to keep the sales team focused on an authentic buyer journey rather than on a product-driven buyer journey, you also need a set of deal velocity plays that anchors each additional sales conversation back to the buyer impact and payoff. Ideally, a buyer's impact is confirmed, reconfirmed, and deepened throughout the entire sales process. The ending of the initial discovery call is used to recap and confirm the buyer's top goals, most important areas of fit, and top impacts from a company's product capability set.

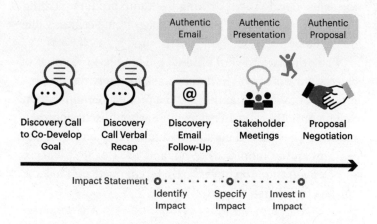

**ANCHORING ON IMPACTS
AND DEAL VELOCITY PLAYS**

If we go back to the Avis Budget example, their impact statement might look something like this:

> We discussed that each employee with a Preferred membership saves on average one hundred minutes of time per trip in their car pickup, drop-off, and expense reimbursement. You shared that you have three hundred employees who rent cars about five times per year. We did a little math, and that's six thousand, two hundred and fifty days, or the equivalent of three full-time employees in productivity gained or employee hassle removed.
>
> You have mentioned how, in employee satisfaction surveys for your road warrior travelers in Sales and Merchandising, the complication of manual travel reimbursements was a big satisfaction killer. You also shared

that Avis Budget's approach to bill splitting, which allows expenses to be digitally and automatically allocated to multiple different accounts, could remove a lot of this pain.

Deal velocity plays continually re-anchor sales conversations to buyer value and impact to keep momentum strong. The three most important deal velocity plays are an authentic follow-up email, the authentic sales presentation, and the authentic proposal.

Deal Velocity Play 1: Authentic Follow-Up Email

The most basic deal velocity play is the authentic follow-up email, as we discussed earlier in the chapter. This follow-up email is not only a great way to audit the quality of your team's skill in running three-part meetings, but also the key to building momentum into the next steps of a buyer conversation.

For the Avis Budget team, using an authentic follow-up email to the discovery call anchored on an impact statement builds momentum in a number of key ways. It differentiates a team's selling style from other vendors—who are more focused on product pitching—by showing active listening skills, anchoring the conversation on the buyer value and impacts, and creating concrete next steps to a partnership. A high-quality email is also a powerful sell-through document to other, indirect decision-makers who don't join the sales conversation with Avis Budget team members. It summarizes key goals, impacts to partnering, and aligned capabilities to quickly engage all decision-makers.

A high-quality follow-up email also helps your sales team spend time on the most qualified buyers—the ones who commit to and complete the "next actions" on the decision road map. When next actions are confirmed and written down in a follow-up email, it creates a very obvious way to evaluate deal quality. Either your buyer commits to the specific requests and follows through so the deal can progress, or they are unwilling or unable to follow through on the request, meaning the deal is likely to stall.

TRADITIONAL AND AUTHENTIC FOLLOW-UP EMAIL

Deal Velocity Play 2: Authentic Sales Presentation

Another important deal velocity play is the *authentic sales presentation*, which anchors on buyer goals and impacts and not on the company's product. Most sales presentations, or "pitch decks" as they are commonly called, make three mistakes:

1　They start with the company story rather than with buyer goals and priorities.

2　They spend too much time on a generic discussion of product capabilities rather than mapping the product capabilities to specific buyer goals.

3　They do not have slides at the end that encourage an intentional conversation on the buyer group's confirmed

You can differentiate your selling by starting each follow-up email by recapping the buyer's success statement and ending the email with the buyer's next committed actions. Most follow-up emails miss both elements.

impacts and their next action steps toward partnering on those impacts.

Sales presentations can go one way or another. Your team's sales deck can reinforce product pitching or they can reinforce an authentic buyer journey by focusing on buyer goals and targeted impacts. If your team builds an authentic sales presentation in a modularized way, they can quickly create a deck before a prospect meeting with an eye to speaking directly to a prospect's goals and target impacts.

There are three key slide templates in an authentic sales presentation. The first, at the beginning of the presentation, is a *buyer goals* slide. It is designed to recap what your sales team member has learned to date about the buyer's goals and target impacts. It also supports further discovery on new goal areas and potential impacts to allow the sales team member to quickly see areas of highest alignment for a buyer group as a whole. The recap slide plays a central role in encouraging your champion and decision group around that champion to co-develop a specific set of goals and impacts that can support a partnership.

The second important slide in an authentic sales presentation is the *buyer impact* slide. This is the best way for your team to end a product discussion or demonstration, by directly connecting a product or service to the buyer's targeted goals and impacts. Your team can show impact with one or two examples of peer buyers who worked with the vendor to successfully advance in their goal area. The success story slide makes the potential impact of a product or service very specific and visceral. Your team can also focus on building a business or ROI case. ROI slides show the specific revenue increases or cost savings at different levels of impact on a buyer's goal area. In either case, the purpose of the buyer impact slide is to give an easy but structured way for the buyer to confirm top areas of goal alignment as well as specific emotional, organizational, or financial impacts that will motivate a new vendor into partnership.

AUTHENTIC SALES PRESENTATION GOES BEYOND TRADITIONAL PRESENTATION

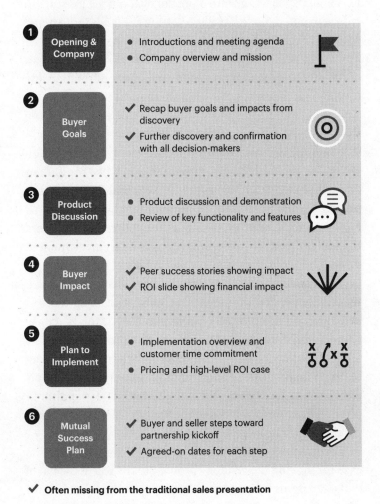

1 Opening & Company
- Introductions and meeting agenda
- Company overview and mission

2 Buyer Goals
- ✔ Recap buyer goals and impacts from discovery
- ✔ Further discovery and confirmation with all decision-makers

3 Product Discussion
- Product discussion and demonstration
- Review of key functionality and features

4 Buyer Impact
- ✔ Peer success stories showing impact
- ✔ ROI slide showing financial impact

5 Plan to Implement
- Implementation overview and customer time commitment
- Pricing and high-level ROI case

6 Mutual Success Plan
- ✔ Buyer and seller steps toward partnership kickoff
- ✔ Agreed-on dates for each step

✔ **Often missing from the traditional sales presentation**

The final key slide in an authentic sales presentation focuses on a *mutual success plan*. The mutual success plan helps your team connect the decision road map questions from an initial discovery call and turn them into a working plan to close a partnership. It also creates the opportunity to prioritize and narrow into the starting phase of a partnership. In chapter 8, we will go into more detail about the mutual success plan and the role it plays in setting the land-and-expand motion. In terms of closing the initial sale, the purpose of the mutual success plan slide is to commit to using the final part of the meeting focused on the buyer value confirmation and the actions a buyer is willing to take to secure that value.

Deal Velocity Play 3: Authentic Proposal

The final deal velocity play for continually anchoring on buyer value is the authentic proposal. Much like the authentic sales presentation, the authentic proposal focuses on the pricing details of the seller's product for the buyer's goals and impacts. Most proposals miss the opportunity to present the dollars spent on a vendor's product as an investment in desired impact rather than just an additional budget item.

The typical proposal cover letter presents like a procurement document for the purchasing office. After some niceties, it focuses on the products being purchased, the purchase price, and the timeline to purchase. The problem with this approach is that a proposal happens before a confirmed intent to buy. The proposal is going to be shared with individuals who need to justify and approve the budget expenditure—often referred to as the economic buyers—in addition to the purchasing office.

The proposal is your team's last opportunity to make the case for moving the vendor's product to the top of the list of budgeted items for purchase. A strong proposal should have a one-page cover letter that follows the same structure as every other authentic buyer interaction. It should lead with the impact statement, which recaps in a sentence or two what has been learned and refined through the sales process about the buyer's goal and desired impact. It should continue with a mapping to the two or three key vendor capabilities that will move the buyer toward that goal. It should conclude by confirming the actions the buyer needs to take to secure the agreed-on value to the partnership.

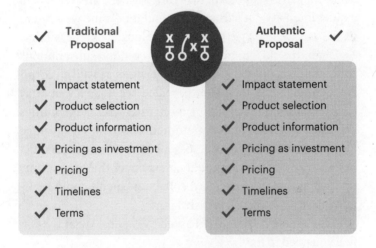

AUTHENTIC PROPOSAL ANCHORS ON IMPACTS AND PRICING AS AN INVESTMENT

✓ Traditional Proposal	✓ Authentic Proposal
✗ Impact statement	✓ Impact statement
✓ Product selection	✓ Product selection
✓ Product information	✓ Product information
✗ Pricing as investment	✓ Pricing as investment
✓ Pricing	✓ Pricing
✓ Timelines	✓ Timelines
✓ Terms	✓ Terms

Digerati Sells into Buyer-Defined Value

Let's now look at how a top digital publisher, which we'll call Digerati, used three-part meeting plays and deal velocity plays. Consistently implementing these plays helped Digerati increase sales productivity and build much broader sales team strength.

"We did it again," is how the CEO of Digerati—let's call her Michelle—started our conversation. It was the first Monday in July after the Q2 sales quarter.

"How bad was it?" I asked.

I was meeting with Michelle that day over coffee in my favorite Boston coworking space. I've spent time in a half-dozen coworking spaces in and around Boston, and this one had the best coffee, the best views, and the best snacks. Michelle and I were sitting near a big window in a common area on the eighth floor and had a great view of the Boston skyline.

"We missed by about fifteen percent in Q2, which puts us in a hole for getting to goal for the year," Michelle answered with a quiet intensity. "It's frustrating, and it tells me we need to fix the way we manage our deals." She looked out the window.

Digerati sold online curriculum content subscriptions to K–12 schools, colleges, and universities as well as corporate training programs. They provided access to a vast array of digital materials, including more than 5,100 digital titles and more than 2.2 million multimedia entries. The average annual subscription cost across all of their customers had been in the $7,500 range, but a new buyer that was setting up its first digital curriculum collection spend could make purchases that ran well into six figures.

"So what went off track?" I asked Michelle. "What is it you feel you need to fix?"

"Well, to start with, I need to figure out how to build broader team strength," Michelle answered, and then paused for a moment and took a sip of her coffee. She looked at me pensively, measuring her words, and continued. "I have a love-hate relationship with my top seller. She is fun, charming, and intuitive about buyers. Quarter over quarter she is our top producer, sometimes bringing in more than fifty percent of our total sales. So, when *she* misses, *we* miss."

At the time of this conversation, Digerati was an emerging growth company with just under $10 million in revenue. It had a sales team of five people, and each team member had their own approach to taking the company's digital products to market. The lack of balance in the team's sales production was quite typical of sales teams that have not developed a shared sales playbook.

The teams I have worked with that rely on each seller to develop their own selling style typically find their top 20 percent of performers produce 60-70 percent of the sales revenue. This is equally true for emerging growth teams and enterprise teams that might have fifty, seventy-five, or one hundred sales team members. Without shared playbooks, there is no mechanism to capture team best practices in ways that raise the performance of all team members.

"So, let me ask a few questions that can help focus performance initiatives for the back half of the year," I said. "Have you created a standard set of discovery questions around buyer goals that can be used to open meetings? And do you expect your team to use the last ten minutes of each sales call to focus on the 'hard questions' regarding the buyer's level of interest in purchasing?"

"No, I wouldn't say we have," Michelle responded. "We tend to do a product demo and talk about the breadth and searchability of our digital reference products. We aren't doing a lot of discovery right now about buyer goals for using digital reference. And our demos often take up the entire time allotted, without an intentional end to the meeting to really qualify the buyer."

"Yeah, both patterns are really common," I said. "So, one thing the team should definitely focus on in the back half of the year is developing skills for running a three-part meeting. Get the team to start each meeting with discovery or confirmation of a buyer's goals, use the middle of each meeting to map your capabilities to those goals, and the end to confirm the level of interest and agree on next actions."

"That makes a ton of sense, but it's new muscle for most team members," Michelle said, now leaning forward and engaging in the conversation more deeply. "How do we get the team to change their style without totally disrupting their deal flow?"

"Great question," I said. "There are sets of plays you can build into a sales playbook that fit right into the flow of their sales work. You can ask each team member to build a cheat sheet of their own discovery questions. You can ask them to take their sales call notes in a three-part meeting structure. You can ask them to use a follow-up email to recap those three meeting parts."

"So, what you're really saying is that you want the team to use best sales practice in each meeting," Michelle said. Her mood had started to shift, with the earlier frustration being slowly replaced by an excitement in new possibilities. "This isn't about doing something different, but sharpening their day-to-day practice."

"That's it," I said. "Sales is really sort of a real time verbal joust. The teams that practice their plays over and over again, inside and outside their deals, perform at a much higher level."

"Okay, I'm sold on the three-part meeting," Michelle said. "What else?"

"Well, running a three-part discovery meeting is the right start, but sales teams often drift back to product pitching and lose focus on buyer goals and impacts as they move through the sales process," I said. "So, it's really important to develop tools for your later sales conversations, whether that's a group demo or proposal call, to help your team continually re-anchor on the buyer goal and impact."

Michelle sat straight up now. "Yeah, I hate that a good discovery call turns into a product pitch in the next call. I join many of the calls with bigger, strategic accounts and I've seen that happen too often. So, you're suggesting that a different kind of presentation deck that might be used in a decision group call, or a different kind of proposal, might solve this problem?

"That's right, but what's key is to work from the sales documents your team is already using and just enhance them," I said. "In your sales deck, you can add first slides to focus on recapping discovery on what has been learned to date about buyer goals, and your last slides to focus on next steps in the decision-making process. And for your proposals, just having a cover letter that again anchors on the buyer's goals will position pricing as an investment in their desired impact rather than as just another cost item."

"So, if I understand correctly, we work from the main sales documents we currently use and create updated versions that focus first on the buyer goal and impact, and align our product specifically with this impact," Michelle said. "That makes a lot of sense. I like that we can work from all our existing material and tweak it in a way to help the team continually refocus on what is in it for the buyer."

"That's exactly right," I said. "The final thing we should talk about is your sales pipeline model. It's easy for the sales team to be optimistic. Are there any concrete buyer actions you force your team to confirm before they can move a deal forward in your pipeline?"

Michelle tilted her head. "What do you mean by a concrete buyer action?"

"Well, I've seen your sales pipeline, and it has many of the traditional stages for moving a deal forward. It flows from discovery to demo to proposal to verbal commitment," I said.

A strong sales process has two to three buyer actions at each stage that are completed before advancing to the next stage. **Buyer actions are a more objective measure of deal progress than seller actions.**

"After an early discovery conversation, the sales team member might ask the buyer to confirm who else would need to be involved in a decision, or who would fund a partnership, or if there is a timeline to consider starting. And in a later sales conversation, the seller might ask if funding has been allocated or if a competitive evaluation of alternatives has been completed."

"I got it," Michelle said, finishing up her coffee and mentally already moving into action with her sales team. "You want each team member to ask questions about their buyer's actions and decision-making process that are sort of 'objective' and could be verified, so they're not relying on their subjective view of the deal."

"That's exactly right," I said. "The best sales processes have one to three actions that a seller needs to confirm at each sales stage before moving the deal forward. These more 'objective' criteria, as you called them, force both sides to intentionally ask: Do we want to keep talking or to move forward? Is it really worth our time? It's a way of creating a decision road map. Either you move forward together or not."

Over several months of practice, the three-part meeting, deal velocity plays, and managing deals around buyer "gives-gets" became ingrained in this digital publisher's sales practice. This resulted in significant performance impacts. The top sales producers continued to produce at high levels, but so did others on the team. Year-over-year growth in individual seller revenue productivity increased by 25 percent over the next twelve months. It was not that the team worked far more deals, but that they got a lot better at closing the deals in their pipeline. The rate of discovery call to closed-won deal conversion increased from 27.5 percent to 35 percent.

As important, the consistent approach to deal management across the team led to the successful onboarding of new sales talent and broader team strength. Michelle's top performer never contributed more than 30 percent of the total team's number in the following year, as other team members raised the quality of their performance.

Sales Playbook: Sales Stage and Exit Criteria Play

As the Digerati and Avis Budget examples show, a key final play for any sales team is a *sales stage and exit criteria* play, which outlines the sequential actions a sales team member and buyer each need to take for the deal to progress. Sales team members often progress deals when they have taken an action like finishing a discovery call or giving a product demonstration or sending a proposal. Buyer actions, however, matter a lot more than the sales team actions in qualifying a deal.

The exit criteria play outlines on a single page the sales team's actions, which I call "gives," and the buyer actions, which I call "gets," that need to happen at each sales stage. The "gets'" should act as stage exit criteria and keep a deal from moving to the next stage until a buyer has taken a specific and concrete action.

In the Digerati example, the team used a basic set of five sales stages:

1 The sales-qualified opportunity, when an internal champion advocates for a vendor.

2 Active evaluation, when the internal advocate is connecting to a stakeholder group.

3 Stakeholder evaluation, when the decision group in the buyer organization is evaluating a vendor.

4   Proposal, when that decision group is evaluating and responding to the vendor proposal.

5   Verbal commitment, when the decision group has committed to working with a vendor pending final purchasing and legal approvals.

Digerati's sales team was asked to confirm a handful of buyer actions at each sales stage before progressing the deal to the next stage. Until they were confirmed, the deal could not progress. The team built consistency in the approach to the sales pipeline stage model, including directly using this model in all individual and team pipeline review calls. During the pipeline calls, sales team members were asked to compare their deals directly with the pipeline stage model, to confirm all buyer "gets" up to the current deal stage, and to identify the actions they were planning to take to secure the buyer "gets" needed to progress to the next deal stage.

The expected buyer actions at each stage should progress along two dimensions. In the first dimension, actions are related to the buyer co-owning the business impact to a partnership. In the Digerati example, value confirmation starts by identifying the most important emotional and financial impact. It might be about how access to digital reference content could reduce acquisition costs and save money, or it might be about increasing usage with ease of remote access for faculty and students. As a deal progresses, Digerati's sales team members work with buyers to quantify potential cost savings and also the number of users or user sessions that might be facilitated.

At Avis Budget, similarly, early discovery focused on identifying the buyer's goals for time savings, traveler convenience, and cost savings relative to their employee travelers. After getting the buyer to confirm their goals and key Avis

Budget technology capabilities to facilitate those goals, the seller asks the buyer to build their own ROI case, in their own worksheet, calculating the number of minutes saved for each of the workflows. Buyers and sales team members work together on building the impact statement that can be positioned to other decision-makers, capturing time and cost savings as well as higher employee ease and satisfaction.

SAMPLE SALES STAGES AND SAMPLE STAGE EXIT CRITERIA

Sample Sales Stage	Sample Buyer Gets/Stage Exit Criteria
Sales-Qualified Opportunity	• Confirms top areas of goal alignment and potential impacts • Identifies champion and potential funder/economic buyer
Active Evaluation	• Identifies all decision-makers and influencers • Secures a stakeholder call with all decision-makers
Decision Group Evaluation	• Confirms evaluation criteria and alternatives • Confirms source of funding
Proposal	• Prioritizes goal areas and rollout plan • Confirms timeline to start
Verbal Commitment	• Confirms company selection

The other dimension for securing buyer actions involves building organizational readiness to purchase, including making sure the right decision-makers are in the discussion, all alternatives have been evaluated, funding exists, and timelines are manageable. In the Digerati example, the early

Qualifying a sales conversation by asking a buyer to verbally confirm they see value and a potential impact in a partnership is good. **Asking them to take concrete actions toward securing that impact is even better.**

actions toward organizational readiness focused on confirming sources of budget and budget decision-making, as well as confirming all the key instructors and other influencers involved in a purchase decision. Later buyer actions focused on confirming Digerati as the preferred vendor, securing alignment with the budget decision-maker, and confirming a timeline to a funding decision.

Selling into Buyer-Defined Value Builds Deal Velocity

In this chapter, you have seen from examples of Avis Budget's corporate car rental programs and Digerati's work with schools, colleges, and corporations how your sales team can build an authentic buyer experience: by beginning and ending every sales meeting focused on buyer goals and impacts.

There is always a pull back to product pitching. Buyers often quickly ask detailed product questions or for product demos. Sellers are most comfortable with their product and product features. They know these things going into the call, whereas the buyer's goals and impacts are uncertain and dynamically changing. The chapter has shown how three-part meeting plays, deal velocity plays, and a pipeline stage and stage gate play can help teams avoid product pitching and support their efforts to continually re-focus on the buyer's goals.

In chapter 8, we will concentrate on strong value discovery and how partnering with a buyer to co-develop an impact statement can lead to higher account values. An authentic buyer journey approach leads to less pricing pressure in proposal or closing negotiations and faster identification of new account expansion opportunities after an initial close.

YOUR NEXT STEPS ON SELLING INTO BUYER-DEFINED VALUE

- **Value discovery cheat sheet:** What are your strategies to quickly get to a buyer's goals and target impact? Do you start with an agenda and then use an authentic commercial? Or do you move directly into value discovery questions?

- **Decision road map cheat sheet:** How do you end each of your sales meetings? What questions do you use to confirm where your buyer sees the most value and the actions they will take next to secure this value?

- **Three-part meeting transitions:** What verbal cues and prompts do you use to support running a three-part meeting? How do you open with a goal, commit to discovery, avoid product pitching, confirm buyer value, and hold time to qualify the buyer?

Go to winalytics.com/theplays for content to help build plays that sharpen your skills in consistently selling to buyer-defined value. Start by building your own approach to three-part meetings and deal velocity plays and then compare notes with your team members.

8

Closing and Expanding on Value

"WHEN IT comes to negotiating deals, we act like we have a commodity product and cave quickly on price discounts," the VP of enterprise sales for a leading business risk analytics company—let's call him Greg—shared with dismay. "I don't get it."

I was sitting in a cafeteria in San Francisco talking to Greg by phone. He was also based in Boston, and I had shared by email that I would be happy to meet up in person when I finished my travel to the West Coast in a few days, but Greg was eager to start our conversation as soon as possible.

Greg had recently been recruited to the company—which we'll call Inspira—as a "disruptor." He was tasked with bringing new practices to a team that was winning based on a unique market position but was underperforming its growth potential. His undertaking was to get the salespeople to change their behavior and to sell business value, not just a product.

"We need to teach our team to always start a negotiation focused on the incredible value we provide," Greg said. "We offer our clients a unique commercial data set and actionable analytics. There is nothing like it in the market, and most customers increase profitability by millions of dollars every year."

Inspira is publicly traded, with more than $1.5 billion in revenue. An important driver of the company's growth is access to a one-of-a-kind data set that combines national and state-level data on macro- and micro-economic drivers of the business environment, including business and consumer purchasing, regulatory risks, and environmental and seasonal risk factors.

The company has three sales teams reporting to the senior VP of sales. Greg runs the enterprise team, focused on large companies whose end buyers are other business or government organizations. One of his peers is a VP overseeing the consumer team, focused on larger companies with individual consumers as their end buyer. His other peer is a VP overseeing the sales team for small- and medium-size companies, who have other businesses as well as consumers as their end buyers.

"Do you guys do negotiation training?" Greg asked, transitioning to the main reason he had asked for a call.

"In our approach, an effective negotiation usually starts at the very beginning of the sales process," I said. "It's about getting the customer to co-define value and impact throughout the sales process. A sales team member is in a much better position to negotiate if the buyer has already heard and internalized an impact or business case multiple times." I stopped and took a sip of my coffee.

"Bingo, that's it," Greg responded. "A lot of sales managers have gotten into this habit of repeating 'hold the line on pricing' to their team and discouraging price concessions. But holding the line on pricing only makes sense if we've set a deep hook around value."

"So, how well is the team anchoring on the business case?" I asked.

"On the whole, the team is definitely leading with product and whiz-bang data analytics rather than a business case, but there are flashes of brilliance." Greg was showing a strong instinct that to be successful as a change agent he would need to identify and build on wins within the team. "I remember a team member who was getting pushback on pricing and he told the buyer, 'That's our best price. You are on the hook for a hundred million dollars in growth this year, and we both know there is no way you get that growth without our analytics.' It sort of reset the conversation by highlighting our value to the buyer, and the prospect closed at our asking price."

Greg paused and then, choosing his words carefully, asked me, "How do we make the pockets of brilliance more consistent and repeatable across the team?"

"Often the sales tools available to a team are very product-heavy rather than helping identify and focus on what the buyer values most," I said. "Let me ask a couple of questions. Do the sales teams have a clear idea of the business outcomes created by your products? Do they have good discovery questions to lead the buyers to those outcomes? And are they expected to identify and quantify business impacts early and often in the sales process?"

"All great questions," Greg responded. He paused as he made notes, and then said, "Those are all gap areas in how we support and enable the team. If they could be addressed, it would definitely move the team forward."

Inspira Focuses on Closing on Value

After this discussion, Greg, his senior VP of sales, his two other VP colleagues, and the sales enablement team began a value narratives project. The focus of the project was to identify the key business goals from Inspira's product suite that could most anchor value and support in holding the line on pricing during buyer negotiations.

The group identified four value narratives around their product suite:

1 Using digital automation to reduce the costs of business risk evaluation.

2 Leveraging analytics to improve pricing to increase revenue.

3 Proactively monitoring exposure to catastrophic business risk.

4 Leveraging business risk data to identify new markets and growth opportunities.

After defining the value narratives, the leadership team brought in frontline sales managers to identify goal, gap, and impact questions—for example:

Goal questions:
- Have you set goals for using risk monitoring to increase prices and revenue?
- Have you set a goal to use proactive or automation risk monitoring to reduce costs?

Gap questions:
- How do you currently collect and ensure accuracy in all categories of business risk?
- Do you have the breadth and quality of data for accurate business risk assessments?

Impact questions:
- How could more accurate risk assessment impact your business costs?
- What would a 1–2 percent increase in revenue be worth?

The sales leadership introduced and trained the sales teams on these questions and then created three new expectations for leveraging business impacts in their buyer conversations:

1   Each discovery call will include a follow-up email identifying specific business goals and targeted improvements on those goals, which Inspira's product could help address.

2   The sales team member will work to build a specific business investment case, with a dollar ROI case, before sending a formal proposal.

3   All business negotiations will begin with a recap of the business case before any consideration is given to pricing discounts or concessions.

Later, after the initiative was introduced to the sales team, I had another call with Greg.

"How are things going six months into this new approach?" I asked.

"Well, we have a lot of very experienced sellers who have been doing things the same way for years," Greg said. "But we're definitely seeing some good signs. At the start of this initiative, most of the follow-up emails I reviewed were product pitches with a series of bullets and attachments on our product capabilities. Now, it seems like almost all the emails identify a specific business goal and target improvement that our products can help advance."

"How about getting a specific business impact and ROI case before a negotiation?" I asked.

"That's still a work in progress," Greg said. "We go in with a quantified business impact more than half the time, and it seems like we are getting a lot crisper on the ROI case. One of my favorites was by a team member who showed a buyer

Until your buyer has defined a specific goal and targeted impacts, pricing should be presented with a ballpark low-to-high range. This allows your team to qualify out budget-constrained buyers while also leaving flexibility to finalize price later.

how we could eliminate sixteen percent of their risk misclassification, which was worth five percent in revenue. Another favorite was from a team member who showed a buyer how we could help add ten thousand new customers in a new market, which would increase revenue by three million dollars."

In six short months, the work by Greg and the sales VPs had helped the team significantly improve how they anchored pricing negotiations on buyer value. At the start of their value narratives initiative, about three-quarters of follow-up emails reviewed by managers included no specific buyer goal and only shared product capabilities. Six months later, three-quarters of follow-up emails identified a specific business goal and target improvement. In addition, nearly 55 percent of pricing proposals had a specific ROI case, and the team had doubled the number of non-price concessions offered, from 1.1 to 2.2 per deal, while holding the line on pricing.

Closing Playbook: Pricing and Negotiating Plays

Building an authentic buyer journey that continually anchors on buyer-defined value helps your team increase deal velocity—meaning, as discussed in chapter 7, that a higher percentage of sales opportunities close, and they close at a faster pace. Not only that, but it also leads to higher account values.

Strong value discovery across a range of all goal areas makes it easier for you to find the goal with the highest urgency, strongest ROI case, and least price pushback and discounting. When you continually re-anchor on the buyer impact or ROI case throughout the sales process, you shift your pricing discussions from being about spending more money to being about investing in achieving an impact the buyer values highly.

In the best closing conversations and pricing negotiations, your buyer has already heard a specific impact statement three or four times. They have heard it recapped during and after an initial discovery call. They have read it recapped in an authentic follow-up email. They have had the opportunity to further co-develop the impact or business ROI case with other decision-makers during a stakeholder call supported by an authentic sales deck. They received an authentic sales proposal before the negotiation that led with an impact statement or ROI case they helped co-develop. All of this reduces friction about price even before negotiations begin.

There are four specific pricing plays that can help support anchoring your sales conversations on buyer-defined value: the ballpark pricing play; the pricing as an investment play; the strategic discounting play; and the non-price concession play.

PHASE OF THE SALES PROCESS

Four Pricing Plays	Phase of Sales Process
Ballpark pricing	Early discovery or discovery
Pricing as an investment	Active evaluation or proposal
Strategic discounting	Proposal negotiation or verbal commitment
Non-price concessions	Proposal negotiation or verbal commitment

Ballpark Pricing Play

Pricing often comes up very early in the buyer discovery phase, as a potential buyer is trying to qualify for themselves if a product is even in reach financially. For early questions on pricing, before a lot of work has been done to identify specific goal-to-capability alignment, I always recommended that your sales team members use a *ballpark pricing play*.

Ballpark pricing focuses on offering a wide pricing range as a way of keeping the conversation open for your team to explore top buyer goals and areas of potential alignment. It allows your team and the buyer to see if the size of the financial investment is even feasible for the buyer.

For example, in a conversation about a product or service with an average contract value of between $15,000 and $20,000, the ballpark response to the question, "How much does your product cost?" would sound something like:

> We have partners at many different investment levels. Some are investing as little as $7,500, while others are paying $35,000. It all depends on the range of ways we are supporting their goals and priorities. So, let me ask—is that a range you could consider? Shall we continue on your goals for talking with us?

The low-end prices are designed to make it easier for the buyer to imagine a financially affordable way to start, while the high end of the range indicates the potential investment in a fully operating partnership.

Pricing as an Investment Play

The most important pricing conversations take place in the stakeholder call or stakeholder evaluation stage. This is when a group of decision-makers, users, and influencers in the buyer organization have agreed to meet with the vendor, learn more about their product or service capabilities, and actually evaluate a purchase. Typically, at this stage, there has already been a discussion of fit with the buyer's goals and identification of capabilities, as well as client success examples that map to those goals.

The discussion in the stakeholder or decision group phase often focuses on alternatives. Why should they choose this vendor over another, or over doing nothing at all? The mistake sales team members make in presenting pricing to stakeholder groups is similar to that made in proposals. The focus is all on the cost of a purchase, rather than where it should be: on the buyer impact that can be achieved with an investment in the vendor.

To focus the buyer on the investment return rather than on the financial cost, the second pricing play I always recommend is *pricing as an investment*. It supports holding the line on the asked-for price in the pricing proposal. Pricing in the context of value means you always start by recapping the buyer's potential value and impact, provide pricing in the context of this value, and then stop to see if your buyer will confirm that the proposed investment is worth the potential value. In the Inspira example from earlier in the chapter, it could sound something like this:

> I'm glad you have brought us to the pricing question. We always think about pricing in the context of your business goals and potential for business value in a partnership with us. I understand your primary business goal this year is risk pricing on your property insurance, and you are targeting a 2–3 percent improvement as a way of lifting property premiums.
>
> We did a little number-crunching based on your property portfolio, and it looks like each 1 percent improvement in risk pricing is worth around $3 million in increased profitability, so the 2 percent low end of your improvement goal would be worth around $6 million. Does that sound right?
>
> To realize that profitability improvement, you would be investing $250,000 with us. Do you believe that investment level is worth the increased profitability?

When you lead your pricing discussions with a restatement of the buyer's value and ROI case, **you remind the buyer that they are investing in something they really care about and not just adding another budget expenditure.**

PRICING AS AN INVESTMENT PLAY

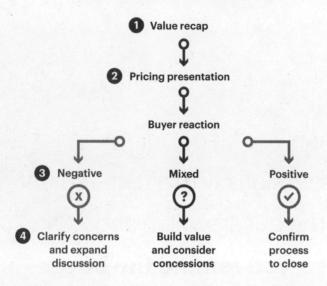

1 Value recap

2 Pricing presentation

Buyer reaction

3 Negative	Mixed	Positive
(X)	(?)	(✓)

4 Clarify concerns and expand discussion

Build value and consider concessions

Confirm process to close

---

1 Recap agreed-on value and impact for the buyer

3 Pause for a reaction: positive, negative, mixed

2 Share pricing as an investment in that value

4 Align next asks with buyer reaction

Stopping at the end of the pricing discussion to let the buyer confirm whether they perceive sufficient value is critical for your team to successfully close a deal. Too often, sales team members never get this direct confirmation, leaving them to wonder whether they are on a path to a closed partnership, and not knowing what actions to take next.

Your buyer will typically respond in one of three ways to the pricing-in-the-context-of-value play. Each requires a different set of actions on the part of the sales team member. The best response is the positive one: "It seems about right," "It seems very reasonable," or "We could fund that investment level." This response allows the sales team member to move into the purchasing process and confirm all the steps to initiating a contract and partnership.

Another possibility is the neutral response. Your buyer might say something like, "I'm not sure I can answer," "We would have to look at our budgets," or "I would have to understand more about the potential impact." In this case, your sales team member needs to continue with clarifying perceived value relative to pricing by identifying areas of highest impact that might justify some level of investment. The sales team member also needs to expand the sales conversation to explore other sources of potential budget.

A final possibility is the negative response. It might sound like, "That seems like a lot," "We definitely do not have that in our budget," or "I'm not sure why we would invest externally when we can do this internally." In this situation, your sales team member needs to go back to square one to reset the buyer's goals for the conversations and see if there are specific impacts or outcomes that could motivate a partnership, even if at a reduced level.

Strategic Discount Play and Non-Price Concessions Play

The third pricing play is the *strategic discount play*, which offers a pricing discount for something of value to the purchasing company and sales team. The strategic discount play is great for evoking a positive reaction to the investment level relative to the return with a buyer who is excited to move forward but wants to get the best pricing available.

The strategic discount play is particularly useful when your buyer has a neutral response to the pricing-in-the-context-of-value play. They may not perceive enough value to agree to move to a purchase. They may have a budget limitation that doesn't allow them to spend at the level requested in the

Your strategic price discounts should be linked to something of significant value to your company. Examples could include a product bundle, a high-volume purchase, a multi-year contract, early payments, or a premium customer brand.

pricing proposal. Or they may just be holding back on their enthusiasm as a strategy to secure a price discount.

In all of these cases, your sales team member can respond with strategic discount options, meaning price discounts that create strategic value for the vendor organization. There is a range of strategic discount options used by the Inspira team discussed earlier in the chapter that your team could also use. These include:

- Giving a bundled discount based on the buyer purchasing multiple different product lines.

- Offering a volume discount for a larger purchase of a product or service.

- Giving multi-year term discounts with the buyer committing in advance to purchasing over multiple fiscal years.

- Offering a time-sensitive discount for early payments that increase your cash flow.

- Giving a strategic logo discount if the buyer is a premium brand that will raise your company's reputation and profile.

Best practice in all of these cases is for your sales leadership to write down for their team the percentage price discount available for each strategic consideration, as well as the total available discount from combining multiple factors. I always recommend that each strategic discount be worth 5–10 percent of the total purchase price, with the total available strategic discount targeting 15–20 percent of the total purchase price. The other best practice is for your sales team members to avoid agreeing to a discount level during a negotiation call. Instead, they should focus on all strategic discounts that a buyer might consider and then have a conversation with their sales manager to confirm the target discount range.

In addition to strategic pricing discounts to handle push-back on pricing, sales teams should consider non-price concessions. In the *non-price concession play*, your sales team member can offer the buyer a positive response to a request for price discount while still holding the line on the pricing proposal. In the Inspira example, non-price concessions include things such as:

- An extended planning and onboarding time frame that can allow the buyer to access a product or service early so they get off to a strong start; these can be presented as "free months."

- Payment terms that offer value by shifting the payment timeline to a preferred point in the buyer's fiscal year, helping with cash flow management.

- Product development input that allows the buyer to shape the product in ways beneficial to their needs and the company's product development road map.

- An additional service like a report, consultation of some type, or additional premium feature offered at no cost to extend the value of the products in the pricing proposal.

- Attendance at a conference offered by Inspira as a way to deepen the buyer's use of the product and provide access to peers.

Closing and Expansion Playbook: The Mutual Success Plan

Building an authentic buyer journey helps create higher account values not only by reducing price discounting, but also by shortening the time frame between an initial closed sale and an expansion sale. As we discussed in a few places already, good value discovery should be broad and deep. The best discovery uncovers two to five different goal areas where the buyer has a gap or pain that they may need help addressing.

Broad goal exploration has a number of important benefits in helping your team close an initial sale. As we discussed in chapter 7, a key measure of success for any sales team is deal velocity—how quickly they can move sales opportunities with a new buyer to closed-won deals and the start of a new customer relationship. Broad goal exploration helps your teams build deal velocity by inviting a variety of decision-makers into the conversation. It makes it easier to identify the goal area with the highest business impact, strongest potential ROI, and least pricing pushback. It also creates multiple potential sources of budget or funding for a new purchase.

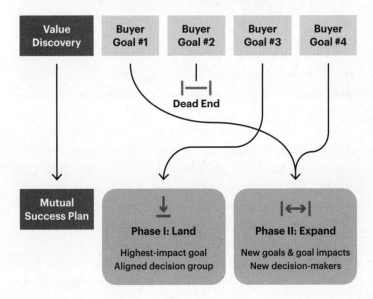

**MUTUAL SUCCESS PLAN
TO LAND AND EXPAND FASTER**

Broad goal exploration also helps raise account values by reducing the time frame from an initial sale to an upsell opportunity. Sales teams handle the initial sales, but then typically collaborate with account management and customer success teams who lead on account expansion. Some sales teams are so focused on the initial sales, they forget that the real value in an account typically comes from a series of upsell opportunities that can expand and deepen the account over time. As we will see below and in chapter 9, broad goal discovery creates a direct connection between your sales team focus on closing the initial sales and account management or customer team's focus on creating a plan to expand the account.

Broad goal exploration, however, also has the risk of creating decision-making complexity, which can slow down buyers and stall deals. It is this need to balance the strengths and risks of broad goal discovery that makes the *mutual success plan* such an important play in the closing playbook. The mutual success plan also bridges into the expansion playbook. It connects closing the initial sales and expansion opportunities that deepen the partnership. A good mutual success plan shifts the buyer-seller relationship from the idea of "closing a deal" as an isolated transaction to a focus on connecting each buyer-seller conversation to the opportunity to continually expand value.

In a classic study on information and decision-making called "On the Pursuit and Misuse of Useless Information," Anthony Bastardi of Stanford and Eldar Shafir of Princeton showed the challenge of information complexity. In this study, two groups of individuals were faced with making the same decision on an everyday activity like enrolling in a college course or taking on credit card debt.

The first group was provided with full information. The second group was provided with the same information but

If you get good at executing a mutual success plan that focuses on immediate needs while not losing sight of other goals, you will close more deals and expand accounts faster.

with a key detail withheld until later. That key detail might be which professor was teaching a course the students were thinking of taking or how much credit card debt an otherwise exceptional applicant for a loan had outstanding. The groups forced to wait for details said no to the course or the loan at a much higher rate. When individuals are made to wait for or have to proactively pursue information, they deem it to be more valuable, even if it isn't particularly important.

For sales representatives and sales teams, this research offers a big red flag for keeping too many different goals or buying options open into the later stages of a buyer conversation. Having a broad and deep value discovery phase in the early stages of a buyer conversation is important to identify the most important and highest impact buyer goals. However, as the conversation works toward evaluation and a financial proposal for a specific set of products or solutions, leaving too many possibilities open leads to worse sales outcomes.

When your buyers have many options left open, they often create their own decision-making complexity by latching onto unanswered questions as well as areas of ambiguity. The alternative to leaving options open is for your sales team to collaborate with each buyer to target one or two specific goal areas to begin a partnership and justify those targeted areas with a clear and meaningful impact or ROI case. According to Corporate Executive Board (now Gartner) research, proactively narrowing the choices available to a B2B buyer can increase purchase ease by up to 86 percent and reduce buying regret by up to 37 percent.

Using a Mutual Success Plan
to Land and Expand Faster

The mutual success plan is best applied when your sales team members get into stakeholder calls and product demonstrations with a group of decision-makers. The focus shifts from a broad discovery across a number of goals and impacts to a mutual success plan that can help prioritize across all these areas. The goal of the mutual success plan is to narrow the focus to a top priority for an initial partnership as well as setting down anchors on goal areas you might return to later. It is a way of clearly capturing and communicating those additional goal areas to account managers and customer success team members who are likely to be involved in account expansion efforts.

There are three ways that a mutual success plan can help you move into the right closing motion with a new partner. The first is by moving from identifying a range of potential goals and impacts to prioritizing and quantifying specific impacts. As discussed earlier, impacts can be emotional, organizational, or financial. An emotional impact taps into a buyer's feeling of relief about a problem being solved or better serving a constituency. A financial impact links to a specific revenue or cost ROI case to justify a budget investment. An organizational impact connects to specific organizational or business road map objectives.

In building a mutual success plan, you will want to gauge the strength of the potential impacts in bringing the decision-making group into the fastest alignment with a desire to partner. Prioritizing goal areas and potential impacts helps you identify and focus on the Phase I goal areas that will be part of an initial partnership. You can also confirm Phase II goal areas that can be revisited after success in Phase I. The

Mutual success requires a good planning process to align your buyer, sales team, and account management or customer success team around **identifying and prioritizing all of your buyer's goal areas.**

goal areas you will want to include in Phase I are those with specific, concrete impacts for which there are no outstanding details or questions that need to be answered in order for the buyer and seller to agree on the impacts. These are areas that can be put into a proposal for a Phase I pricing negotiation without the risk that outstanding information will cause the buyer to pause.

Second, a good mutual success plan helps you lay out the steps to move through the decision-making process, identify all of the decision-makers on the buyer's side, and clarify legal and procurement processes to get to a signed agreement. The sales team member and buyer need to work together to build this stepwise plan and assign working data for each key step.

On the buyer side, the plan will be co-developed by an internal champion who partners with your sales team member to manage the internal process of building readiness to purchase. The champion is often the one who leads initial discovery and sees an emotional, organizational, or financial benefit from working with the sales team member and the vendor.

The champion will help plan steps to get in front of the right decision-making group. This group will include users who benefit from adoption of a product or service. Users often think about their specific work process or work areas, and focus on gaps that a product or service can help solve. They often think more about the emotional than the financial or organizational impact. The decision group is also likely to include an economic buyer who is responsible for authorizing the budget expenditure to secure a purchase and is often motivated by a financial or organizational impact that justifies a budget investment.

The decision group may also include technical evaluators, who look at how new products or services work within their existing processes, technologies, and workflows. These individuals are often motivated only by avoiding disruption to existing processes, so they need to be persuaded by others that the benefits of the impacts versus the disruption trade-offs merit considering something new.

Beyond the decision group, the mutual success plan should also support identifying steps in a legal and contract review as well as steps in the procurement process. The mutual success plan helps with running the decision processes in parallel as a way of reducing the time between agreement with the decision group to move forward and actually being able to begin a partnership.

Third, a good mutual success plan helps focus buyers on the strength of a company's product or service relative to alternatives. In building a mutual success plan, the sales team member and their internal buyer champion are moving from the question of fit with a buyer goal and targeted impacts to a question of relative fit compared to other alternatives being considered.

To establish relative fit, it's important to directly ask the champion and decision group questions like, "Are you considering other alternatives?" "Can those alternatives deliver the same impact we have discussed?" and "What do you see as our strengths and the strengths of the alternatives relative to your goals?" The earlier you understand where you stand on relative fit, the better off you will be in adjusting your sales conversation and knowing where to best spend your time.

Burning Glass Leverages a Mutual Success Plan

Now let's turn to a compelling example of how a mutual success plan can be used to support the goals of landing faster as well as setting up account expansion. Ellen Mayes, VP of institutional partnerships at Burning Glass Technologies, explained their value well in a conversation with me: "There are lots of things a buyer may want to do, but we have to help them identify and address the most pressing thing now. I always say, 'You can't eat a whole elephant in a bite.'"

As I spoke with Ellen, I thought of how many salespeople with the prospect of a big commission on the horizon will try to engineer a big sale right away. They forget that a mutual success plan can be used to support the goals of landing faster as well as setting up account expansion. But I wanted to hear Ellen's reasoning. "Oh, that's interesting," I said. "What makes you say that?"

"I have many buyer conversations where there are three or four different goal areas the customer wants to address, and they can get overwhelmed or freeze up in trying to figure out where to start," Ellen said. "This isn't good for getting an initial close. It can lead to stalls. I work with these buyers to use the first goal area to lay the foundation for the other areas."

Before joining Burning Glass, Ellen was at Cengage Learning, leading a team focused on selling and servicing digital education content for higher education partners. She had directly experienced the disconnect that could emerge in the large gap between all the content titles a potential buyer was interested in and those they could actually purchase.

Burning Glass Technologies is the world's leading labor market analytics company and provides real time data on jobs and skills trends to companies, governments, and colleges, tracking about 3.4 million unique, currently active openings. Burning Glass's institutional sales team works with colleges and universities to apply this real time data to a number of goal areas, including helping with undergraduate enrollments, graduate enrollments, academic program development, and a more intentional career search.

The breadth of campus goal areas the Burning Glass platform can address is both a strength and a weakness. There are many buyers from different parts of a campus who can be engaged, but the breadth of appeal can also lead the Burning Glass team to end up in product demonstrations with groups from four or five different areas of campus, all with different goals. Rather than leading to a tight product demonstration with momentum into a proposal and closed sale, the breadth of discussion can lead to a lively discussion that lacks actionable outcomes and causes drifting interest post-demo with a lot of loose ends.

"Can you say more about how a mutual success plan can help avoid deal stalls and turn the breadth of the Burning Glass platform into a more consistent strength in positioning upsells?" I asked Ellen.

"I always want to do broad initial discovery to identify multiple different use cases that might support a partnership," she replied. She began to tick off thoughts on her fingers. "That may mean bringing stakeholders from four or five different departments into one or more product demonstrations. However, I always lead these stakeholder demonstrations with a focus on identifying the one or two use cases that 'need to be solved' right now. I start to talk about those high-urgency items as Phase I."

"That makes sense," I said. "And how do you make those high-urgency items actually translate into a Phase I closed sale?"

"That's easy. I focus the stakeholder group on a process to get these Phase I items to the finish line," Ellen said with the cool confidence of someone who had already done it hundreds of times. "It's really about creating a simple 'closing checklist' of things that need to be completed, personalizing ownership, and setting target dates for completion. That closing checklist would include contract reviews, legal, IT, and procurement sign-offs."

"And how do you make sure that Phase II goals actually stay in focus and come back into the customer opportunity as part of an upsell opportunity?" I asked.

"Good question," Ellen said. "It's important in the sales process that we talk about Phase II midterm goals as building on the foundation of Phase I goals. This makes it easier to hand off Phase I and Phase II goals in a connected way to the customer success team. This is where a mutual success plan comes in. It supports documenting Phase I and Phase II goals, metrics, and key decision-makers so the customer success team can manage each relationship around key goal areas."

"And once it goes over to the customer success team, what is the prompt to revisit the Phase II goals?" I asked.

"We have agreed-on check-in points for a more strategic account review," Ellen said. "These are different from the regular account calls focused on implementation and product training. Having that Phase I and Phase II document makes it possible to use the strategic calls as a 'soft sell' to come back to the Phase II goals. We revisit the customer goals, share successes with that customer to date and also bring in stories about how other, similar customers may be using the platform."

The shift to a mutual success plan with a Phase I and Phase II had some immediate benefits for the Burning Glass team. First, it led to an increased number of sales that closed within eight to twelve weeks, rather than the more typical six-month sales cycle, as the sales team quickly focused on a use case with a strong impact. Second, it helped shift to a focus on continual value expansion, which supported expanding the number of upsell opportunities.

Expansion Playbook: The Authentic Account Plan

Account planning is a decades-old business practice, originally developed by the J. Walter Thompson advertising agency in London in 1968. It is the process of nurturing and growing existing customer relationships. Having a strong account plan and account planning process is a key driver of B2B growth. It connects and focuses the activity of the sales, account management, and customer success teams on deepening the value of existing customer relationships in ways that offer value to the customer and increased revenue opportunities to the vendor.

Traditional account planning considers buyer value one of a variety of elements that go into the account planning process. All of the major sales methodologies mentioned in chapter 7 that focus on high-dollar-value enterprise selling have an account planning process. The traditional account planning process goes through six or seven sequential steps:

1 Conducting industry analysis

2 Determining customer's key initiatives, goals, and challenges

3 Establishing current position and current customer purchasing

4 Identifying competitors

5 Examining customer relationships and assessing stakeholders

6 Developing strategy

7 Action planning

The *authentic account plan* play, in contrast, anchors everything on buyer value. In our work with go-to-market teams,

A traditional account plan considers a buyer's goals as one of several elements to identify expansion opportunities. **In an authentic account plan, by contrast, the buyer's goals anchor all other elements.**

we find that keeping buyer value as the "north star" of your account-deepening efforts can dramatically simplify the account planning process and also keep value-added conversations at the center of customer interactions. I always recommend an account planning process with three major steps:

1 Review the state of the mutual success plan developed in the sales process.

2 Build a prioritized list of opportunities for expanding value for both the customer and the vendor.

3 Make an action plan around this prioritized opportunity list.

Step one in the authentic account planning process, like most account planning processes, is to *assess* the state of a customer's key initiatives, goals, and challenges as captured in the mutual success plan during an initial deal closing. This review of the mutual success plan reminds your team members responsible for account expansion of the full range of customer goals that have been discussed. It helps assess the level of achievement against these goals and can also suggest new goal areas to explore.

The focus of this first step in authentic account planning is identifying a list of specific initiatives and goal areas that align with a company's own value narratives, and then understanding the specific departments and units in the customer's organization that might engage with those value narratives. It is the intersection of the value narratives and the customer's organizational structure that begins the second step in the authentic account planning process.

The second step focuses on developing a prioritized list of *expansion opportunities* that will increase value for both the customer and the company. It is here that the authentic account planning process deviates from the traditional planning process. The prioritized opportunity list comes from four sections of the plan, as follows, which the selling team member should create with these guiding questions:

1 **Critical goals and initiatives:** What has been achieved against the customer goals and initiatives at the start of the partnership? Which of these goal areas are still a priority? What new goal can be surfaced on changed marketing and internal circumstances?

2 **Opportunity canvas:** What is the list of all the new expansion products and services that I could sell to this customer based on their initiatives and goals?

3 **Evidence of success:** Where do I direct evidence of success and value creation for the goal area I am targeting to expand the account? Is that evidence from work with customers or a peer?

4 **Relationship network:** Where do I have existing relationships with users and buyers for each opportunity on my list? Or, where can I quickly establish those relationships?

This is where the authentic account plan is very different from a traditional account plan. The traditional account plan often leads with products, focusing on questions like, "What products has the customer not purchased yet?" and "How are my products most different from those of my competitors?" If it doesn't lead with products, it might lead with relationships, focusing on questions like, "How can my existing relationships introduce me to new contacts with purchasing power?" All of these are good questions and are included in an authentic account plan, but the authentic plan differs by anchoring on direct evidence of success with the customer or with a peer customer.

TRADITIONAL VERSUS AUTHENTIC ACCOUNT PLANNING

✓ **Traditional Account Planning**

✓ **Authentic Account Planning**

Traditional Account Planning

- Industry analysis
- Key initiatives, goals, and challenges
- Current position and current customer purchasing
- Identification of competitors
- Customer relationships and stakeholder assessment
- Strategy development
- Action steps

Authentic Account Planning

Step 1: Mutual Success Plan

- Phase I: Tactical handoff
- Phases I & II: Goals

Step 2: Value Expansion

- Critical goals & initiatives
- Full opportunity canvas
- Evidence of success
- Relationship network

Step 3: Action Steps

The list of expansion opportunities in the opportunity canvas is prioritized based on evidence of potential customer achievement in a new goal area. In the current buying environment, it is not just new buyers but also your existing customers who are busy and often overwhelmed with too much information. Efforts at engaging them with an expansion opportunity are much more successful if you can point to a specific goal you can help achieve, a gap you can assist in overcoming, or a specific impact that will result from an expanded partnership. The quality and likelihood of success with an expansion opportunity, much like the initial opportunity, come from using three levels of value discovery to identify a specific, actionable improvement.

To go back to the Burning Glass example, a university that has had success using the company's real time labor market data to improve graduate recruiting in its business school might be approached for an expansion opportunity for graduate recruiting in the engineering school or undergraduate recruiting with the enrollment management office. The Burning Glass team members would identify the right new contacts through existing customer contacts. In asking for an introduction or making a direct outreach to these new contacts, the team member would present evidence of success working with that university's business school team as well as with peer universities' engineering schools or undergraduate enrollment offices.

The third and final step in creating an authentic account plan is to *identify action steps* around the prioritized list of opportunities. The action steps involve identifying the new buyers that need to be developed, the value narrative that will be put in front of each buyer, and the evidence of helping the buyer with goal achievement.

To go back to the Inspira example, to create their expansion plans, account executives begin by listing all customers that have a gap in the product purchasing process and assigning a dollar amount to the gap. This is the opportunity canvas. They then prioritize each of the larger dollar opportunities based on alignment with one or more key goal areas or value narratives.

They ask: Is there evidence we can help this customer with digital automation, risk pricing, proactive renewals, or targeting new customers? For each opportunity that has good evidence for helping in new goal areas, the account executive then builds out the picture of their relationship network, identifying key relationships that exist, relationships that need to be developed, and the opportunities that might exist to cultivate these new relationships.

Continually building an authentic experience by reconnecting to what the buyer values most is key not only to an initial sale—it also needs to be at the center of the sales, account management, and customer success work around account expansion. A focus on selling more product to existing customers, without first anchoring back to the buyer's goals, can lead things off track for both the customer and the sales team member.

I am reminded of the value of an authentic account plan from work with a team at Lexmark Government Solutions (LGS).

Lexmark Experiences the Value of an Authentic Account Plan

"This large county in Florida is going to make my year," Joe said excitedly. Joe is an account manager at Lexmark selling to state and local governments.

Joe was sharing one of the top deals for the sales quarter as part of a monthly team meeting focused on building the LGS sales team's skills at being a trusted advisor. Joe's district manager, Kevin Stanford, who led account managers in the southeastern states, also joined the meeting that day. The initiative was focused on growing customer accounts faster by shifting the team's sales and account management conversations to focus on buyer goals first, then LGS's product. The initiative had been launched by the vice president responsible for leading the entire sales team. The monthly meeting brought together a group of nine frontline sales managers to discuss important deals and directly develop new sales strategies and tools for their work with their teams of account managers.

On a rotating basis each month, three of the frontline sales managers would invite an account manager to present a customer account. We were sitting that day in an open conference room at the LGS office in Washington, DC. Half of the frontline managers were sitting in the conference room together; the other half joined by videoconference. Kevin was in the conference room and Joe joined online.

"The CIO is my buddy at this point," Joe continued. "We talk every two weeks. He's introduced me to the major revenue-generating departments, including the police, water and sewer, and tax collection, as well as the largest operating groups like the health, planning, and training departments. We've already completed our managed print services assessment in six departments and identified a bunch of potential process improvements."

LGS offers print and content services to more than fifteen hundred government organizations. They provide printers, copiers, and software solutions to optimize and automate processes for document output and information management.

"It's excellent to hear you have gone so wide in the organization to set up a really big account over time," Kevin said. Then he continued, modeling for his frontline sales managers the question-led style he wanted to encourage in their own team: "Let's go back to some of the key types of discovery we've agreed on for the trusted advisor model. I'm wondering if the CIO has shared his top priorities for automating document output. If budgets end up being limited, where will he invest first? Which of the departments is most motivated? Where do we have the most relevant evidence of success?"

Joe didn't have an answer, and, in fact, Kevin had hit exactly on the critical flaw in Joe's deal. Too often, sales representatives listen to their buyers with "happy ears" and pursue every possible purchase to increase the dollar value of a deal.

Sometimes the pull of a big commission can lead salespeople to try to engineer a big sale right away. **Large expansion sales, however, typically only work if you do the legwork of confirming goal fit and alignment with multiple individual buyers.**

Not collaborating with customers to identify the strongest possibilities for expansion opportunities can lead to disappointment for a sales or account management team member and frustration for the customer.

Joe did close a deal with this large county in Florida, but it was a $75,000 deal with the department of water and sewer rather than the $500,000 deal that Joe had hoped for and which would have brought in six major departments all at once. In a later debrief with Kevin and the LGS frontline manager team during one of the monthly trusted advisor meetings, Joe recognized that his strategy of going wide to six departments had not anchored on what the buyer valued most, so he committed to adjusting his strategy.

"I've gone back to the CIO to share how we've already decreased printing by ten percent for the department of water and sewer," Joe said. So everyone in the conference room and online could see it, he shared a short on-screen presentation of his new approach to capturing customer goals and building a case for an expansion sale. "I recapped for him our earlier discussion on the opportunity to do the same in the police health, planning, and training departments. I also gave him examples of how LGS helped reduce document output for these departments for other large county governments. I shared with him that I knew the folks in health and planning, but was interested in his thoughts on which department was currently focused on upgrading their print infrastructure."

"This is a great direction," said Kevin, his whole face lighting up as he saw Joe put in practice the strategies he and frontline sales managers had been coaching. "And how did the CIO respond? Was he open to providing you the names and contacts in the other departments?"

"Yes. The CIO really appreciated the specific examples of how we had helped other large counties like his," Joe said.

"He told me that the planning group was very focused on a five-year strategic plan and would likely not respond, but that my health department contacts would be interested. He also shared the names of the training department individuals who were leading an initiative to digitize all training and reduce print output to what was most necessary."

Kevin stood up at this point, leaned forward slightly across the conference table, and gave Joe a virtual high five directed at the video monitor.

Joe's efforts definitely paid off for him, the customer, and the LGS team as a whole in moving toward their sales goal. His next deal with the county government was $175,000, as the department of water and sewer added another $25,000 to their initial purchase based on success to date, and the health and training departments purchased $150,000 in printers and print services. Joe was now halfway to his goal of $500,000 in purchasing from this Florida county. The county did not single-handedly make Joe's year, but his work on building an authentic account expansion plan did cover a big part of his sales quota.

Closing and Expanding on
Buyer Value Key to Account Value

The examples of Inspira's business analytics, Burning Glass's real time labor market data, and Lexmark's managed print services show how sales, account management, and customer success teams can use an authentic buyer journey to increase account values.

Pricing proposals and closing conversations get to the desired price for a product and service more often when they are linked back to a specific buyer goal and impacts. The pricing proposal works best when positioned as an investment to achieve something the buyer cares a lot about rather than just an additional budget line item.

Similarly, account expansion activities are most effective when they are organized around finding new areas to partner on the customer's goal achievement. The authentic account plan is anchored on the idea that expansion opportunities should always be connected back to evidence of goal achievement. It is those opportunities with the strongest likelihood for goal achievement that should be prioritized for action steps.

In chapter 9, we will look at how customer success organization can become a revenue driver by identifying the elements of an authentic buyer journey that are most important in each target market segment. Moving from a focus only on renewals to one that includes building the customer voice specific to each market segment leads to faster segment growth.

YOUR NEXT STEPS ON CLOSING AND EXPANDING ON CUSTOMER VALUE

- **Pricing as an investment:** Do you confirm buyer value before finalizing a buyer price? In a proposal conversation, how do you position your product or service's price as an investment in something the buyer values?

- **Mutual success plan:** How do you capture all buyer goal areas when closing an initial sale to support later account expansion? What is the account management or customer success process to bring customers back to these goal areas?

- **Authentic account plan:** How well do you capture and prioritize a customer's top goal areas to support account expansion? How do you use evidence of success on goal achievement to engage new decision-makers?

When you connect buyer value across an initial sale and an expansion sale, your account values grow quicker. Get more resources at winalytics.com/theplays to build plays that help land and expand faster around customer value.

9

Customer Success as a Revenue Driver

"WE HAVE a massive market opportunity for our connected worker application for manufacturing workers," Lawrence Whittle, CEO of Parsable, told me as we opened our conversation by videoconference. "More than eighty percent of employees around the world do not work behind a desk. Many work in manufacturing plants. They all could benefit from our solution. But the size of the opportunity presents a real go-to-market challenge."

On the wall behind Lawrence hung a banner for the World Economic Forum. He had been a member of the Forum's Centre for the Fourth Industrial Revolution for years and had contributed articles to *Forbes* magazine, *Newsweek* magazine, and the Forum's agenda. Lawrence was not only the CEO of a rapidly growing company but also an expert in his own right on the manufacturing sector served by that company.

"Why a challenge?" I asked. "You guys started the market for connecting frontline workers in manufacturing with digital tools. How could a really big market be anything other than good news for you?"

"Well," Lawrence replied, "the reality of our business is that while there are"—he gestured with one hand—"maybe two hundred and fifty common processes across all types of manufacturing, there are"—he held up both hands and splayed all his fingers—"thousands of industry-specific processes for each type of manufacturing. It's in the processes specific to their industry where manufacturers gain the most benefit from digitizing."

Parsable is a rapidly growing provider of digital workflow applications for manufacturing plants. Its solutions help manufacturers improve safety, productivity, and quality. The company's Connected Worker platform can replace thousands of paper-based work instructions that typically sit on a shelf in six-inch binders. Additionally, it facilitates the sharing of a huge amount of tacit knowledge in the heads of experienced workers that is not even on paper.

Parsable's Connected Worker technology allows work instructions to fit right into the day-to-day work of employees on the manufacturing production lines. It works with any mobile device and operating system, and offers real-time, how-to guidance with step-by-step instructions on any manufacturing operation in the plant. It also collects new human execution data on how work is being done and how manufacturing workflows can be improved.

"I see," I said. "So you really need to think about growth in this big market in terms of specific types of manufacturing sectors?"

Parsable Positions Customer
Success as a Revenue Driver

"Correct," Lawrence said. "After winning key accounts across a number of manufacturing sectors, we began to see account expansion with our food and beverage customers, as well as paper and packaging manufacturers. In food and beverage, it was our close collaboration with Heineken first, then Coca-Cola and Carlsberg, that allowed us to identify a robust set of safety procedures, manufacturing operations checklists, and standard operating procedures for a food and beverage manufacturing line."

"So, these were customers and also partners, it sounds like," I said.

"That's right. Our key to scaling was thinking very differently about customer success," Lawrence replied.

I was beginning to get a full view of how his distinctive combination of business and manufacturing expertise allowed him to create a unique vision for Parsable's growth.

"We needed to go beyond the idea of customer care focused on implementation and renewals. The big shift was to focus the customer success team on proactively identifying new manufacturing safety use cases that could support expansion in each manufacturing sector. Identifying more uses to keep manufacturing workers safe was good for the worker, for the manufacturer, and for us."

"That's interesting," I said. "That's a much more strategic way of thinking about customer success. It isn't just satisfying customers to make sure they renew, but partnering to look for expansion opportunities that increase business value to the customer and revenue from the account for Parsable."

"That's right," Lawrence said. "We focus on a team selling model across sales, account management, and customer success. Our sales team focuses on identifying two to three manufacturing processes where we can get to quick, measurable proof of the value. Together, account management and success focus on selling the vision of all the processes where we can help by drawing on examples of work with other, similar companies in the sector. Our goal is tripling the number of manufacturing operations covered in the first year."

"That is rapid account growth," I said. "Your sales, account management, and customer success team members are going to need to work together really effectively with a good process for managing accounts. They also need a shared understanding of what you call 'the vision for success' in each manufacturing sector."

"Yes," Lawrence said, making a gesture of strong agreement, "that all needs to be true. We want our account management team to understand that they are the quarterback of the account. They need to work with customer success to ensure high levels of satisfaction so a customer renews, and also so they can identify expansion opportunities by using their deep knowledge of customers. It's often the customer success team member that sees an additional customer need first. They need to share that knowledge with sales team members, who will start an expansion sale opportunity with the customer."

"So the role of customer success is to advocate for the customer," I said, "and that includes introducing new manufacturing operations or processes that have helped their peers in the same manufacturing sector. That's where the identification of industry-specific processes becomes so important."

"That's a great way to put it," Lawrence said. "Introducing a customer to a new manufacturing process that has worked for their peers is customer advocacy. It is a win-win on both sides."

Parsable's focus on a more strategic approach to customer success helped the company double its revenues in a single

When you introduce a customer to new goal areas that have delivered value for peers, it is the highest form of customer advocacy: **it brings customer care and account expansion into alignment.**

year. This was a particularly impressive feat, given that the company had already surpassed the $10 million threshold in annual revenue. The key to this rapid growth was the focus on partnering with customers to identify new manufacturing processes that increased customer value while expanding Parsable's account value. Most companies have a net revenue retention rate of 120 percent, meaning that their average customer renewal is worth 20 percent more than the previous year. Parsable used the strategic customer success model to achieve a net revenue retention rate that was more than triple this best-in-class benchmark.

Customer Success as a Third Revenue Team

Customer success has, in a few short years, become a third revenue team, with the same standing as sales and marketing. The most important part of a customer success team's role as a revenue driver is managing customer renewals. A high renewal rate is among the strongest indicators of the health and profitability of any business. This is particularly true for a subscription-based business. Given the impact of renewals on growth in a subscription business, it is not a surprise that the emergence of the customer success manager role has moved in lockstep with the rise of the "subscription economy," a term coined by Tien Tzuo, founder and CEO of subscription-management platform company Zuora.

The subscription economy started with software as a service (SaaS) in the late 1990s as software companies moved away from a pricing model that focused on a large upfront license payment and smaller ongoing annual maintenance fees toward annual software subscriptions. After the subscription model took hold in software over more than a decade, it then began to take hold in business services like accounting, training, and benefits, as well as in personal services like home cleaning, personal styling, and pet care. Now we see subscription models across the consumer landscape, with subscription options for every kind of consumer good from candy to clothes to cigars.

To understand the importance of renewal rates to the growth of a business, we can do a mental experiment on three companies that are almost exactly the same except for their customer renewal rate. Let's call them Company A, Company B, and Company C. All three sell the same product in the same market; have the same cost structure across sales, marketing, customer success, product, and operations; and successfully add $1 million each in new customer revenue each year for five years.

The only difference between the three companies is that Company A has a 90 percent renewal rate, Company B has an 80 percent renewal rate, and Company C has a 70 percent renewal rate. That difference in renewal rate means that at the end of five years, Company A achieves $24.7 million in revenue, Company B reaches $18.8 million, and Company C lags behind at just $14.2 million. Company A not only grows 74 percent faster than Company C and 31 percent faster than Company B, but also has more predictable cash flow that allows it to make strategic and proactive investments to target even faster growth and higher profits.

Customer success was developed as a key revenue center on equal standing with marketing and sales to manage this customer renewal process. By tracking individual customer satisfaction, engagement, and utilization, the customer success team can help companies proactively manage them to increase renewal rates. Proactive management means identifying and reaching out to customers with a higher risk of not renewing, confirming and troubleshooting key customer priorities, and looking for incremental upsell opportunities.

Customer renewals or repeat sales are the lifeblood of any business. The rise of the subscription economy has driven the growth of customer success teams as a third go-to-market team on equal footing with marketing and sales.

Customer success, like customer service, sits in the post-sale phase of the buyer journey, but the two teams engage customers in very different ways. Customer service teams are tactical and reactive. Their job is to train new customers and walk customers through the tactical steps of getting their account set up. On an ongoing basis, customer service reacts to issues and problems that are stopping a customer from getting value from a product. They also respond to questions and inquiries about how to use a product or service.

Customer success, by contrast, should be proactive and strategic, focusing on aspects of a product or service that can help a customer meet their business goals. They consult with customers to develop a full understanding of the customer's business challenges, needs, and goals. They use this understanding of goals to be proactive in managing customer relationships, sharing use cases, benefits, and features that can help support the achievement of identified goals. Alongside helping advance and expand buyer goals, customer success also continually identifies key individuals in the buyer organization, aligning different goal areas to specific influencers and decision-makers who care the most about each goal.

While many customer success teams have done a good job of being more strategic and proactive when it comes to customer renewals, the majority of these teams have not realized their potential as revenue drivers. In our example above, Parsable has figured out what many companies fail to understand: that customer success should be a strategic growth driver. For top-performing teams like Parsable, there are three distinct areas in the customer success playbook:

- Renewal plays that drive higher renewal rates and more repeat business.

- Expansion plays that make customer success an active participant in account deepening.

- Segment growth plays that make customer success an active participant in supporting peer reference and referrals, which are critical to the growth of any business.

CUSTOMER SUCCESS AS REVENUE DRIVER

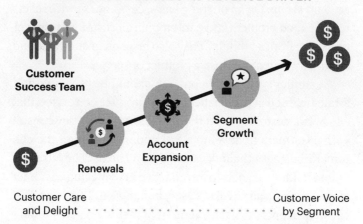

Customer Success Playbook: Renewal Plays

The foundation for all of the renewal and expansion work done by a customer success team is a *renewal and expansion metrics dashboard*. The dashboard gives a quick snapshot of account health, talking points for progress toward the customer's goals, and notes about any conversations concerning renewal. It also provides quick benchmarks to other clients. A dashboard like this can help your customer success team members start their customer conversation without having to do deep account research. The metrics part of the dashboard contains a small handful of the most important indicators to show if your customers are using and getting value out of the product or service.

The ideal number of metrics is three to five, so the list is manageable to produce before the business review call, easy to bring into the review for discussion, and meaningful in comparing across customer accounts. A longer list of the possible metrics I have seen teams use includes:

- Total number of users, as an indicator of the scale of account penetration.

- Number of unique departments with users, to track the breadth of account penetration.

- Percent of users that are active, with the definition of "active user" being specific to the product or service.

- User satisfaction survey score or net promoter score, which is a cross-company and cross-industry measure of satisfaction based on likelihood to recommend.

- Number of customer support tickets, time-to-resolution on tickets, and number or list of any outstanding tickets.

- Number of total trainings on a customer account or number of trainings in different departments.

Because renewals support business growth, most companies have developed their entire customer success playbook around a series of plays to secure higher renewal rates. The foundational plays for renewals is the *account review call*. This can be a Zoom call, a phone call, or an in-person meeting. Regardless of format, your team's goal for a business review call should be to roll up from tactical, ongoing support that focuses on answering customer questions, troubleshooting customer issues, or sharing resources and training on new functionality. The business review focuses on the status of the account, current level of engagement and utilization, and opportunities to improve on both. For some companies and their customers, this review is conducted quarterly and, thus, is referred to as the quarterly business review. For other companies and their customers, a quarterly pace of business reviews is too frequent and can feel more like a chore than value added on both sides. In either case, though, the focus and purpose is a high-level review.

The key performance indicators in a renewal and expansion dashboard can help your customer success team put their accounts in renewal bands or segments. It is the renewal band that identifies the account status and determines the timing and focus of the business review call. I have typically seen teams use either three renewal bands—green, yellow, and red—or five renewal bands—green, blue, yellow, orange, and red.

THREE REVENUE TEAMS, ONE REVENUE ORGANIZATION

Three Renewal Plays	Elements of Play
Promotor Call	• Confirm received value • Explore new goal areas and new users • Ask for internal or external references • Invite into thought leadership
Utilization Call	• Reconfirm customer's initial goals and target impacts • Identify user group tactics to boost utilization • Introduce internal and peer best practices • Reprioritize goals and users for higher utilization
Detractor Call	• Openly acknowledge challenges • Explore tactics and strategies to reset relationship • With engagement reset, reignite excitement

Accounts in the top two bands, green and blue, are typically in "promoter" mode—they are very happy with the service, very likely to renew, have multiple internal advocates, and are often open to supporting account expansion activities. Accounts in the middle bands, yellow and orange, are typically in "utilization" mode—they have had some good experiences and usage, but their level of usage or survey satisfaction level suggests risks for non-renewal, and they probably have a mix of internal promoters and detractors. Accounts in the bottom band, the red zone, are in "detractor" mode—they may not be actively using the service, are not satisfied with what they have used, probably have no strong internal promoters, and are likely non-renewals.

Your team will want to focus each business review call on either a *promoter call*, a *utilization call*, or a *detractor call*, depending on the account status.

Promoter Call Framework

The *promoter call framework* focuses first, of course, on confirming that the renewal is on track. The focus then goes back to a company's value narrative to look for opportunities to harness the promoter energy to support expansion into the promoter's organization as well as into peer organizations. Your team's discussion during a promoter call should cover a set of the following topics:

- Confirming the value areas that lead to satisfaction, utilization, and a likely renewal.

- Exploring new goal areas or value narratives that might extend the customer relationship.

- Exploring other departments or buyers interested in experiencing similar value.

- Giving opportunities for product input to increase impact on value.

- Asking a promoter if they are open to contributing to thought leadership, including potentially giving a testimonial, writing a blog post, or speaking in a webinar or at a conference.

- Asking a promoter if they have peers at other companies who might be interested in experiencing similar value.

When your team brings a call with a promoter account back to an authentic customer journey by re-anchoring on the customer goals and impacts, it's much easier to make customer "asks" about referrals and thought leadership. That is, when your customer success team member starts by getting the customer excited about how the partnership has met their needs and provided value that did not previously exist, it is a lot easier to ask about new goal areas, internal or external referrals, or thought leadership contribution. All of these asks are now put in the context of "sharing and deepening the value" that the customer has already experienced.

Your customer success teams typically will shy away from directly selling on new opportunities that emerge from a business review call with a promoter account. And they do not need to be in a position to sell. They can instead work with a sales team member to turn these new internal or peer opportunities into a sales conversation—and, with success, into a proposal and contract—but the customer success team member should, during the business review call, be open to "soft selling." The culture of customer success is typically strongly against the idea of selling because it can interfere with being a customer advocate. When you start from a position of an authentic buyer journey and re-anchor on buyer goals, however, soft selling is now consistent with customer advocacy. As Lawrence Whittle from Parsable put it, "Introducing a customer to a new process that has worked for their peers is customer advocacy. It is a win-win on both sides."

Utilization Call Framework

The goal for customer success is always to thrill and delight customers and therefore to move all or most accounts into "promoter" renewal bands. However, there will always be a number of accounts that are not yet solidified renewals. In the business review for these accounts, your team needs to focus on a *utilization call framework* designed to secure higher levels of usage and satisfaction. There are several possible reasons your customers may not be fully implemented and using a product or service to the highest level possible. There may be an undetected misfit in the sales process, with the customer not fully understanding what they've bought or not having a clear enough sense of what problem a product or solution can solve. Even with a clear sense of why they've bought, the customer may be struggling to get their team to put time and effort into effectively using a new product or service. There may also be a gap in the training, implementation, or onboarding process.

Regardless of the reasons that have led an account to be at a less-than-ideal level of utilization, your team needs to take the focus of the business review call right back to the authentic buyer journey to re-anchor on a buyer's goals and the targeted impacts expected from the product or service. Any internal promoters of the product or service should be active participants in the utilization play. The ideal structure your team can use for a business review call with a utilization-level account would focus on:

- Reconfirming the customer's goals and target impacts for their initial purchase.

- Exploring ways to deepen product or service utilization with specific users, and particularly internal promoters, or in specific departments to support achievement of these goals and impacts.

- Exploring new goal areas or value narratives—which may not have been covered or were covered insufficiently in the initial sales process—as a path to higher utilization and satisfaction.

- Sharing best practices and success stories from peer customers to help the customer on the call understand goals and implementation from a peer perspective.

- Reprioritizing the customer goals and user groups, from all the items discussed in the business review call that are most likely to have the quickest positive impact on usage and satisfaction.

The utilization account play shows just how important an authentic buyer journey is in connecting sales to customer success's renewal and expansion work. The authentic buyer journey is most important in having consistent value narratives used by both sales and customer success. The value narratives make it possible for both groups to ask a buyer, and then a customer, about their goals, communicate about the company's capabilities, and speak to peer success stories in very similar terms.

The repetition of value messaging and specific language of success in the two phases of the buyer journey builds a customer's confidence in their relationship with a company and makes it easier to discuss and reprioritize goal areas that can increase satisfaction and usage. More specifically, the mutual success plans and account plans discussed in chapter 8 are critical sales tools to close both new and expansion opportunities. However, they are also critical customer success tools that enable team members going into business review calls to have a deeper understanding of the customer's reason for purchasing, as well as all potential goal or value areas explored in the sales process.

Detractor Call Framework

When a customer account is in the lowest renewal band, typically the red zone, they are in "detractor" mode. These customers typically are not effectively using a product or service and also exhibit signs of dissatisfaction or likelihood of not renewing. There is likely no internal advocate or promoter of the product, only detractors who are not satisfied. For this type of customer, I always recommend a *detractor call framework* that starts with the customer success representative simply "falling on their sword," as the saying goes, and acknowledging that things are not going well. This is a way of opening up a return to the authentic buyer journey, by seeing if the open acknowledgement will get a dissatisfied customer to re-engage in a constructive conversation about aligning with their goals and target impacts.

The structure I recommend for the business review call with a detractor account follows this sequence:

1 First, openly acknowledge that things are not on track by asking questions like, "How did we miss in meeting your needs?" or "Are there specific things that are causing frustration?"

2 Then, ask directly about things that might improve the relationship, with questions like, "How can we better meet

your needs?" "Are there training opportunities that would help?" and "Are there different users we might engage or is there different functionality we can explore?"

3 Finally, seek to reignite enthusiasm by anchoring back to the authentic buyer journey and asking some version of "Is there one thing we could focus on together that would get you excited?"

Again, in the business review call with a detractor account, the tools used to build an authentic buyer journey in the sales phase are also critical to the customer success team's effort. The mutual success plan and the account plan give the customer success team member a head start in identifying that "one thing to focus on" to re-energize the account. The peer success stories used in the sales process can also be used by customer success to explore goal areas that might reignite enthusiasm. When I work with customer success teams, I also ask them to find their two or three favorite customer success stories that support a promoter call by introducing expansion opportunities, but also to find two or three customer stories to support a detractor call by introducing examples of really strong clients who may have gotten off to a rough start and then recovered to strongly value the company's product or service.

Customer Success Playbook: Expansion Call Framework

Renewal plays and renewal key performance indicators are, and should be, the foundation of any customer success playbook. From our earlier thought experiment with companies A, B, and C, which were exactly the same except that they

Your customer success team has the best vantage point on expansion opportunities. Beginning each business review call with rediscovery on key customer goals and initiatives makes identifying new expansion opportunities feel customer-centric.

had 90 percent, 80 percent, and 70 percent renewal rates, respectively, it is clear that renewals and repeat business are the foundation of growth for any subscription-based company. However, many customer success teams under-emphasize the role they should play in account expansion. Many customer success teams think of their role as primarily "customer care" and shy away from anything "sales-related" that would compromise this role. And your customer success team is probably no different.

The challenge with this approach is that your customer success team is better positioned than any other team to identify account expansion opportunities. These expansion opportunities often come directly out of the team's work in implementing and training new customers, helping these customers broadly deploy a new product or service, and making sure that the customer is unlocking all product or service benefits. It is usually during these conversations that a customer is most open to sharing ways to deepen their goal attainment.

One of the powerful outcomes of building an authentic buyer journey is that it brings into alignment your customer success team's role as an advocate for their customers. Identifying expansion opportunities around a goal and an impact that bring deeper value to the customer and higher account value to the company is good for both sides. A partnership between your customer success team, on the one hand, and your sales or account management team, on the other, focuses customer success on identifying new areas of customer value, and sales or account management on turning these areas of potential value into commercial opportunities.

At the heart of the *expansion call framework* are the same tools used during the business review call, the promoter call, and the utilization call. Value discovery questions are used to surface buyer goals, gaps to achieving those goals, and buyer impacts that might motivate an additional investment. The mutual success plan during the sales process and an authentic account plan developed to support account expansion can both come into play. They are used to identify new ways to extend an existing goal area, explore other department use cases, identify new buyers who might be interested in the identified goal area, or identify a new goal area that might be of interest to current users as well as potential new users. Success stories with peer customers are used to introduce those expansion opportunities in familiar language and make them actionable.

You can sometimes have an expansion call play and a promoter account play in the same call with one of your customers, but this is not typical. When it does happen, a customer success team member typically leads the first part of the discussion to review the partnership to date and reconfirm top areas of value and top buyer impacts, and the sales or account management team member then builds on this success to date to explore expansion opportunities with the existing buyer group or a new buyer group. Typically, however, the promoter call and expansion call happen in sequence. Again, your customer success team member leads the account review, identification of buyer value, and surfacing of new areas for partnership as part of the promoter call play. A separate expansion call is then scheduled and led by sales or account management to focus on deeper value discovery around these new goal areas. The separate expansion call is also an opportunity to bring in new user groups, as well as more senior economic buyers, to have a business conversation rather than an account state conversation.

Customer Success Playbook: Segment Growth Plays

Customer success starts to become a strategic growth driver when it looks beyond individual customer renewal and incremental upsells to identify the patterns of goals and impacts for buyers in specific target segments. Your customer success team is best positioning to build what I call your *segment growth* plays.

In my experience working with go-to-market teams, the most dramatic growth shifts happen when a team gets very good at mapping value to each of their target market segments. New buyers are most interested in hearing from their peers and about your success with other customers are who just like them. So, when you create playbooks around the goal achievement of peers most important to buyers in the same segment, you get faster segment growth and faster overall revenue growth. This means you craft versions of value narratives to capture a more specific story about segment value, identify the aligned capability statements, and build client success stories for each market segment.

There are two specific customer success plays central to faster segment growth: the customer voice by segment play and the peer referencing play.

Customer Voice by Segment Play

Companies often brand themselves around their most prestigious clients in their target market—for example, "We work with Harvard" or "We work with Amazon." However, in reality, all markets are micro-segmented. While your potential buyers may be impressed by the company's work with top brands, what they really want to hear about is your work with peer organizations who are just like them, and the specific ways a company has helped these peers with their goal achievement.

Building use cases by segment means that your sales and customer success teams can continually position your company as a strategic partner able to solve multiple related problems for a potential buyer. With this approach, buyers hear goals and pains, discovery questions, capability talk tracks, and customer success cases that are all developed from experience with other buyers like them. They hear segment-specific messages in the sales process, in the onboarding process, and in the ongoing account review and account-deepening processes. The repetition of segment-specific language makes it easier for a buyer to understand and engage with expansion options.

Going back to the Parsable example from earlier in the chapter, let's say a bottle manufacturer wants to know that the Parsable team has expertise in manufacturing operations overall and then specifically for bottle manufacturing processes. They want to hear the Parsable team speak to how their Connected Worker platform can be used to support a funnel process for pouring large amounts of molten glass into models, or a settleblow process that allows compressed air into the molds to finish forming the necks of bottles. Similarly, a paper and packaging manufacturer wants to hear how the Connected Worker platform supports the multi-step process used to remove water from the fiber and pulp to create a uniform consistency, as well as the processes for drying and finishing paper or cardboard.

The Torchlight example from chapter 6 provides another helpful illustration of the value of building a buyer voice by segment. You may remember that Torchlight sells a caregiver platform for human resources departments. The platform can be positioned as a benefit to employees who manage a dependent elderly parent or a child with special educational or behavioral needs. Torchlight works with companies in the financial services, biotechnology, pharmaceuticals, and

Building a customer voice by segment with peer success stories in language specific to that market **creates familiarity and leads to faster new buyer engagement.**

manufacturing sectors, as well as with hospitals, universities, and professional services firms. While all Torchlight buyers are interested in considering a caregiver platform for their employee caregivers, their specific reasons and goals vary by market segment.

Many of Torchlight's manufacturing and pharmaceutical buyers are interested in the benefits of caregiver platforms to help shift-based employees better manage their benefit costs, and reduce attrition among contingent employees. They are really most interested in hearing about "bread and butter" issues in managing costs and helping workers in difficult life circumstances. By contrast, professional services and financial services firms that have difficulty recruiting and retaining women leaders and managers due to caregiving responsibilities are most interested in hearing "evocative" language about how access to a caregiver platform can give them a recruiting and retention edge with these target populations and become a central tool in their talent pipeline development. Human resources managers at each type of firm may be impressed that Torchlight has Amgen, Dell, and Johnson & Johnson as clients, but they are much more likely to buy or expand their relationship when they hear language and value propositions strongly aligned with their own concerns and the concerns of their direct peers.

Peer Reference Play

Building a buyer voice by segment is the start of deeper growth in target market verticals. Activating "evangelizers" by segment to support direct and indirect *peer reference plays* is as important. New buyers are most likely to engage when they hear from peer evangelizers that have had a strong positive experience with the company. Customer success is in the best position to identify these peer evangelizers and also to ask for participation in thought leadership activities like testimonials, blogs, and webinars that the marketing team can manage and use to build reputation and awareness. The knowledge about top customers by segment who might be well-suited to support and participate in these efforts comes from working directly with customers on training, looking for ways to deepen customer value, and working with customers on new expansion goal areas.

However, most companies never really build a robust buyer voice by segment or peer reference that can be actively put back into the market expansion effort in a targeted way, and they therefore miss this powerful growth opportunity. This is because most companies fail to develop a process to secure marketing and customer success collaboration for this exact purpose. To effectively build the buyer voice and peer references in each target segment, customer success and company leadership need to prioritize having their teams roll up from their day-to-day work supporting customer usage to focus on identifying cross-customer patterns.

Typically, this becomes a priority when either marketing leadership or the revenue leadership overall recognizes an opportunity to grow faster through peer referencing and commits to harnessing the power of peer evangelizers. Once this commitment has been made, there are four key steps to building organizational muscle around peer referencing:

1 Identifying the most important target growth segments to harness peer referencing.

2 Identifying the three to five most successful customers in this segment for success stories.

3 Add and revise segment success stories every one or two quarters.

4 Build an internal referral list from these success stories.

Peer referencing is your easiest strategy to engage new buyers in any target market segment. Most companies do not have a well-developed process to make peer referencing repeatable.

Your first step is to build deeper segment growth. Have your marketing and customer success teams identify the most important segments that can grow faster through peer referencing. Your target growth segments need to have a handful of strong existing customers who are already evangelizers. These are customers who can act as strong advocates for the product or service and are willing to act as referrals and to have their stories shared with other potential buyers in the sector as examples of successful client outcomes. Target growth segments also need enough other potential buyers to build a segment growth pathway. Typically, a target growth segment should have hundreds of other peers as potential buyers.

Once you have identified target growth segments, your next step is to build the buyer voice by segment. Take a deep dive into your three to five most successful customers in each segment. You can capture these stories in a video testimonial or a success story or in a one-on-one referral conversation with another potential customer. Your stories should capture the problem that the customer had, the range of use cases addressed by your product or service, and, most importantly, the before-and-after case for the specific impacts the customer achieved. Ideally, these impacts can be quantified into a business case or financial ROI, but the impacts could also be organizational or emotional. It is in writing down the goals and impacts for top customers in a segment that the buyer voice by segment typically emerges. It sits with customer success to identify the goals and impacts, but it is typically the marketing team that formalizes these success cases into formal case studies for the website, as well as for verbal success story snippets and slides that can be incorporated easily into sales calls.

Your third step in building the buyer voice by segment is to commit to a revision cycle. This should occur either quarterly (every ninety days) or twice a year (every 180 days). Your decision on this is really dependent on the volume of clients you work with and the time it takes for your product or service to generate a meaningful impact. As a rule of thumb, your pacing should be aligned to the goal of identifying two or three new customer success stories for each key target market segment per revision cycle. The revision cycle means that customer success and marketing sit down together to pull out and revise their segment use case and payoff examples. The working session should focus on identifying new top customers in each segment, as well as any new goal areas or impacts for the existing top customers. The output of the working session is a revision of the buyer voice by segment, as well as the addition of new case studies and success stories.

The fourth and final step in the peer referencing play is to develop formal and informal peer referral programs. Informal peer referrals happen when a company lists all of its buyers in a specific market segment or sector. These lists of a company's "segment footprint" can be used in outreach emails or discovery call talk tracks to build quicker familiarity. Formal referral programs involve directly asking buyers to identify peers for outreach. Usually, a referral request can take the form of a simple question like, "Which of your peers might be interested in learning about our work together? Or about the success we have had together?" Formal peer reference programs may involve incentives or discounts, but often it is just the satisfaction of being a leader using a new solution that will motivate peer referencing.

Plus Delta Partners Drives Growth with a Peer Reference Play

In thinking about capturing both the voice of the customer by segment and customer references to drive strong business growth, I am reminded of a discussion with Beth Nelson, Plus Delta Partners's chief client officer. Beth was sitting that day on the enclosed porch of her home in Maryland as we spoke by teleconference.

"Early in the company's history, we had a great list of liberal arts colleges and midsize private universities as referenceable brands," Beth said. "We had really strong evidence that we could raise fundraisers' productivity by twenty-five to thirty percent at places like Pomona College, Haverford College, and Loyola Marymount University, among others. But these client names get almost no attention from the large research universities, which have ten times the budget for professional development."

Plus Delta Partners has become the leading provider of professional development services to fundraisers in the higher education, nonprofit, and medical fundraising fields. As chief customer officer, Beth was in a unique position to accelerate Plus Delta's segment growth. She had spent several years as a Plus Delta senior consultant directly fulfilling professional development engagements for clients. She also served as a fundraising executive and leader at both Lafayette College, a small liberal arts college, and Temple University, a large public research university. She knew this world from a number of perspectives.

"From those humble beginnings," I said, "you now work with several dozen of the large public research universities [like Michigan State, Ohio State, and University of North Carolina at Chapel Hill], as well as top private universities [like Cornell, Duke, and Rice]. So how did that evolution happen?"

"Well, it took us probably a year and a half to land any research universities at all," Beth said. "Fundraising leadership at the research universities would get excited about our training approach, saying things like, 'We love that you focus on ongoing skills development and coaching sessions rather than single-day training sessions.' Then, as we would get deeper into the conversation, things would stop. They could not imagine how our training model for teams of twelve to fifteen fundraisers would scale to work with their teams of one hundred to three hundred fundraisers."

"So, if I hear you correctly, they were interested in your approach," I said. "But in your language they hear, 'This works for small fundraising teams, but not enterprise-scale teams.' Is that right?"

"That is exactly right," Beth said raising both her hands in a gesture of agreement. It was clear that she understood the nuances of value and language for fundraising teams in different segments. "Despite this objection, we eventually did find partners like Duke, Michigan State, and Northeastern who would take a chance on us," she continued. "Then we looked at how these research universities actually used our training program."

"From what I know about the training world, I'm guessing they wanted to see how an initial investment could scale and sustain," I said.

"That's correct," Beth said. "In each case, they were interested in using our cohort model designed for twelve to fifteen people to focus on manager skill development. So, that allowed us to go to many other large research universities and talk about our program as a manager development tool that would help recruit and retain top-quality manager talent and support the productivity of their entire fundraising team. Within a couple of years, we had dozens of research university clients."

"That's cool. Same product, different packaging—a subtle language shift—and a big growth result," I said. "Did growth happen the same way when you moved into medical fundraising?"

In each market segment, you can partner with your top customers to build your customer voice. Use your top customers' words and language to make small adjustments to help your message really land with their peers.

"Yes, it did," said Beth. "There was a slight bit of product development we had to do, since, for many, the focus in medical fundraising is on grateful patients and community rather than on alumni, who are the main focus of college and university fundraising, but the product stayed ninety percent the same. Again, it was mostly different positioning—a new skin on the same product—and watching how first customers used the training program."

"So, if I hear you correctly, a central element of Plus Delta growth has been selling forward from one sector peer to another," I said. "I'm curious to hear about the pattern in medical fundraising."

"As it turns out," Beth said, "one of the primary things medical fundraisers wanted to improve was communication and collaboration between the senior fundraiser staff and their doctors." Beth had not worked in medical fundraising but had gotten good at capturing language and value specific to each type of fundraising segment. "Medical fundraisers are typically very experienced and sophisticated fundraisers. They do not perceive that they need training, but they often have difficulty engaging and getting medical staff's attention."

"So, in this case it was more an organizational skill set than an individual skill set you were developing," I said.

"For the most part, yes. It was a lot easier to sell our program as fixing an organizational problem. If we sold our program as fundraiser skill development, the senior fundraisers would have folded their arms and said, 'We don't need this.'" Beth imitated the gesture as she spoke. "So, we sold it as an organizational solution and then used our cohort training model to also train for individual skills in exactly the same way we did with colleges and universities."

Plus Delta's success in capturing the voice of the customer in these three very different fundraising segments helped it to consistently achieve 40 percent and higher year-on-year revenue growth for more than five years. As they diversified from initial clients among liberal arts colleges and midsize universities to research universities and medical centers, the company was very careful to build out success cases to validate its approach and ROI outcomes in each of these three core segments. They are now taking a similar approach as they extend into other segments in the nonprofit space, including advocacy/rights, environment/animal advocacy, media, and museums and the arts.

Customer Success as a Key to Renewals and Revenue Growth

The examples of both Parsable's digital workflow application for manufacturing operations and Plus Delta's professional development service for fundraising professionals show the critical role that customer success teams play in driving faster revenue growth through an authentic buyer journey.

Compared with marketing and sales, customer success is a relatively new go-to-market team. The importance of customer success has increased in lockstep with the rise of the subscription economy and the importance of customer renewals to a strong growth trajectory. Anchoring your customer conversations on an authentic buyer journey helps customer success play an important role not only in renewals but also in partnering with sales to surface expansion opportunities. It also helps them partner with marketing to build buyer voices by segment and peer referencing programs that lead to deeper market segment growth. By anchoring on customer goals first while maintaining a focus on customer care, the work of customer success stays in alignment with sales and marketing, and the coordinated effort of all three teams contributes to increasing the pace of upsell and reference opportunities.

In chapter 10, we will move from a focus on the playbooks that build an authentic buyer journey within individual go-to-market teams to looking at cross-team processes and metrics. Top-performing teams not only have strong playbooks within individual go-to-market teams, but directly connect these playbooks to form a single revenue organization and an authentic, seamless buyer journey.

YOUR NEXT STEPS ON CUSTOMER SUCCESS AS A REVENUE DRIVER

- **Renewal plays:** How do you identify and segment customers by renewal and expansion likelihood? What are your renewal plays to expand promoter accounts, build utilization in accounts with usage gaps, and remedy dissatisfaction?

- **Customer voice by segment:** How well do you identify and use your top customers in each target market? What approach are you taking to building customer voices by segment and peer reference programs?

Renewals are the lifeblood of any business, but there is no conflict between the customer success team leading renewals and at same time feeding expansion and segment growth. Go to winalytics.com/theplays for resources to help build plays that turn customer success into a revenue driver.

PART III

Organizational Supports for an Authentic Buyer Journey

10

Three Revenue Teams, One Revenue Organization

"**I** ALWAYS FIND myself in these funny roles of needing to build a business-to-business revenue organization inside a company that began with a consumer focus," said Ben Robinson, SVP of sales at Zeel. "To not get lost in the more established, consumer-focused part of the company, you have to be really good at getting B2B sales, marketing, and success teams to execute as one, integrated organization."

I was talking with Ben that day in his home office by videoconference. There was a feeling of calm focus that pervaded his physical environment: the room had high ceilings, and directly behind him was a floor-to-ceiling glass wall that looked out onto a well-kept, colorful garden.

Zeel helps its customers increase health and reduce stress with a range of health services, from high-quality massages to yoga, mindfulness, and assisted stretching. Customers include individuals as well as employees who receive a health benefit from a Zeel-partner company. Ben leads the B2B group, called Zeel@Work, which delivers employee wellness services both in-person and online to its business customers. "So, what is the biggest challenge?" I asked Ben. "Is it getting the whole revenue organization synced up on content and messaging? Or is it having clear rules on buyer handoffs, and creating aligned incentives?"

Ben sat back for a moment to consider. "Well, getting the Zeel@Work team synced up on messaging has been pretty straightforward," he said. "Our team sells to corporate HR buyers with messaging that targets 'increasing wellness, decreasing cost.' It's very similar to the messaging that our consumer team uses, which focuses on wellness as a path to a happier and healthier life. On the business side, we really just add well-known research that employee stress costs US businesses $300 billion each year, and that wellness programs can reduce health care costs by eighty-six percent. So, there was no real issue there."

Zeel@Work Builds an Aligned B2B Revenue Team

"Okay, and what about the handoff points and incentives? That must be different from the consumer side of the business," I said.

Ben grimaced ever so slightly and then said in a measured tone, "Yes, that took some work, particularly in the prospecting playbooks to support marketing-to-sales handoffs. The first marketing campaigns run by the consumer marketing team ... well, they really didn't work at all for our business-focused sales team. We had way too much variability in leads, some good, some really bad. Since seventy percent of our leads are inbound, we needed to really work with the consumer marketing team to optimize their lead generation efforts for our team."

"How did you do that?" I asked. "I know marketing usually wants to get credit for all the leads they generate, and sometimes sales teams are really picky about working only the 'best' leads."

Ben nodded. "We definitely had that tension here as well. So it became really important for both sides to agree on clear rules of the road." I could see the expertise that had made him a successful B2B leader in an environment with a stronger business-to-consumer focus. "We started by agreeing to a set of clear targets for campaigns. We focused on companies with more than five hundred employees in geographies we served, with that effort concentrated in just three target industries: technology, professional services, and legal firms."

"Okay," I said, "so that helps narrow the campaign focus, but how did you make sure the leads handed to the sales team were something close to an ideal buyer?"

Ben leaned forward and, with emphasis in his voice, said, "In addition to the three rules on the company target, we added two more rules at the contact level. We agreed that the contact had to be in a director-level role or above and had to show a pattern of engagement that involved two or more activities, things like an email open, a clicked link, a webinar registration, or a content download."

"So, that's how you got alignment on the handoff from marketing to sales," I said. "How about from sales to customer success? How did you create a smooth handoff from the sales team member getting a signed agreement with a new customer to the group responsible for onboarding and supporting your corporate buyers?"

"On the customer success side, we started with a clear process of communication between the teams." Ben now started to show how much he had truly learned about building end-to-end go-to-market processes that would in turn create a stronger buyer experience and faster revenue growth. "We built four sales stages in our customer relationship management [CRM] system, where we manage all our new customer deals. Sales team members manage a deal from stage one, which is an initial discovery call, to stage four, which is closed won. An account manager then takes it forward into an account deepening phase. We ask our sales team members to attach all their notes on a closed-won deal to the account to ensure a smooth transition."

"Hmm," I said, and I might have raised an eyebrow. "I've worked with a lot of sales teams, and they all seem to spend as little time as possible in CRM. How did you ever get the sales team to spend time adding notes for the success team?"

"Great question," Ben said with a broad, celebratory smile. "We also changed incentives for the sales team members by compensating them on any upsell deal closed by an account manager within twelve months of the initial sale. This motivated the sales team to do really good discovery on all potential places a new buyer could use Zeel@Work, and to hand off really good notes. At first, my CEO was not a big fan. He called it 'double dipping.' But as he saw the results come in, he became more comfortable with the approach."

"That's cool. It's a great approach to team collaboration that also builds a strong understanding of buyer goals, which is the best way to find expansion opportunities quickly and deepen account value," I said. "Last question. When you think about aligning the revenue organization, does it mean marketing, sales, and customer success all report to someone in your role?"

"It could be organized that way," said Ben. "In my last role, I had end-to-end revenue responsibility with all three of those teams reporting to me. With Zeel, I currently have sales and customer success. We draw on central marketing, and we expect to get our own marketing team when we get a bit bigger. More important than the organizational structure are the cross-team communication and incentives that keep the buyer at the center of our focus as responsibility for engaging with them moves from one internal team to the next."

Three Revenue Teams, Three Revenue Cultures

A single, cohesive revenue organization is key to building an authentic buyer journey. It can help your go-to-market teams increase the pace of all revenue-generating activities, from sourcing and closing new opportunities, to increasing account values, to increasing the pace of market development in target market segments.

In the previous chapters, we talked about how a value narrative playbook can help your go-to-market teams create a consistent and authentic buyer and customer journey. We have also shown how the value narrative playbook acts as a shared messaging framework across your go-to-market teams and can guide the creation of team-specific playbooks for prospecting, sales, account management, and customer success. A value narrative playbook creates the overarching philosophy and approach to customer value creation. Playbooks specific to each go-to-market team then put the authentic buyer journey into practice with plays that guide and direct each buyer interaction.

As the Zeel example shows, building a consistent value narrative framework is one key to a cohesive revenue organization. The other is building cross-team revenue processes and measurement to create shared accountability for an authentic buyer journey across three very different teams. Sales, marketing, and customer success each have their own

Value narratives create a common story and language about buyer value across sales, marketing, and customer success departments, but **for an authentic buyer journey to take hold, you need to have cross-team processes and performance measures.**

personality and culture. Sales is stereotypically focused on earning more incentive compensation and putting points on the boards by closing date. Marketing is filled with "brainiacs" who can turn a clever phrase and also crunch numbers. Customer success has those "nurturing" types who want to care for customers.

In my work with revenue leaders, the tensions between sales and marketing have long been a topic of discussion. The classic tension is around lead quality. As I mentioned in my conversation with Ben, marketers often want sales teams to work all of the leads being generated, from content downloads, to event leads, to "hot" leads generated by demo requests. Sales people want to spend time only on well-qualified leads. Another common challenge is around messaging. Marketers think in terms of building messaging that appeals to customer categories or segments. Sales people focus on language that helps build excitement and commitment in individual buyer conversations. There are also cultural tensions. Marketers tend to be analytical and data-oriented, and have a project-focused working style, whereas sales people focus on relationships, are action-oriented, and will drop everything to focus on progressing or closing a deal.

More recently, I am seeing revenue leaders additionally focus on effective partnerships between sales and customer success teams. As noted in chapter 9, the rise of the subscription economy has made renewals and upsells an even more critical foundation of growth. This has led more and more companies to develop a customer success team as a third revenue team, on par with marketing and sales. Many companies are shifting responsibility for ongoing customer care and growth of a customer account from an account manager in a sales organization to a customer success manager who focuses first on customer interests and customer care.

THE REVENUE ACCELERATION PLAYBOOK

332 ·THE REVENUE ACCELERATION PLAYBOOK

The growing role of customer success managers and teams has led to a few points of tension in managing customer relationships. Customer success first focuses on customer implementation and making sure that customers are fully unlocking the value of a company's product or service. Account managers within the sales organization think less about implementation and more about how the customer experience with the product may lead them to want more products. Customer success managers focus first on customer loyalty and renewal. Account managers on the sales team think about upsells and expansion opportunities.

The focus on incentive compensation and financial success is a key cultural tension between sales on the one side and both marketing and customer success on the other. From looking at our customers' compensation structures, we can say that sales teams often derive 40-50 percent of their total compensation from commissions on closing deals. In contrast, almost no marketing teams have any form of incentive compensation, and for most customer success teams, renewal or upsell-based incentives are typically 10-15 percent or less of total compensation.

Three Revenue Teams, One Revenue Organization

In an increasingly buyer-centric world, cross-team processes and measures that can help your marketing, sales, and customer success teams partner on anchoring buyer goals first, even as a buyer or customer transitions from one internal team to the next, are necessary for creating an authentic buyer journey.

In a stereotypically dysfunctional revenue organization, each go-to-market team acts separately. Leads are thrown over the wall from marketing to sales regardless of how they fit with a buyer profile that is likely to progress to a value-added sales conversation. New customers are pushed from sales to customer success without much coordination. Sales team members are the image of charm and attentiveness right up until the deal closes, at which point customers are often left to fend for themselves. Each new customer then needs to re-educate their customer success representative on all the information shared with their sales contact. Existing customers are cared for by customer success team members, but these experiences are never organized into a customer voice framework that can be shared with other internal team members so that everyone can gain a fuller understanding of customer use cases and help other buyers and customers get the most out of a product or service.

In contrast, revenue teams like Zeel@Work's, which are focused on creating an authentic buyer journey, partner across go-to-market teams in managing customer transitions. Leads transition from marketing to sales based on the likelihood of a value-added sales conversation. Sales has incentives and a process to do deeper buyer discovery and share those notes with customer success to support a smooth customer transition. That same deep buyer discovery supports expansion opportunities that deepen customer value while increasing revenue from the customer account. Customer success stories for top clients are captured by the team in coordination with marketing to help peer buyers understand how and why to adopt a product. This, in turn, helps increase the pace of new buyer deals in specific target markets.

One increasingly common approach to building a cohesive revenue organization is designing the C-suite to include a chief revenue officer (CRO) role. The CRO is responsible for all revenue-generating departments, including marketing, sales, and customer success. The CRO is a relatively new role, having emerged in Silicon Valley in the late 2010s, but it's growing rapidly. A quick search of the number of job listings for executive-level CRO roles with end-to-end revenue responsibility versus listings for senior VPs of sales or chief sales officers with responsibility only for sales revenue suggests that CROs now account for almost one-third of job listings for the B2B revenue leader.

THREE REVENUE TEAMS, ONE REVENUE ORGANIZATION

As we saw in Zeel's case, more important than the organizational structure in making collaboration the norm across your go-to-market teams is creating a different set of measures and incentives. Traditionally, marketing, sales, and customer success teams are measured based on department-level activities that contribute to revenue growth. Each team has a set of activity metrics around their core areas of focus. For example:

Marketing teams are evaluated on engagement of new prospects, with metrics like:
* How many campaigns do they run to engage the market?
* What is the rate of opens, clicks, or downloads resulting from these campaigns?
* How many qualified contacts result from the campaigns?

Sales teams are evaluated on success in sourcing and closing deals, with metrics like:
* How many new discovery calls do they conduct?
* How many new opportunities came from those calls?
* How many opportunities progress to proposals and closed-won deals?

Customer success teams are evaluated on customer engagement, with metrics like:
* What is overall customer satisfaction?
* What percentage of customers renew?
* What percentage of customers purchase an upsell?

These department-level activity measurements are important to keep each of your revenue teams effectively making their individual contributions. They do not, however, help you build deeper collaboration across teams to ensure an authentic buyer experience. They also do not support the kind of collaboration that leads to faster revenue velocity. And, in fact, these department-level metrics can make the problem of cultural conflict within a revenue organization worse by encouraging each team to focus exclusively on their specialization area. The single-minded focus on department specialty hurts both the buyer and revenue growth.

Four Parts to Revenue Velocity

If you want to build a one-revenue-organization philosophy to drive faster *revenue velocity* across your go-to-market team, the key is adding onto the department-level metrics a new set of metrics that highlight key drivers of an authentic buyer journey. Revenue velocity for your go-to-market teams is driven by four constituent parts: *prospecting velocity*, *deal velocity*, *account velocity*, and *segment velocity*.

Of these four, deal velocity is the only one that sits completely within a single team—your sales team. All three of the other drivers of revenue velocity sit across two of your go-to-market teams. Your marketing and sales teams jointly own prospecting velocity, meaning the pace at which prospecting campaigns produce not just qualified leads but, more importantly, new discovery calls and new quality opportunities. Your sales and customer success teams jointly own account velocity, or the time from an initial sales transaction to upsell transactions. Your customer success and marketing team jointly own segment velocity, or the pace at which customers in different segments reference, refer, and evangelize the company to segment peers.

Whether your go-to-market team has a CRO or an overall revenue leader or three separately led revenue teams with VP-level leaders, the addition of cross-team metrics focused on revenue velocity builds greater consistency in an authentic buyer journey. The cross-team measures go beyond a focus on department-specific activities to zero in on the quality of these activities in deepening the fit with a buyer's key goals and target impacts. That deepening of fit can be measured only by looking at successful movement across the three teams in the revenue organization.

Traditional department-level activity measures are important, but it is cross-team measures that **build deeper collaboration to keep the buyer at the center as they transition from marketing to sales to customer success.**

Prospecting Velocity

To see cross-team processes and metrics work in practice, let's start by looking at marketing and the marketing-to-sales lead handoff. Quality leads that open the way to new buyer conversations are the lifeblood of growth for any company. Traditionally, marketing teams focus on the volume of leads from a wide variety of sources, including website leads, content-driven leads, email promotions, webinars, and trade shows. They tend to measure their success and want credit for "buyer engagement" that results from these activities—things like email opens, clicks, booth swipes, and website traffic.

Traditional marketing metrics definitely build brand impression and a company's market presence, but they may not generate actionable sales leads. Sales teams are laser-focused on working the best leads, ones that fit with a known buyer profile and are willing to commit to getting on the phone to discuss a potential partnership.

MARKETING METRICS AND PROSPECTING VELOCITY METRICS

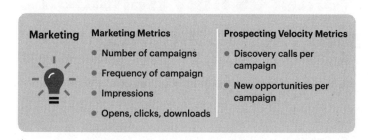

Marketing	Marketing Metrics	Prospecting Velocity Metrics
	● Number of campaigns	● Discovery calls per campaign
	● Frequency of campaign	
	● Impressions	● New opportunities per campaign
	● Opens, clicks, downloads	

As in the Zeel example earlier in the chapter, you will produce more quality opportunities faster if your sales and marketing teams agree on measuring the impact of marketing campaigns on opportunity creation and not just buyer engagement. This begins with agreeing on what constitutes a qualified lead. As at Zeel, your marketing and sales teams need to reach agreement on:

- Target titles or buyer roles
- Employee or revenue size of the buyer's organization
- Market segment or sector focus
- A buyer action that demonstrates interest

The buyer action could be engagement with a prospecting campaign, download of content, participation in a webinar, or a request for information.

Getting to alignment on what constitutes a qualified lead, however, is hard to do in the abstract. Sales and marketing teams can sit together in a room and speculate on the right buyer role, size of organization, and target segments, but "best guesses" may or may not be accurate. Much better than relying on opinions is to generate actual market data.

In chapter 6, we discussed how a key commitment within the prospecting playbook is to use prospecting campaigns to actively test which qualified leads turn into potential buyers at a faster rate. Your sales and marketing teams need to agree on measuring prospecting velocity: the pace at which prospecting campaigns produce not just qualified leads but also, more importantly, new discovery calls and new quality opportunities. This means setting up ways to measure the number of new discovery calls and deals that come from each one hundred or one thousand contacts in a campaign or an engagement tactic.

If your team commits to measuring prospecting velocity, then each prospecting campaign becomes an opportunity to test a key buyer goal area from your company's value narrative playbook. That buyer goal area can be tested against your key target buyer personas and market segments. I usually recommend teams build quarterly or ninety-day campaign

Prospecting velocity measures the connection between campaign leads and new opportunity generation. It is the only way your marketing team really knows which campaigns are effectively engaging buyers around their goals.

test plans with four to six different value messaging tests by persona and segment, and then hold monthly check-in meetings for marketing and sales to review prospecting results and make adjustments to the campaign strategy.

If you commit to head-to-head comparison of prospecting campaigns, you can generate evidence on which categories of qualified leads convert at the highest rate to an initial discovery call and which progress from an initial discovery call to a sales-qualified opportunity. Running these marketing tests helps a company make sure it is staying strongly focused on an authentic buyer journey and inviting the right prospects into value-added discovery calls.

In chapter 6, we looked at two examples of how marketing and sales worked together to run prospecting tests and accelerate prospecting velocity from a qualified lead to a qualified opportunity. One of the company examples highlighted was Torchlight, the provider of a digital caregiver platform sold to HR departments as an employee benefit. The company knew that its key value narratives were around employee retention and lower benefits costs. The team's prospecting tests focused on identifying which of their target market segments—financial services, professional services, biotech, and manufacturing—had the strongest engagement with each message. They measured engagement not just by opens, clicks, and responses, but also by commitments to first meetings. The team identified and doubled-down on their marketing and campaign investments in the areas of greatest success. This commitment to measuring prospecting velocity and agile adjustments led to a 61 percent increase in first-meeting production in just twelve months.

The other example of success with measuring prospecting velocity was AdmitHub, the company that uses an AI-based conversational messaging platform to help colleges and universities achieve their enrollment goals. AdmitHub knew that its strongest market segments were second- and third-tier large research universities as well as regional public universities that served the vast majority of first-generation college students and underrepresented student populations. Their team's market tests focused on identifying which executive leaders at these universities—including VPs of enrollment management and of success, and provosts—would engage at the highest rate, and what value messages they found most engaging. The prospecting tests involved 3,500 contacts over a six-month period, which doubled the number of discovery meetings set with senior leaders and significantly raised the rate at which first meetings led to closed-won deals.

Account Velocity

The second new area for cross-team measurement is account velocity, which connects sales and customer success. Sales teams are traditionally measured on deal velocity, which means the rate at which new sales opportunities move to closed-won deals, the average time it takes to move to closed won, and the value of the closed-won opportunities. However, measuring success in closed deals does not encourage your sales teams to think about developing customer value in ways that maximize overall account value. For your sales team, connecting forward to build an integrated revenue organization means thinking beyond the first close. It means that they are also thinking about account velocity, or the time frame to the first upsells and the overall increase in account value in the first twelve months after the initial close.

Measuring account velocity changes the relationship between your sales and customer success teams. No longer is the focus on sales doing an initial discovery to get an initial deal closed that will be handed off to customer success for care and renewal. Instead, your sales team's focus will shift to doing as deep a discovery as possible during the sales process to identify multiple potential goal areas, and then to effectively handing off information on all buyer goal areas to customer success. This will enable your customer success team to work quickly toward the second, third, and fourth upsell opportunities that expand customer value while also expanding account value.

SALE METRICS AND ACCOUNT VELOCITY METRICS

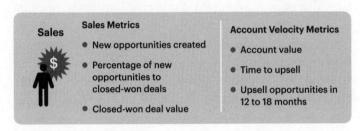

Adding account velocity measures to your deal velocity measures is a great way to anchor the focus on an authentic buyer journey in both sales and customer success teams. When your sales and customer success teams are both responsible for account value over the first twelve months, you achieve deeper and broader buyer goal discovery. This joint accountability also encourages better customer handoffs, a stronger onboarding, and deeper connection to key influencers and decision-makers within the buyer's organization.

In the Zeel example earlier in the chapter, we saw how changing sales incentives to include account velocity measures changed salesforce behavior. The team was no longer thinking about just the velocity of their own close but also that of the account managed by the customer success team. A key contribution they could make to faster account expansion was identifying and capturing in their notes a broad range of potential use cases for Zeel@Work employee wellness services for each new customer account.

In chapter 9, we saw how Parsable moved to a team-based selling concept across sales and customer success. When a sales team member approaches a manufacturer about the company's Connected Worker platform to replace thousands of paper-based work instructions, the team member's goal is not to try to sell everything, but to start with a handful of manufacturing operations or processes. The goal is to prove the value of this Connected Worker platform and, once that value is clear, to triple the number of manufacturing processes covered in the first twelve months. Both the sales and customer success team members are rewarded and incented based on the twelve-month value of the account. Parsable used this joint focus on account velocity to achieve a world class net-revenue-retention rate that was more than triple the 120 percent year-over-year account growth considered to be a best-in-class benchmark.

Segment Velocity

The third new area for cross-team measurement connects customer success and marketing. Customer success teams play a critical role in maintaining a company's growth trajectory through their work on renewal and incremental upsells. While this work is critical, it is actually not the customer success team's most significant contribution to overall growth. Even more important to dynamic growth is the team's role in building segment velocity.

Account velocity links the initial close to expansion closes and the twelve-month value of an account. It encourages your sales and customer success teams to think broadly about customer value and goals.

CUSTOMER SUCCESS METRICS
AND SEGMENT VELOCITY METRICS

Customer Success	Customer Success Metrics	Segment Velocity Metrics
	• Renewal rate	• Segments with evangelizers
	• Upsell opportunities	• Segments with 3+ evangelizers
	• Account value	• Percentage of referral leads

Segment velocity is the pace at which customers in different segments reference, refer, and evangelize a company to their segment peers. Very few companies recognize or incent the critical role the customer success team plays in building reference value, segment-specific success stories as well as developing customers who can evangelize to other customers. As discussed in chapter 9, what your new potential buyers want to hear more than anything else is the voice of their peers who already work with your product or service. Specifically, they want to hear how the product or service helps their peers with their goal achievement. Segment velocity is hard to measure directly, but if you decide to move in this direction, there are a few key proxy measures related to building the customer voice by segment that can be used to incent and reward the customer success and marketing teams to focus on segment velocity.

The best proxy measures for account velocity are:

1 The total number of a company's key market segments covered by these client success stories, and how many can be directly used in sales or customer calls. This is the simplest measure.

2 The number of market segments with a critical mass of three to five success stories. This starts to build a picture of

consistent success and deeper understanding of the customer voice in that target market segment.

3 The total number of new sales opportunities that come from existing customer references. While it is hard in this case to get specific to a market segment, looking at the total number of reference opportunities relative to opportunities generated by inbound marketing activities or outbound prospecting activities can be a good measure of success in cultivating evangelizers.

If you commit to building your customer voice by segment, it will lead to deeper market segment growth. This makes it easier for each of your go-to-market teams to anchor new buyer engagement on outcomes that have been achieved with current peer customers. Rather than leading with a company-centric message around a product, the focus is on leading with a customer-centric message concentrated on demonstrated goal achievement with peers that will engage and build trust with new buyers.

In chapter 9, we saw how Plus Delta Partners used a targeted segment growth strategy to achieve 40 percent growth for five years. The company very intentionally tailored the language used to describe its cohort-based professional development program for fundraising to align key value drivers for liberal arts colleges, then large research universities, then academic medical centers. Plus Delta also identified peer evangelizers to build success stories that could be used to engage new potential buyers. The focus on building a segment voice and segment references allowed Plus Delta to grow rapidly and very profitably. The company did not need to make new product investments as they moved from one market segment to another.

We also saw the power of the customer-voice-by-segment and peer-referencing-by-segment in building segment velocity

Segment velocity measures the pace that current customers evangelize to segment peers. It encourages your customer success and marketing teams to partner in building a segment voice and references that engage new peer buyers.

in our Mursion example, in chapter 2. Mursion's immersive VR training is a transformational approach to training on soft skills like leadership, customer service, sales, and diversity and inclusion. In building more than a 250 percent year-over-year growth trajectory, it was not the product but the voice of current customers that led the way and built buyer engagement and excitement. Mursion has consciously developed success stories that can be used in its prospecting, sales, and customer success departments for each of its target market segments. Prospecting and sales engagement for professional services, financial services, retail, manufacturing, and other key sectors was led with stories about success with peers in the same market segment. The company has also created compelling content for their website, blogs, and white papers with active contributions from customers and thought leaders in these segments.

HubSpot's One Revenue Organization Supports Exceptional Growth

HubSpot offers a software suite that helps businesses grow by more effectively managing marketing, sales, and service processes. It is one of the most successful companies in recent history, growing from nothing to $100 million in revenue in six short years, and then to just under $900 million in revenue by year fifteen. As I learned from Mark Roberge, HubSpot's senior VP of sales and service and then CRO from 2007 to 2016, one of the many reasons for their success was their one-revenue-organization approach around buyer goals and outcomes as a key foundational principle.

"One key to our success was starting with the customer outcome," Mark told me. "We answered the question, 'What is a good lead?' by looking at customer success and asking which customers had the highest lifetime value and what goals led them to become customers."

I was speaking to Mark by phone that day. He was in transit from visiting with the leadership team for a Stage 2 Capital portfolio company. Stage 2 was a venture capital fund that Mark had founded a few years ago after leaving HubSpot. It focused on investments in B2B software companies.

"So, if I'm hearing you correctly," I said, "the question you asked to focus your go-to-market efforts was, 'Where is the highest level of alignment between customer value and value to HubSpot?' How did that impact the way you developed your market and team?"

"It led us to think differently about how we measured the success of each go-to-market team and the revenue organization as whole," Mark said. He paused before he continued, "Most companies try to figure out which leads they close at the highest rate and focus their sales and marketing investments in those areas, but there is often not a direct correlation between leads that close at a higher rate and sales success. It is the close rate in combination with revenue per customer that shows the highest return on investments."

"That makes good sense," I said, "but how do you get your demand gen team to turn off the leads from the less productive segments? They usually want to get credit for all leads."

"Your instincts are right, and that was an area of learning. The first business development representative [BDR] compensation plan at HubSpot was based on how many meetings a BDR set for sales executives. It was awful," Mark said with a self-deprecating laugh. "I remember those sales reviews. If a sales executive was at or above plan, they would praise the heck out of the discovery meetings coming from their BDR, and if a sales executive was below plan, they would blame the quality of the discovery meetings."

Mark and the HubSpot team quickly learned that focusing on traditional activity measures for the marketing and demand gen team did not lead to a great outcome. So, in addition to the traditional activity measures around campaigns, calls, leads worked, and so on, they implemented a cross-team measure of prospecting velocity that created a focus on higher-quality buyers.

"That first plan was a blunt instrument," Mark explained. "So, we changed the compensation plan to focus not on meetings but on *productive* meetings, and made revenue and customer lifetime value key drivers of the BDR compensation plan."

"Okay, that explains how you build alignment on revenue production at the front of the pipeline," I said. "How did you handle the other key element of lifetime value, which is the pace of upsells and cross-sells?"

"Good question," Mark said, with a twinkle in his eye. "There is a funny story in that. To build account value, I told my sales team that they would get paid twenty percent more on expansion revenue than on the first revenue. They said to me, 'Mark, you are crazy! You're going to encourage us to tee up five opportunities and only close the first one?' And I responded, 'Go for it.'"

Again, Mark and the HubSpot team realized that focusing the sales team on only the traditional sales measures of success—deals worked, deals closed, and deal value—would lead to a suboptimal outcome. So they added an account velocity measure that focused the sales team on doing deep discovery that could lead to not just an initial sale but many follow-on expansion sales. Prioritizing account velocity over deal velocity was part of the secret sauce of HubSpot's growth story.

"I wanted them to use the sales process to surface all kinds of problems that might not be part of the original sales transaction," Mark said. "The broader discovery could lead to rapid upsells and expansion deals that would increase the value of the account. From an enterprise point of view, it really didn't matter if those deals were closed as part of the initial transaction or part of an upsell three, six, or even twelve months later."

"You were way off of the traditional compensation path," I said. "You arrived at an approach that strongly aligned the customers, sales team members, and customer success team member incentives."

"That's right," Mark said. "Sales compensation plans typically incent sellers more for the first revenue from an account than for follow-on revenue, so the seller tries to convince the buyer to purchase as many seats up front as possible. This behavior puts sellers and buyers at odds with each other, elongates sales cycles, decreases close rates, and, most importantly, creates a substantial churn risk for the selling company, with so many seats purchased before the product is tested in a smaller environment."

Mark's focus on aligning incentives toward revenue velocity across the demand generation, sales, and customer success organizations helped HubSpot acquire ten thousand customers in sixty different countries and grow to $100 million in revenue between 2007 and 2013.

One Revenue Organization and Revenue Velocity

The examples of Zeel's employee wellness services and HubSpot's marketing and sales software show that an authentic buyer journey needs to be supported by linked processes and measurements that cut across the revenue organization.

The sales, marketing, and customer success teams each have different but complementary roles to play in building an authentic buyer journey that leads to faster revenue growth. Marketing teams are evaluated based on engagement of new prospects. Sales teams are evaluated based on success in sourcing and closing sales deals. Customer success teams are evaluated on customer satisfaction, engagement, and renewal rates. Measuring and incentivizing these department-level activities without additional cross-team measures can make the problem of cultural conflict within a revenue organization persist or, worse, can encourage each team to focus on their specialization area in ways that lead to slower growth.

The key to building a one-revenue-organization philosophy is adding to the department-level metrics a new set of metrics that highlight key drivers of an authentic buyer journey and contribute to revenue velocity. Marketing and sales need to jointly own prospecting velocity, or the pace at which prospecting campaigns produce new discovery calls and new quality opportunities. Sales and customer success need to jointly own account velocity, or the time from an initial sales transaction to upsell transactions. Customer success and marketing need to jointly own segment velocity, or the pace at which customers in different segments reference, refer, and evangelize the company to segment peers.

In chapter 11, we will move from a focus on process and measures to one of developing the team skills that build an authentic buyer journey. Top-performing teams do not just develop playbooks, they also continually practice as individuals and teams so they can revise their playbooks. It is the continual iteration of playbooks to capture new best practices that keeps a go-to-market team sharp in responding to buyer goals and target impacts as well as adjusting to new market and competitive circumstances.

YOUR NEXT STEPS ON
BUILDING ONE REVENUE ORGANIZATION

- **Prospecting velocity:** How well are you measuring the link between marketing campaigns and sales opportunities? What are the simplest metrics you can put in place to start making this connection?

- **Account velocity:** How effectively are you connecting a first closed deal to twelve-month account expansion? What metrics could help focus sales and customer success on broad value discovery?

- **Segment velocity:** Have you set goals for generating peer success stories and references in your target market segments? How can you use performance measurement to anchor this as a goal for customer success and marketing?

An authentic buyer journey starts with anchoring on buyer goals and accelerates with cross-team measures that keep the buyer at the center as they transition from marketing to sales to customer success. Visit winalytics.com/theplays to get resources to build the plays that help these cross-team measures.

11

Team-Based Skills Development

"WHEN I joined DealerRater, our biggest threat to growing revenue in a predictable way was not necessarily market competition, but recruiting and retaining talent," Bobby Gaudreau, DealerRater's VP of sales and marketing, told me.

I was sitting that day with Bobby at a conference table in DealerRater's offices, in a common area near the kitchen. The common area was outfitted appropriately with pictures of classic cars. Bobby related that DealerRater had just completed a recapitalization with a large private equity firm, and, despite its leadership position in the market for car dealer reviews, it was struggling to retain talent. Another company, also in the car dealer space, was poaching Bobby's top talent. They were not competitors, but they sold to the same buyer.

Bobby's challenge has become increasingly common in the knowledge economy, where a company's employees, and the way these employees interact with buyers and customers, can be more important than the company's product itself in creating competitive advantage.

"We would typically hire a class of five new reps every few months," Bobby continued. A grimace replaced his normally enthusiastic smile. "We would hire people, onboard them, train them in the industry, and then, every three to four months, this other company in the car dealer space would come after our top reps with a thirty percent higher base, stock options, and significantly more perks, such as catered meals, free parking [in Cambridge], rotating taps of beer and coffee, a very attractive space, and so on."

The other company in the car dealer space was also located in Cambridge, one of Boston's many tech hubs. They had to address their own challenges of attracting and retaining top product and engineering talent, as they were physically located on the same campus as HubSpot and blocks away from Google.

"We had a lot of conversations internally about what to do," Bobby continued. "Our private equity owners, who were preparing to position the company for an acquisition, asked us not to raise salary levels. Since we couldn't match the salary offers, we focused instead on developing a pipeline of sales talent."

Bobby stood and walked over to refill his glass at the water cooler. He absent-mindedly ran his finger around the frame of one of the classic car pictures, then, walking back and standing at the end of the conference table, continued: "We would say to our top recruits or producers, 'Listen, we're not going to be able to match the other company's offer, but we are going to make big investments in building your skills so that after a year or two here, you'll be able to jump a couple of levels on the career ladder here or somewhere else. This can be your springboard.'"

There are many reasons job candidates or new employees may not take the highest-paying job offer, particularly younger and early-career employees without family and child obligations. DealerRater was using access to better training and accelerated career development as an incentive to retain top talent in a competitive market. For other companies, the added incentive might be mission or better and more secure benefits, or increased autonomy and flexibility in a working situation.

DealerRater Competes with a Team-Based Skills Model

"To make the case that we could be the springboard, we needed to walk the walk and give a credible story on turning them into a modern seller," Bobby said, still standing. He leaned forward and put both hands on the conference table. "They needed to hear, throughout the entire recruiting process, that there was 'something different going on' here at DealerRater. To do this, we had to build a different kind of skill development program from the one our team had experienced elsewhere."

As we discussed in chapter 2, the US market for corporate learning and training is huge, variously estimated to be between $87 billion and $142 billion. Until a decade or so ago, more than 90 percent of this training investment took the form of formal, instructor-led programs delivered either in classrooms or online. This classroom-based training, however, has what social scientists call high "learning retention failure." That is a fancy way of saying that little of what is taught is remembered and used on the job.

"Our recruits had all been through what I call 'one and done' training. These were one-time workshop sessions that led to excitement but had no impact," Bobby said. "In our reimagined training program, we focused on how to use best

If your team is going to be successful in creating an authentic buyer journey, you need to **create a team-based learning model that supports the continuous identification and sharing of top team practices.**

practice playbooks, individual coaching, and team-based training to meaningfully change our team members' skills in ways that helped them improve their performance. We also took a very different approach from other sales methodology training. We focused less on closing and more on building great discovery that guided buyers to goals and impacts, thereby building a natural momentum to a close."

As Bobby and the DealerRater team recognized, the traditional types of sales training programs have a very big gap in that they lack the effective buyer discovery that starts every sales conversation focused on what the buyer cares about most.

"I wanted our employees and new recruits to understand that our success was going to come from understanding our buyers really well," Bobby said with a confident smile. "Our buyers are auto dealers who invest in our community to build their brand reputation. I wanted to recruit people who were excited to have value-added conversations with our auto dealer partners and who enjoyed the process of meeting their needs rather than just showing up and pitching a product."

DealerRater is the industry-leading automobile dealer review site and is owned by Cars.com. At the time of this conversation, the company had just under six thousand dealer partners in North America, and fourteen million visitors a month submitting dealer reviews, which was 48 percent more dealer-specific reviews than all other consumer reviews and social media sites put together. Well before being acquired by Cars.com, DealerRater had pioneered the market for auto dealer reviews and ratings. However, when Bobby joined, new entrants to the dealer review market with widely recognized brands like Autotrader, Edmunds, Yahoo, and Yelp were starting to offer dealer reviews, and DealerRater's sales started to decline.

Bobby's strategy for building a modern sales team by focusing on the promise of deep skills development and faster career progression worked. The strategy was particularly effective in taking early-career sellers and shifting them from average performance to top performance, with the typical seller increasing their performance 15–25 percent year over year. Over two years, the sales and marketing team shifted from declining sales to 20 percent average gains. The shift set up DealerRater to grow into a $20 million business and be successfully acquired by Cars.com.

The DealerRater example shows that, in the current buyer environment, building an authentic buyer journey depends not just on a new set of go-to-market playbooks, processes, and measurements, but also on having a different approach to developing the skills of go-to-market teams. Sales and customer success teams, in particular, who spend the most time with customers, need to continually sharpen their discovery, positioning, and qualification skills to stay ahead of an ever-changing buyer environment.

In my work with go-to-market teams, we have found that a *team-based skills development model* leads to the highest levels of performance across the entire team. The team-based model starts with the shared playbooks. Having team-level playbooks for content marketing, prospecting, sales, and customer success allows team members to go to market in a similar way and makes it easier for the departments to directly learn from one another. The team-based skills model also includes team-based learning sessions, direct application in buyer or customer work, and individual coaching and skills reinforcement.

The team-based skills development model fixes three big problems in the traditional skills development model to create higher levels of performance:

1 In traditional skills development, learning retention is a huge problem. Team-based skills development fixes this

with playbooks that make it possible to practice and hone skills outside of buyer or customer interactions.

2   Traditional skills development is based primarily on a workshop model that misses the opportunity for social learning, which research from cso Insights shows leads to innovation and top performance. A team-based learning model builds peer-to-peer learning around playbooks to identify and share team best practices.

3   Traditional skills development lacks the personalization to support building targeted individual skills while addressing skills in playbook implementation. Adopting a team-based skills development model helps each team member achieve their top performance potential.

Bringing Skills into Practice

One of the biggest problems in traditional skills development programs, as we saw above, is learning retention failure. Dr. Art Kohn and a team of researchers at Portland State University developed an estimate that adult learners in traditional learning settings forget approximately 50 percent of new information they encounter within an hour, 70 percent within twenty-four hours, and 90 percent within weeks. Importantly, their research also showed that, for the sake of information retention, what you do *after* learning material is more important than what you do *while* learning material.

Sales, marketing, and customer success teams are typically introduced to new marketing or sales enablement material through workshop sessions. At your company, team workshops are probably used to introduce a new messaging approach, new product positioning information, new lines of discovery inquiry, or new product concepts to use with buyers and customers. The new messaging or discovery materials are then shared electronically and put in a shared folder after the training, and go-to-market teams are expected to immediately shift the way they talk to buyers and customers.

TEAM-BASED SKILLS MODEL

Playbooks
- Capture top plays
- Consistent practice

Team Training
- Peer-to-peer learning
- Play innovation

Team-Based Skills Model

Individual Coaching
- Individual voice
- Skill strengths/paps

The problem is, without structured coaching feedback and a playbook to practice in the context of real buyer conversations, this learning is not very sticky. To go back to our analogy from chapter 5, it would be like handing a football team a new playbook, never giving them the chance to practice or get coaching on how to implement the plays, and then expecting them to run these new plays in their next live game with an opponent. Just like a football team, go-to-market teams need to practice before live calls with buyers and customers, and again between calls to get better.

In chapters 6 to 9, we looked at how playbooks specific to marketing, prospecting, sales, account management, and customer success are foundational to bringing an authentic buyer journey into practice. If you build playbooks specific to each revenue team and provide plays that guide and shape interactions at each phase of the buyer journey, you will have a much higher level of consistency and quality of execution in team members leading each buyer or customer interaction by putting goals first and product second.

These same revenue playbooks can also build the foundation of your team-based skills development model. Standardizing discovery questions, capability talk tracks, client success stories, and other content assets helps your whole team get more consistently to best discovery and messaging in each buyer and customer interaction. If every member of a go-to-market team is left to develop their own messaging and discovery approach, the buyer experience becomes very ad hoc and subjective. Without effective playbooks, each buyer or customer communication is based more on the individual go-to-market team member than on the way the company wants to position and engage buyers around value.

With shared playbooks, each team member has their own voice and style, but your team as a whole has a shared way to go to market and engage buyers and customers. Marketing, sales, and customer success teams master best practices when they apply playbook tools directly and continually into their prospect, buyer, and customer conversations. Playbooks make direct application to buyer and customer conversations easier and more sustainable by aligning with each type of buyer interaction. As we have seen throughout the chapters on team-specific playbooks and plays, the playbooks essentially create a road map with signposts: if you are prospecting to new buyers, start here; if you are working on better discovery during an initial call, start here; if you are working on a closing call, start here; if you are onboarding a new client, start here; if you are looking to expand an existing account, start here; and so on.

In the DealerRater example earlier in this chapter, a key outcome of building shared playbooks was developing consistency in discovery questions and messaging around a dealer's ability to manage their reputation and the reputation of their staff. Before the playbooks were developed, there were a variety of approaches to engaging new buyers, all focused on different aspects of the dealer review product. Some focused on using reviews as an innovative approach to advertising, others on managing reviews across all digital and social channels, and still others on building stronger connections to sales staff. The playbooks brought the best approaches together and guided team members in ways that helped them all improve faster and deliver a more consistent buyer journey.

For DealerRater, the shared playbooks focused the whole sales and marketing team on discovery around reputation management and building a customer review culture. Before starting to pitch their product in sales calls or prospecting emails, the team used playbooks, which guided them to always start with questions to understand the buyer's goals and gaps regarding review management. Through the team-based skills development process, the team developed a shared set of questions that covered questions like:

- Did the dealer understand the relationship between positive reviews and dealership visits?

- Was the dealer currently able to put the voice of their top customers in front of other customers?

If you build playbooks to guide authentic buyer interactions, you also need to practice the plays. **A sports team would never get on the field without practicing, but many go-to-market teams do exactly that.**

- Did the dealer want to build familiarity with their staff before a potential car buyer came to the dealership?

Each team member might have different questions or words, but the important thing was that DealerRater's sales playbook emphasized starting every call by "committing to discovery" around questions that were most likely to build engagement with the auto dealer as a potential buyer of DealerRater's service. The sales playbook also emphasized using every call to get the buyer to confirm the elements of the platform that were most important to them. Team members were encouraged to write down their top discovery and buyer qualification questions and to practice them on their own, with a teammate, or with their boss before important sales calls.

Shared playbooks are the foundation for top performance, but playbooks by themselves do very little to drive higher levels of performance. Higher levels of performance come from the consistent application of playbook best practices in the day-to-day work of the sales and customer success team members. The repetition of the same questions in practice sessions and on live sales calls helps to build mastery more quickly. When sales or customer success team members test different discovery questions and success stories, they can figure out more quickly the language and value narratives that work best with the buyer.

Team-Based Learning and Innovation

The second gap in traditional training that a team-based skills model fixes deals with the social aspect of learning. Individual practice helps go-to-market team members build familiarity and fluency with new messaging or discovery concepts, but it is the social, peer-to-peer learning that creates opportunities for the whole team to excel.

Team members can crystallize top practices and help each other achieve top performance when they:

- See how others apply the same playbook concepts.
- Understand what works and does not work.
- Find new word choices or phrases that make plays their own.

At DealerRater, the forum for team-based innovation was a fifteen-minute stand-up meeting every morning with the sales and marketing team, during which one or two team members would report on a deal they were working on. Sometimes the meeting focused on prospecting campaigns that led to first discovery meetings as a way of better understanding which campaign messages, content assets, and types of outreach were most effective. Other times, the focus was on good discovery during first calls to understand which questions were really landing. More topics included qualifying questions that got the right group to the next call, high-impact follow-up emails that were helping a champion build the case with other decision-makers, or pricing conversations that kept the focus on buyer value.

The topics for DealerRater's daily stand-ups varied but were all designed to focus on team learning and innovation around the playbooks. They provided a quick hit each day on which elements of the playbooks were working and not working. They allowed each team member to hear other team members' voices and language choices to decide which elements aligned best with their own style. It was this team-based approach to capturing best individual practices, particularly from the top 20 percent of performers, and

If you want high levels of execution around an authentic buyer journey, you need to create opportunities for individual and team practice. **It is the repetition in practicing playbooks that supports mastery.**

making them accessible to the whole team that had the greatest performance impact. Many of the middle performers on the team raised their performance by 15 percent, 20 percent, or more by incorporating and modeling the practices of the top performers.

Many other sales or customer success teams also allocate part of a standing weekly team meeting to learning and sharing best practices. Others have biweekly or monthly team meetings that focus just on specific playbook practices. Rotating participation among team members in these team-based learning formats helps nudge newer and less experienced team members to share and get feedback on their playbook practices. Some senior or top performing team members might be inclined to "hoard" their best practices; rotating participation makes this more awkward and less likely. It recognizes senior and top performer team members for their ability to share skills and practices with the whole team and act as peer-to-peer mentors.

The strongest empirical evidence of the impact of social learning in the go-to-market world comes from CSO Insights managing partners Jim Dickie and Barry Trailer, who produced a study of more than one thousand companies, called "Anatomy of a World-Class Sales Organization." The study showed that the go-to-market teams in the top quartile of sales performance used a shared set of best practice processes and tools, ongoing feedback to each salesperson on effectively operating these shared processes and tools, and continual updates to tools and processes to adjust to shifting market conditions.

Team-driven innovation is an important aspect of social learning that is supported in a team-based skills development approach that uses playbooks. Until messaging and discovery frameworks are written down, the social aspect of learning and sharing does not work. The purpose of writing down playbooks is to capture individual best practices for each type of buyer interaction and make them accessible to the whole team. Once playbooks are written down, innovation and agility in putting them into practice begins. Good playbooks provide flexibility and options around best practices so each team member can find their own voice and style. As playbooks are used with buyers and customers, each team member finds the questions, talk tracks, and content assets that work best for them individually. They identify language or word choice revisions that lead to higher buyer engagement. This direct application is then shared as "stories from the field" during team-based training to help capture and socialize best practices.

A key best practice in DealerRater's approach was focusing on cross-team learning sessions that brought together the sales and marketing teams. Cross-team learning sessions are a key ingredient to the cross-team processes and metrics we discussed in chapter 9 that anchor an authentic buyer journey. The DealerRater daily stand-ups focused on one of the most important parts of regular cross-team learning, which is understanding the qualitative aspects of prospecting campaigns that lead to the highest prospecting velocity or the highest number of first meetings. The sales and marketing teams at DealerRater jointly reviewed their prospecting campaigns and plays to see which of their value stories and which content worked for each type of buyer. The outputs of these joint meetings then led to revisions and updates to the prospecting campaigns and playbooks.

The second type of important cross-team learning deals with account velocity, or the time between an initial sale and follow-on sales, as well as the twelve-month value of the account. In chapter 2, we saw that Mursion moved to industry-specific teams focused on health care, financial services, professional services, technology, and telecommunications to accelerate the pace of account expansion for their immersive VR training platform. These industry segment teams combined prospecting, sales, and customer success team members, but a primary purpose was to accelerate the pace of innovation in its expansion playbook. By moving to vertical teams, Mursion found their sales and customer success team members could learn more quickly about the connections between leadership, diversity and inclusion, and customer service training in their specific vertical segments and could identify expansion opportunities faster. These sales and customer success learning sessions then fed into the expansion playbooks and specifically led to the development of new success stories and discovery questions to guide existing customers toward an expansion pathway.

The third important type of cross-team learning is around segment velocity, or the pace at which customers in each target market segment become evangelizers who support "selling forward" to peers in the market segment. In the Parsable example in chapter 9, we saw how the customer success team worked closely with key customers in the food and beverage industry, as well as in the paper and packaging industry, to identify the most important manufacturing processes and operations in each sector. They captured manufacturing use cases in the sector-specific language of the customers to build a customer voice by segment. The customer success team then partnered with marketing to embed this information in website snippets and metrics, as well as in customer success stories, which would engage other buyers in the segment.

By approaching skills development with a team-based skills development model that incorporates social learning, companies can build continual improvement into their go-to-market approach while also helping individual team members be their best. Peer-to-peer modeling and coaching helps team members develop a level of mastery above individual practice sessions. Cross-team sharing and collaboration builds knowledge from shared experience.

Individual Skills Coaching

A third gap in traditional training that a team-based skills model fixes is around individual skills development and coaching. Just like in sports, every player on a go-to-market team has a different style and their own strengths and challenges in how they operate shared playbooks. Regular coaching interactions can help your individual team members put shared playbooks into practice in a way that emphasizes their strengths and manages their weaknesses. It helps them put the playbooks into their own voice and individualize their working style. It allows your team members to experiment and make adjustments to their own practice as they continue learning from peers.

There is strong empirical evidence that individual skills development around shared playbooks and processes significantly increases performance. Research by the Sales Management Association and Sales Executive Council, now part of Gartner, has shown that regular coaching can raise the performance of individual sales team members by 17–19 percent. According to these studies, there is no other sales enablement investment that comes close in terms of ROI on dollars spent. However, individual skills coaching is also the hardest part of a team-based skills model to execute. Playbooks can be developed in a project-oriented way by a small working group. Team-based learning sessions can be set up as regularly recurring calendared meeting invitations. Individual skills coaching, by contrast, requires deep personalization and ongoing commitment.

Team-based learning that captures and shares best team practices for playbook execution is a key driver of improved performance. It allows the entire team to benefit from the practices of the top 20 percent of performers.

Many sales and customer success leaders mistake regular reviews of their teams' work—seeing how they engage with prospects, buyers, and customers—for targeted skills coaching. However, targeted skills coaching is different. It focuses on improving individual skills that will have the most impact on an individual team member's performance. What's important is that the manager and individual team member reflect on the team member's performance effectiveness, agree on the most important skills to improve, and then use buyer and customer conversations intentionally to improve these skills. Where an external third party is involved in coaching, that individual should also be part of the discussion of the most important skills to focus on for each team member.

In my work at Winalytics, there are two main skills-coaching plays that help teams and members coach more effectively. The first is using a *core skills matrix* that outlines the most important skills needed for a team to effectively operate a shared playbook. Managers often struggle with the question, "What skills should I coach?" Developing the core skills matrix for the operation of a playbook begins to answer this question and, more importantly, supports a direct dialogue between a manager and each of their team members. For each role and for a whole team, the core skills matrix helps managers and individual team members understand the key skills they need to be successful.

For a sales team, there are typically eight to ten core skills that are key to sales performance achievement. These include:

- Prospecting
- Buyer discovery
- Presenting and mapping capabilities
- Anchoring on buyer-defined value
- Qualifying deals

- Managing a decision process and decision-makers
- Negotiating and closing deals
- Forecasting
- Account development and account expansion

For a customer success team, there are typically six to eight core skills directly related to customer satisfaction, renewal, and upsells. These skills include:

- Demonstrating deep product knowledge
- Effective training and implementation
- Relationship and account management
- Understanding and managing customer expectations
- Internal team management
- Buyer value discovery
- Presenting and mapping capabilities
- Anchoring on buyer-defined value
- Account development and account expansion

The other key skills-coaching play is creating an agreed-on list of *coaching formats*. I have seen three main coaching formats:

1 Document reviews, which can include reviews of emails, presentation decks, or proposals.

2 Call reviews, which may include initial discovery calls, stakeholder calls with a group of decision-makers, pricing and proposal calls, or account management and upsell calls.

3 Role-playing, which can cover just about any type of sales, account management, or customer success conversation.

My experience is that most teams arrive at just three or four coaching formats that work well with the team's style and primary modes of buyer and customer engagement.

Individual coaching can focus on role-play, call reviews, or document reviews. Your teams will experience more successful coaching if you **identify two to three consistent coaching formats and use them repetitively.**

The DealerRater team, for example, relied heavily on coaching call role-playing as it was building a new approach to buyer discovery and buyer qualification. Their coaching focused on the middle 60 percent of performers. Individual team members were paired with an external coach or a manager to identify specific skills to focus on during role-playing. The team developed a set of what they called "ready-made" roles to support each manager in coaching more effectively. In their daily stand-up meetings, the DealerRater team relied on document reviews for team learning. Individual team members shared prospecting emails, discovery call follow-up emails, pricing proposals, and buyers' responses to each.

In the AdmitHub example from chapter 6, by comparison, the team relied very heavily on call reviews, as they tried to engage senior university leaders by optimizing their messaging on the impact of AI-based conversational messaging. Recorded calls reviewed by team members, a manager, and an external coach became a way to build skills for buyer discovery, deal qualification, and securing the buyer commitments needed to build deal velocity to a close. The team also ran a weekly call that focused on dissecting just one recorded call. Borrowing from the Navy SEALs' concept of an after action review, the team review focused on a handful of questions about how well the call was planned and executed, what went off track, and what could have gone better.

Apptio Transitions Through Growth Phases with a Team-Based Skills Approach

"When Apptio moved into a high-growth mode and started to expand from a team of fifteen strategic sales executives to one that eventually reached several hundred, we had to figure out how to scale a skill development system," said Larry Blasko, Apptio's CRO. "We had a few different sales processes in place and it was causing confusion."

Apptio is the market leader for technology business management solutions. It offers a suite of tools to help companies plan, manage, and forecast their information technology spend. Apptio was founded in 2007 and was acquired twelve years later by Vista Equity Partners after reaching several hundred million dollars in revenue.

I was speaking to Larry by videoconference that day. Behind him, on his bookshelf, were pictures and mementos from his successful decade-long run at Apptio. Larry had been Apptio's VP of sales, then senior VP of worldwide sales, then CRO as the company grew from several million to several hundred million in sales. This type of success across so many growth phases is almost unheard of in any type of company, but particularly in technology companies. Larry had an uncommon blend of laser focus on a few goals and flexibility in strategies for getting to those goals.

"Say more about the different systems you had in place and the reason you adopted each," I said. I wanted to hear more about his unique professional trajectory.

"The original team liked the MEDDIC [metrics, economic buyer, decision criteria, decision process, identify pain, and champion] sales methodology, which had a strong focus on identifying a specific pain and specific metrics that demonstrate value," Larry said. "As the team grew, we adopted and trained on the proactive selling methodology. It included a very tactical set of techniques for structuring meetings, doing good buyer discovery, and qualifying to the next meeting. It was simple and practical and appealed to a broad group of sellers."

"So," I said, "it sounds like you started with a sales methodology that helped with qualifying and forecasting deals, and then added a second approach that had a very practical set of plays for managing specific buyer interactions."

Larry nodded. "That is a good way to summarize it. Those two worked together because one was sort of top-down and the other was more bottom-up. Then, about a year and a half ago, we were acquired by the private equity firm Vista Equity Partners. They have their own proprietary value-selling method, which they expect all of their acquired companies to adopt."

"So, now you had three different methodologies, three different sets of terms and concepts," I said. "That must have been really confusing for the team."

"If we had stayed with three sets of terms, then, yes, it would have been confusing," Larry said with a small wary chuckle. "But we didn't. We moved toward a single, integrated blend." I was getting to see how blending focus and flexibility had helped him scale Apptio's revenue organization. "We developed a modified version of the Vista value-selling method. We mapped the team's existing practices from all three sales methodologies, so we had a single process and set of tools. Then we identified twelve core skills associated with our modified Vista value-selling approach and had managers train their team members on these core skills."

"Was this disruptive, to switch the team over to a new, modified sales process? I'm guessing it took some time," I said.

"We were actually able to move pretty quickly since so much was familiar. And we used a targeted skills coaching program to maintain the team's performance in spite of the transition," Larry explained.

"Say more about the skills coaching program," I said. "I've seen so many skills coaching programs get started with great fanfare only to die out because managers don't really know what to focus on, or managers and sales team members disagree on where to focus."

"That's a great point, and you are exactly right that implementation and alignment are key," Larry said. "We asked each of the sales team members to score themselves on the twelve skill areas. We also asked the sales manager to score each team member. Then we targeted individual skills coaching in the areas where both gave low scores or areas of big discrepancy. This scoring process helped everyone quickly understand the twelve core skills and create alignment in each manager-sales team member relationship."

"That was a smart way to transition the team quickly," I replied. "After that, on an ongoing basis, how did you keep the team sharp in practicing each of the skill areas? Did you agree on a format for ongoing skill coaching?"

"Yes," Larry said. "We use weekly team-based deal reviews to reinforce all aspects of the value-selling method. Sales team members don't know in advance if they'll be called on, and if they are called on, they don't know which deal they'll be asked to review. The practice encourages each team member to update the deal stage weekly and stay sharp on the tools and skills they need to advance deals from one buyer phase to the next. The specific area to focus on in coaching is also refreshed each quarter by the seller and manager."

Apptio grew by an average of 43 percent year over year through this growth period, even as the go-to-market team added several hundred members, and the sales team made its transition through three different sales methodologies. Key to their success was committing to a team-based skills development approach. Each new sales methodology was treated not as a replacement but as a supplement to an updated sales process and set of tools. Individual skills coaching was used to anchor each team member's skills development. A weekly cadence of team meetings and peer learning created accountability to continue to sharpen and use skills.

Team-Based Skills and an Authentic Buyer Journey

DealerRater's dealer review product and Apptio's technology business management software show how a team-based skills model is a key support for an authentic buyer journey.

The team-based skills development model fixes three big problems in the traditional skills development model:

1 In traditional skills development, learning retention is a huge problem. Team-based skills development fixes this through playbooks that support practice.

2 Traditional skills development is based primarily on a workshop model that misses the opportunity for social learning, which research has shown propels innovation and top performance.

3 Traditional skills development lacks personalization that builds individual team members' strengths through feedback and coaching.

In chapter 12, we'll conclude with a few simple strategies to move into action on an authentic buyer journey individually or as a team.

YOUR NEXT STEPS ON
TEAM-BASED SKILLS DEVELOPMENT

- **Skills matrix:** Do you have a list of the top skills for success as a sales, account management, or customer success team member? How do managers and team members identify skills they want to work on together?

- **Coaching formats:** What formats do you use to support regular team learning sessions? What formats do you use for individual and cross-team coaching?

A team-based skills model is key to the consistent and high-quality execution of an authentic buyer journey. For supplementary resources to help build plays that support a team-based learning model, visit winalytics.com/theplays.

12

Into Action on an Authentic Buyer Journey

T HANKS FOR being on this journey with me. I was a revenue leader for more than a dozen years, and I've spent
the last seven years providing go-to-market revenue acceleration consulting. While I've honed my process over the
years, this is the first time I've written down the end-to-end
approach for creating an authentic buyer journey.

After hearing about and buying into the benefits of shifting
from a product-led buyer journey to an authentic buyer journey, many revenue leaders ask me, "How do I get started?"

One easy way is for your CEO and whole executive leadership team to *read this book together.* Use that shared reading
experience to assess how connected and authentic your buyer
journey is currently. You can use time together in your senior
leadership meeting to consider and discuss some simple
questions, such as:

- Are we all messaging our buyer and customer value in the
  same way?

- Would that be obvious if we each gave our short elevator pitch?

- How are we connecting our buyer experience across marketing, sales, and customer success?

- Do we have playbooks that bring an authentic buyer journey into the day-to-day work of our go-to-market teams?

A second strategy is to visit my website (winalytics.com/theplays) and download supplemental materials for this book to support an audit of your go-to-market playbook. On the site, you'll find some examples and worksheets to help you build out initial playbooks. There are also materials that can help you develop value narratives that align with your buyer personas, as well as templates for prospecting, value discovery, buyer qualification, account planning, and renewals that align to an authentic buyer journey.

A final strategy is to conduct a *value narratives audit* of your sales, marketing, and customer success teams to see how much consistency you already have within and between go-to-market teams in how they express buyer value. This is an activity that involves each frontline go-to-market team member and their frontline manager. It brings immediate benefits in terms of clarifying and building consistency in your team's value messaging and deepening your buyer engagement and ability to qualify buyer conversations. In the aforementioned supplemental materials, there is a worksheet with instructions on how to conduct the value narratives audit.

In the opening chapter of this book, I shared how I personally experienced the impact of switching from a product-driven to an authentic buyer journey when I bought my Brookline condo in 2002. Now, almost twenty years later, and as I finish writing this book, we have a new home in Jamaica

Plain, another suburb of Boston. One of the early projects in this new home was to paint some of the all-white walls.

We had two color consultants come over a few weekends to give us painting options. Both started with the "get to know you" pleasantries, the house tour, and congratulations to us as the new owners. The first consultant then pulled out their color palette, put it on the kitchen counter, and walked us through all our color options. The second consultant walked us back through the house and asked a number of questions to help them understand why we wanted to paint sections. The questions included things like, "Where do you think adding color would make the most difference to you?" "What hours of the day do you use this room and your kitchen?" "How do you want the main living and dining room areas to make you feel?" "What's important for your lifestyle while in your home?" "Do you use your home to entertain? How often?" These questions got us into a thirty-minute discussion before we even talked about color.

Can you guess who we're going to work with? *Boom*—it is that simple!

Start by letting your buyer tell you what they care about most and where your product might make a difference. Using an authentic buyer journey can make selling more effective for anything—even when you're selling a complete commodity like paint!

Acknowledgments

DEVELOPED IDEAS for *The Revenue Acceleration Playbook* incrementally over almost two decades, first as a revenue leader and then as a sales and revenue acceleration consultant. The book itself was my "pandemic project." It took me about a year of constant framing, writing, and rewriting to fully flesh out the revenue acceleration playbook as it is written in these pages.

Like any good consultant, I have gained much of my success from working with really smart people, absorbing their ideas, and integrating them into my own unique approach.

I have several old bosses to thank for letting me build my revenue leadership experience. Tom Dretler took a chance on an "ex-academic" to give me my very first revenue leadership role at Eduventures. Mark Miller recruited me to serve as CEO of CollegiateLink and to lead that company's revenue acceleration and then successful acquisition. Guy Hart allowed me to act as his revenue leader and guide as Plus Delta Partners entered into a sustained growth spurt.

Several key clients in my first five years at Winalytics were foundational partners in building out different aspects of the revenue acceleration playbook. Thanks to Mike Sweet, Bobby Gaudreau, Mark Guthrie, Adam Goldberg, Drew Magliozzi,

Kirk Daulerio, Brian Ruhlmann, Jason Prybylo, Mark Atkinson, Brentt Brown, Christina Yu, Glen Brooks, Deric Peterson, Phil Charland, Mark Malaspina, and Ian Giddings, among others.

There are also a number of revenue leaders who took time out of their busy schedules to be interviewed about their growth strategies and practices and then shared comments and revisions on their stories. Thanks to Jarin Schmidt, Ilana Fischer, Adam Ellingson, Rachael Hawkey, Bob Ruffolo, Marcus Sheridan, Rogier van Erkel, Rick Hall, Chris Coad, John Hawkins, Ellen Mayes, Lawrence Whittle, Beth Nelson, Ben Robinson, Mark Roberge, and Larry Blasko.

Several team members at Winalytics helped me clarify and simplify the concepts in *The Revenue Acceleration Playbook* to make it easier to implement and adopt. Thanks to Steve Brown, Tim Hawk, and John Hope for their thought partnership. Thanks to Alice Fackre for her partnership in building our original Insight Series and copyediting the entire first draft. Jim Quinn was an excellent partner on the interviews with revenue leaders for the stories in the book. Thanks to John Brissette for building *The Revenue Acceleration Playbook* into visually accessible iconography.

My book coach, David Meerman Scott, did an amazing job of taking an analytical writing style and making it more story-driven. He also acted as a guide, advisor, and friend in keeping me motivated through the arduous process of writing a first book. My editor at Page Two, James Harbeck, also deserves credit for pushing me to tell stories in ways that were more accessible, with stronger emotional anchors.

Thanks to my parents for their continued support, input, and enthusiasm for every single project I take on.

The biggest thanks go to my wife, Ann-Marie; son, John Henry; and daughter, Anna, who indulged my pandemic project and hours of weekend writing with their love and support.

Notes

Chapter 2: The Revenue Impact of
an Authentic Buyer and Customer Journey

"Almost a decade ago..." Mark Lindwall, "Why Don't Buyers Want to
Meet with Your Salespeople?" Forrester, September 29, 2014,
go.forrester.com/blogs/14-09-29-why_dont_buyers_want_to_meet_
with_your_salespeople/.

"Sales teams overshare..." Nicolas Toman, Brent Adamson, and Cristina
Gomez, "The New Sales Imperative," *Harvard Business Review* (March–
April 2017), 118–25, hbr.org/2017/03/the-new-sales-imperative.

"In fact, a recent article..." Sarah MacKinnon, "Stop! We're
Overwhelming B2B Buyers in a Content Marketing Tsunami and
It's NOT Helping Them Buy," Medium, July 2, 2019, medium.com/
swlh/stop-were-overwhelming-b2b-buyers-in-content-marketing
-tsunami-and-it-s-not-helping-them-buy-55fd1faa1763.

"Both have developed their immersive..." Kevin D., Shannon L., Dagmawit
W., Stephie B., Ivana, contribs., "US Corporate Training Market; Part
1: Market Size and Growth," Wonder, July 17, 2019, askwonder.com/
research/industry-outlook-us-corporate-training-market-yb9scv8ol.

"Each company first launched..." Salento was founded in 2020 as a
merger of two separate companies in the training space. After the
merger, Salento carried forward the immersive VR platform of one
of the companies, which had first launched in 2014.

"Nearly a decade later, Mursion..." Maxine Kelly, "FT Ranking: The
Americas' Fastest-Growing Companies 2021," *Financial Times*, April
13, 2021, ft.com/americas-fastest-growing-companies-2021?hss_
channel=lcp-6414748&utm_content=162206234&utm_medium=
social&utm_source=linkedin.

Chapter 3: Value Discovery as the Foundation

"This sales truth was impeccably documented..." Rackham and a team
of forty researchers in the 1970s and '80s collectively observed
35,000 sales calls done by 10,000 sales people in twenty-three
countries over twelve years.

Chapter 4: Value Mapping and Value Confirmation

"To have a strong content strategy..." "2019 Content Preferences Survey
Report," Demand Gen Report, December 2019, demandgenreport
.com/resources/reports/2019-content-preferences-survey-report/.
"Several years ago..." Unfortunately, additional research did not turn up
the exact figure. We reached out to Aberdeen Strategy & Research for
confirmation of the percentage but did not hear back by the press date.

Chapter 6: Prospecting as a Trusted Advisor

"SalesLoft has shown that..." See Stuart Leung, "You Never Call Me
Anymore: The Case for Sales Phone Calls Over Email," *Salesforce*
(blog), February 12, 2014, salesforce.com/content/blogs/us/
en/2014/02/email-vs-phone-calls-business.html; Ken Krogue,
"31 Inside Sales Must Haves for Driving Leads, Appointments, and
Sales," Presentation at High Velocity Sales Tour, August 30, 2012,
slideshare.net/insidesales/high-velocity-tour-citrix-ken-small;
"Videos in Sales Emails Increases Reply Rate by 26%," *SalesLoft*
(blog), October 11, 2018, salesloft.com/resources/blog/video
-sales-emails-increases-reply-rate/; and Juliana Nicholson, "How
We Increased Sales Opportunities 4X with Video: A HubSpot
Experiment," *HubSpot* (blog), July 5, 2017, blog.hubspot.com/
marketing/video-prospecting.

Chapter 7: Selling into Buyer-Defined Value

"There are more than fifteen different sales..." According to a post from
Lucid Charts, there are more than fifteen major sales methodologies.
See Lucid Content Team, "Choosing the Right Sales Methodology
for Your Organization," *Lucidchart* (blog), August 15, 2019,
lucidchart.com/blog/choosing-the-right-sales-methodology.
"My personal preference..." For a post on this, please see: Jacco van der
Kooij, "BANT and Beyond: Advanced Sales Qualification for SDRs
& AEs," Sales Hacker, December 20, 2020, saleshacker.com/bant
-sales-qualification-new-era/.

Chapter 8: Closing and Expanding on Value

"In a classic study on information..." A. Bastardi and E. Shafir, "On the Pursuit and Misuse of Useless Information," *Journal of Personality and Social Psychology* 75, no. 1 (1998): 19–32, doi.org/10.1037/0022 -3514.75.1.19.

"According to Corporate Executive Board..." Toman, Adamson, and Gomez, "The New Sales Imperative."

"Account planning is a decades-old..." Cristina Sánchez-Blanco. "J. Walter Thompson: The Origin and Development of Account Planning," *Journal of Historical Research in Marketing* 12, no. 1 (2019): 173–91, doi.org/10.1108/JHRM-09-2018-0041.

Chapter 10: Three Revenue Teams, One Revenue Organization

"A quick search of the number..." For example, at the time of writing, a search of job postings on Glassdoor shows 861 chief revenue officers and 1,419 senior vice presidents of sales or chief sales officers positions. Or, a search on job postings on Indeed shows 2,225 chief revenue officer roles and 4,678 senior vice presidents of sales or chief sales officers positions.

Chapter 11: Team-Based Skills Development

"As we discussed in chapter 2..." Kevin D. et al., "US Corporate Training Market."

"Dr. Art Kohn and a team..." "Dr. Art Kohn Explains How to Achieve the Optimal Learning Experience with Boosts and Bursts," NASBA, CPE *Monitor Newsletter*, October 1, 2017, nasbaregistry.org/cpe-monitor -newsletters/dr-art-kohn-explains-how-to-achieve-the-optimal -learning-experience-with-boosts-and-bursts.

"The strongest empirical evidence..." "Anatomy of a World-Class Sales Organization," produced by Jim Dickie and Barry Trailer, CSO Insights, February 26, 2015. slideshare.net/FrankTroppe/anatomy ofaworldclasssalesorganization-55829689.

"Research by the Sales Management Association," "Supporting Sales Coaching," Sales Management Association, November 2015, salesmanagement.org/web/uploads/pdf-renamed-by-uzzal/89f5 f8ff556f7a60adf7f1a78eac94c1.pdf; Matthew Dixon and Brent Adamson, "The Dirty Secret of Effective Sales Coaching," *Harvard Business Review*, January 31, 2011, hbr.org/2011/01/the-dirty-secret -of-effective.

Index

114–15; value discovery cheat sheet, 218; value mapping and content strategy, 104–5, 106–7, 109; value mapping and product discussions, 99–100
Tzuo, Tien, 292

utilization call framework, *298*, 302–4

value confirmation: about, 97, 112, 114–15, 121; in authentic, three-part meetings, 210–12; Avis Budget's experience, 202–3, 205; Research Solutions's experience, 115, 117–20
value discovery: about, 84, 94, 263; across buyer and customer journey, 78–79; in authentic, three-part meetings, 207–8, 210; in authentic campaign narratives, 175–76; Avis Budget's experience, 202–3, 205; broad value discovery, 67–68, 208; buyer engagement from, 60, 62; CeriFi's experience, 79–80, 82–84; Credly's experience, 57, 59–60, 64–65, 67; expansion call framework and, 307–8; impact statements, 72–73, 73–74, *74*, 74–75, 77, 84; next steps, 85; process of, 62–65, *63*, 67; True Fit's experience, 89, 91–94; value mapping and, 89, 91–94, 96; in value narrative playbook, 65, 67, 68; Whisps's experience, 69–70, 72–73
value discovery cheat sheet, 217–19, 245
value mapping: about, 96, 120–21; in authentic, three-part meetings, 210–12; Avis Budget's experience, 202–3, 205; content marketing and, 102–7, *105*, 109–12; IMPACT's experience, 109–12; next steps, 121; product discussions and, 96–97,

99–100; True Fit's experience, 87–89, 104–5, 106–7, 109, 114–15; value discovery and, 89, 91–94, 96
value narrative playbook: about, 19–20, 40, 173, 329; consistency across buyer and customer journey, 78, 102; pitfalls avoided by, 41, 43; team-level playbooks and, 127–28. *See also* authentic buyer journey; playbooks; team-level playbooks; value confirmation; value discovery; value mapping; value narratives
value narratives: about, 27; Aginity's experience, 125–27; buyer personas and, 74, 127–28, 130–32, *132*; expansion campaigns and, 192; next steps, 52
value narratives audit, 384
van Erkel, Rogier, 115, 117–18, 119, 120
velocity. *See* deal velocity; revenue velocity
voicemails, 181–82

Walsh, Bill, 136
Whisps, 69–70, 72–73
white space campaigns. *See* expansion campaigns
Whittle, Lawrence, 287–88, 289–90, 302
Winalytics, 15
work satisfaction, 16

XANT (InsideSales), 171

Yu, Christina, 23, 26–28

Zeel: about, 325–26; account velocity, 343–44; alignment across revenue organization, 326–29; cross-team processes and measurement, 333, 334; prospecting velocity, 338–39

About the Author

BRENT KELTNER, PhD, is president of Winalytics LLC and creator of Winalytics's revenue acceleration and sales growth methodology. Winalytics works with customers from growth stage to enterprise in a range of industries, including the education, human capital, SaaS, business operations, retail, and marketing communications sectors. Before starting Winalytics, Brent successfully scaled growth as a revenue leader in both early-stage and enterprise companies. He began his career as a PhD social scientist and qualitative researcher at Stanford University and the RAND Corporation. He has published articles on go-to-market strategy in the *MIT Sloan Management Review*, *California Management Review*, and the *Financial Times*.